Global Guidance Principles for Life Cycle Assessment Databases

A basis for greener processes and products

'Shonan Guidance Principles'

Acknowledgements

Producer

This Guide has been produced by the UNEP/SETAC Life Cycle Initiative

Supervision and Support

Guido Sonnemann (UNEP), Bruce Vigon (SETAC), Sonia Valdivia (UNEP) and Mireille Rack (UNEP)

Editors

Guido Sonnemann (UNEP) and Bruce Vigon (SETAC)

Authors

For Chapters 1-5 and 7-8 the authors are listed in the following order: Chair of Work Group, Co-Chair of Work Group, the Work Group Members (in alphabetical order) and the Liaison Member. The Executive Summary has been prepared by two lead authors together with the whole leadership team listed in the following order: Chair and Co-Chair of Work Groups in numerical order and the Liaison Members in alphabetical order.

Executive Summary: Bruce Vigon (SETAC), Mary Ann Curran (US EPA-ORD), Guido Sonnemann (UNEP), Hongtao Wang (Sichuan University, China), Andreas Ciroth (GreenDeltaTC), Clare Broadbent (World Steel Association), Martha Stevenson (World Wildlife Fund), Atsushi Inaba (Kogakuin University, Japan), Angeline de Beaufort (Independent Consultant), Jim Fava (Five Winds International), Laura Draucker (WRI), Mark Goedkoop (Pré Consultants), Martin Baitz (PE International AG), Rolf Frischknecht (ESU Services), Stephan Krinke (Volkswagen), Nydia Suppen (Center for Life Cycle Assessment and Sustainable Design – Mexico, CADIS), Bo Weidema (Ecoinvent), Marc-Andree Wolf (EC JRC)

Prologue: Guido Sonnemann (UNEP)

Chapters 1 & 8: Guido Sonnemann (UNEP), Bruce Vigon (SETAC), Martin Baitz (PE International AG), Rolf Frischknecht (ESU Services), Stephan Krinke (Volkswagen), Nydia Suppen (Center for Life Cycle Assessment and Sustainable Design – Mexico, CADIS), Bo Weidema (Ecoinvent), Marc-Andree Wolf (EC JRC)

Chapter 2: Hongtao Wang (Sichuan University, China), Andreas Ciroth (GreenDeltaTC), Pierre Gerber (FAO), Charles Mbowha (University of Johannesburg, South Africa), Thumrongrut Mungcharoen (Kasetsart University and National Metal and Materials Technology Center, Thailand), Abdelhadi Sahnoune (ExxonMobil Chemical Co.), Kiyotaka Tahara (National Institute of Advanced Industrial Science and Technology, Japan), Ladji Tikana (European Copper Institute), Nydia Suppen (Center for Life Cycle Assessment and Sustainable Design – Mexico, CADIS)

Chapter 3: Clare Broadbent (World Steel Association), Martha Stevenson (World Wildlife Fund), Armando Caldeira-Pires (UNI Brasilia, Brazil), David Cockburn (Tetra Pak), Pascal Lesage (CIRAIG, Quebec, Canada), Ken Martchek (Alcoa Inc.), Olivier Réthoré (ADEME, France), Rolf Frischknecht (ESU Services)

Chapter 4: Atsushi Inaba (Kogakuin University, Japan), Angeline de Beaufort (Independent Consultant), Alberta Carpenter (NREL, US), Fredy Dinkel (Carbotech AG), Ivo Mersiowsky (DEKRA Industrial on behalf of PlasticsEurope), Claudia Peña (Chilean Research Center of Mining and Metallurgy), Chiew Wei Puah (Malaysian Palm Oil Board), Greg Thoma (The Sustainability Consortium), Marc-Andree Wolf (EC JRC)

Chapter 5: Jim Fava (Five Winds International), Laura Draucker (WRI), Greg Foliente (CSIRO, Australia), Henry King (Unilever), Joon-Jae Lee (KEITI, Korea), Toolseeram Ramjeawon (University of Mauritius), Sangwon Suh (University of California, Santa Barbara, USA), Reginald Tan (National University of Singapore), Bo Weidema (Ecoinvent)

Chapter 6: Sonia Valdivia (UNEP), Guido Sonnemann (UNEP), Bruce Vigon (SETAC), Atsushi Inaba (Kogakuin University, Japan), Mary Ann Curran (US EPA-ORD), Mark Goedkoop (Pré Consultants), Bo Weidema (Ecoinvent), Surjya Narayana Pati (National Council for Cement and Building Materials, India), Cássia Maria Lie Ugaya (Federal Technological University of Parana, Brazil)

Chapter 7: Mary Ann Curran (US EPA-ORD), Mark Goedkoop (Pré Consultants), Scott Butner (Knowledge Systems Group, Pacific Northwest National Laboratory, USA), Katsuyuki Nakano (Japan Environmental Management Association for Industry), Greg Norris (Harvard University, USA/ Sylvatica), Surjya Narayana Pati (National Council for Cement and Building Materials, India), Cássia Maria Lie Ugaya (Federal Technological University of Parana, Brazil), Sonia Valdivia (UNEP), Martin Baitz (PE International AG)

Steering Committee

Co-Chairs: Guido Sonnemann (UNEP), Bruce Vigon (SETAC)

Members: Clare Broadbent (World Steel Association), Mary Ann Curran (US EPA-ORD), Matthias Finkbeiner (TU Berlin, Germany), Rolf Frischknecht (ESU Services), Atsushi Inaba (Kogakuin University, Japan), Aafko Schanssema (PlasticsEurope), Martha Stevenson (World Wildlife Fund), Cássia Maria Lie Ugaya (Federal Technological University of Parana, Brazil), Hongtao Wang (Sichuan University, China) and David Pennington (EC JRC)

International Scientific and Professional Review Panel

Peer Review Committee **Co-Chairs:** Reinout Heijungs (CML Leiden University, The Netherlands) and Michael Hauschild (Technical University of Denmark)

Peer Reviewers: Pablo Arena (University of Mendoza, Argentina), Terrie Boguski (Harmony Environmental LLC), Joyce Cooper-Smith (University of Washington, USA), Amy Costello (Armstrong World Industries), Shabbir H. Gheewala (King Mongkut's University of Technology, Thailand), Jean-Michel Hébert (PwC), Walter Klöpffer (Editor-in-Chief of the International Journal of Life Cycle Assessment), Yasushi Kondo (Waseda University, Japan), Todd Krieger (DuPont), Kun-Mo Lee (Ajou University, Korea), Deanna Lizas (ICF International), Martina Prox (IFU Hamburg, Germany), Isabel Quispe (Catholic University of Peru), Gert van Hoof (P&G)

Technical Editor

David Evers

Editing, Proofreading, Design and Lay-Out

Mimi Meredith (Coordinating Editor of SETAC Books), Larry Kapustka (Books Editor for SETAC), Winifred Power, Serge Miserez

Photography and Graphics

Scott Butner, Shutterstock images, iStockphoto, Sue Dobson, Jason Pearson (TRUTHStudio)

Printing

Imprimerie Escourbiac

Contributors

The authors would like to thank everybody who has contributed to the development of the 'Global Guidance Principles for LCA Databases'. In particular, the authors would like to thank Mike Levy (American Chemistry) for his overall insights and Pablo Cardoso, Charlotte Collin, Pascal Lesage, Annie Levasseur, Claudia Peña, Hongtao Wang, Ping Hou and Gil Anderi for the translation of the executive summary into French, Spanish, Chinese and Portuguese. Moreover, the authors would like to thank the Ministry of Economy, Trade and Industry (METI), the host organization, and the Society of Non-Traditional Technology (SNTT) for providing logistical and organizational support for the workshop in Japan. Finally, the authors would also like to thank the sponsors of the UNEP/SETAC Life Cycle Initiative (please see a complete list at the end of the publication).

Table of Contents

Chapter 1 The Context for Global Guidance Principles for Life Cycle Inventories 41

Chapter 2 Development of Unit Process Datasets 53

Chapter 5 Adaptive Approaches

Chapter 6 Cooperation and Capacity Building

List of Figures and Tables

List of Figures

List of Tables

Abbreviations and Acronyms

Acronym	Full Explanation
AIST	National Institute of Advanced Industrial Science and Technology (Japan)
APIs	aggregated process inventories
API	application programming interface
CAS	Chemical Abstracts Service
CPC	Central Product Classification
DBMT	database management team
DQI	data quality indicator
EC	European Community, European Commission
EEIO	environmentally extended input output
E-PRTR	European Pollutant Release and Transfer Register
ERP	Enterprise Resource Planning
FAO	Food and Agriculture Organization
GHG	greenhouse gas
GIS	geographic information system
IEA	International Energy Agency
IGES	Institute for Global Environmental Strategies (Japan)
IGO	intergovernmental organization
ILCB	International Life Cycle Initiative Board
ILCD	International Reference Life Cycle Data System
IMD	independently managed database
IMF	International Monetary Fund
IOA	input-output analysis
IOT	input-output table
IPCC	International Panel on Climate Change
ISIC	International Standard Industrial Classification
ISO	International Organization for Standardization
IT	information technology
JEMAI	Japan Environmental Management Association for Industry
JLCA	LCA Society of Japan
JRC	Joint Research Centre (European Commission)
LCA	life cycle assessment
LCC	life cycle costing
LCI	life cycle inventory analysis
LCIA	life cycle impact assessment
NACE	Nomenclature Générale des Activités Économiques dans les Communautés Européennes
NAICS	North American Industry Classification System
NREL	National Renewable Energy Laboratory (US)
OECD	Organisation for Economic Co-operation and Development
POCP	photochemical oxidant creation potential
RDF	resource description framework
REC	renewable energy certificate
S-LCA	social and socio-economic life cycle assessment
SEEA	socio-economic and environmental assessment
SETAC	Society of Environmental Toxicology and Chemistry
SME	small and medium-sized enterprises
TRC	Technical Review Committee
UNEP	United Nations Environment Programme
UNFCCC	United Nations Framework Convention on Climate Change
UNSPSC	United Nations Standard Products and Services Code
UPI	unit process inventory
URI	uniform resource identifier
URL	uniform resource locator
USEPA	United States Environmental Protection Agency
VOC	volatile organic compound
WBCSD	World Business Council for Sustainable Development
WHO	World Health Organization
WRI	World Resources Institute

Foreword by UNEP

Nearly 20 years after the Earth Summit, nations are again on the Road to Rio, but in a world very different and very changed from that of 1992. Then we were just glimpsing some of the challenges emerging across the planet, from climate change and the loss of species to desertification and land degradation. Today, many of those seemingly far-off concerns are becoming a reality with sobering implications not only for achieving the UN's Millennium Development Goals, but challenging the very opportunity for close to seven billion people to be able to thrive, let alone survive. Rio 1992 did not fail the world—far from it. It provided the vision and set in place important pieces of the multilateral machinery to achieve a sustainable future.

A transition to a green economy is already under way, a point underscored in UNEP's Green Economy report and a growing wealth of companion studies by international organizations, countries, corporations and civil society. But the challenge is clearly to build on this momentum. A green economy does not favor one political perspective over another. It is relevant to all economies, be they state or more market-led. Rio+20 offers a real opportunity to scale-up and embed these "green shoots".

Life Cycle Assessment, or LCA, is a crucial tool standardized in the ISO 14040 series for changing unsustainable consumption and production patterns and making products greener. More and more institutional and individual consumers want to understand the world behind the products they buy. They want to know about the environmental impacts and the resources used throughout the life cycle of products. This type of product sustainability information is revealed through Life Cycle Assessments studies. Carbon footprints are just one piece of information provided by LCA databases, which detail the amounts of energy, materials, land and water consumed or emitted into water, air and soil. In this way, comprehensive environmental information on

processes and products over their life cycle is made easily accessible. Generating reliable LCA data is one of the challenges society is facing in its transition to a low-carbon, resource-efficient 21st-century Green Economy.

Understanding, quantifying and communicating the environmental impacts and resource consumption of products is part of the solution to continuously reduce their impacts and increase their benefits to society. Indeed, UNEP's Life Cycle Initiative, launched with the Society for Environmental Toxicology and Chemistry (SETAC), has been promoting life cycle management as a key area in terms of the sustainability challenge since 2002. The Life Cycle Initiative has published a number of relevant reference documents since then, such as the Life Cycle Management Business Guide to Sustainability and the Guidelines on Social LCA.

Promoting the powerful and flexible tool of Life Cycle Assessment and the holistic concept of Life Cycle Management is no easy task, and here I would like to congratulate the Life Cycle Initiative and its experts and partners for bringing to governments, business and civil society an important piece of work in the sustainability jigsaw puzzle. This new publication, Global Guidance Principles for LCA Databases, provides a missing reference document to account systematically for the resources used and emissions generated by different processes, the aggregation of these data at the product system level and their management in databases. In this way it supports a far more intelligent understanding and trajectory towards sustainable development that reflects the needs of a planet that will be home to more than nine billion people by 2050.

Achim Steiner
UN UNDER-SECRETARY GENERAL
AND EXECUTIVE DIRECTOR UNEP

Foreword by SETAC

One of the key objectives of the UNEP/SETAC Life Cycle Initiative is to foster a globally accepted life cycle assessment practice that builds on the concepts and methods in the standards developed by the International Organization for Standardization (ISO).

With technology and processes advancing at a breathtaking pace, products and services have become increasingly diverse in their sources of materials, manufacturing and assembly locations, areas of use, and points of final disposition. To accurately reflect this diversity, data must be available for areas where the activities embodied in a life cycle assessment (LCA) actually take place. Databases, as repositories of this information, are being established at a rapid pace. Datasets contained within these systems must meet increasingly rigorous criteria if they are to be consistent and exchangeable among users worldwide.

To that end, the United Nations Environment Programme (UNEP) and the Society of Environmental Toxicology and Chemistry (SETAC) organized an intensive workshop to develop global guidance on databases for LCA. The Pellston format, established at the first such SETAC workshop held in the 1970s in Pellston, Michigan, USA, and used now for decades, strives for a consensus approach among a diverse group of experts. Some 50 such workshops have been conducted in various parts of the world. For the LCA Databases Guidance workshop, a select group of 48 participants from 23 countries worked for a week to draft the document you have in hand. Strict groundrules on the conduct of the workshop and the participation of the attendees were enforced to allow for an open, honest, objective, and individual (rather than organizational) forum.

We anticipate that the resulting publication will serve to promote consistent practices for data collection, dataset development, and all aspects of database management. Given its forward-looking perspective, implementation of the recommendations and anticipation of enhancements in information technology will enable the life cycle community to be proactive in serving the data and database needs of the users well into the future.

Mike Mozur
GLOBAL EXECUTIVE DIRECTOR
SOCIETY OF ENVIRONMENTAL TOXICOLOGY AND CHEMISTRY

Executive Summary

Global Guidance Principles for Life Cycle Assessment Databases

As products and services have become more geographically diverse in their resources, manufacturing and assembly operations, usage, and final disposition, the need for LCA users to obtain data that accurately and consistently measure the resource consumption and environmental aspects of those activities has never been more acute. Providing a sound scientific basis for product stewardship in business and industry and for life cycle–based policies in governments ultimately helps to advance the sustainability of products and society's economic activities. For the past two decades, databases have been developed, maintained, and updated by different general database providers, by academics and researchers, by industry sector database providers, and by industry internal groups. The primary basis for development of global guidance principles is the belief that agreement on recommended practices for data collection, modelling, aggregation, and insertion in databases exists for a large percentage of the aspects to be addressed. Thus, the workshop that resulted in this global guidance principles document focused on getting consensus on aspects where prior agreement was not achieved.

Background

In early February 2011, forty-eight participants from 23 countries gathered in Shonan Village, southeast of Tokyo, Japan, for the Workshop on Global Guidance Principles for Life Cycle Assessment Databases, a Pellston workshop (informally to be known as the "Shonan Guidance Principles Workshop") to develop principles for creating, managing, and disseminating datasets for the purpose of supporting life cycle assessments (LCAs) of globally produced products and services. The Pellston format, established by the Society of Environmental Toxicology and Chemistry (SETAC) in the 1970s and used since in some 50 workshops worldwide, strives for a consensus approach among a diverse group of experts. Strict groundrules on the conduct of the workshop and the participation of the attendees were enforced to allow for an open, honest, objective, and individual (rather than organizational) forum. The results of the workshop presented in this report reflect only the views of its participants.

The vision for the workshop was to create guidance that would accomplish the following:

- serve as the basis for improved dataset exchangeability and interlinkages of databases worldwide;
- increase the credibility of existing LCA data, generate more data, and enhance overall data accessibility; and
- complement other data-related initiatives at the national or regional level, particularly those in developing countries and where more prescriptive guidance has been developed.

Approach

To ensure the validity of these global guidance principles, workshop participants were selected for their technical expertise as well as their geographic representation and their perspective in the "data supply chain". The final mix of participants consisted of a balance of data and study providers (primarily consultants and industry associations) along with data and database users, including intergovernmental organizations (IGOs), government, industry, nongovernmental organizations (NGOs), and academics. Here the emphasis was on development and access to datasets within databases, because there is already a set of International Organization for Standardization (ISO) standards on methodology and conduct of LCAs.

Participants were organized into six topical tracks, based on responses to a series of eight stakeholder engagements held around the world during the preceding 18 months. Issue papers were prepared for each area, and previously published information was extracted into a database for use in preparing these papers and for consultation during the workshop. Topics for the work groups, along with the goals for each, included the following:

- Unit process data development: Defining a data collection approach and mechanism that results in unit process datasets with the desired quality attributes and adequate documentation, specifying data modelling requirements to accurately transform raw data into unit process datasets, and collaborating with the review and documentation group to address verification and transparency issues.

- Aggregated process data development: Defining and validating procedures and requirements for combining unit process data into multi-process datasets, specifying requirements on additional information to be provided with such datasets to users to allow determination of suitability, and collaborating with the review and documentation group to address verification and transparency issues.
- Data review and documentation: Providing detailed analysis of requirements and procedures for review of datasets prior to their acceptance into databases, overall management roles and responsibilities for database managers, and description, along with dataset development work groups, on necessary documentation for primary data and supplemental (metadata) characteristics.
- Adaptive LCA approaches: Addressing data demands and aspects of LCA questions accessible with non-conventional methodologies, such as environmentally-extended input-output table-based techniques, time-dynamic LCA, spatially explicit LCA, and hybrid methods.
- Integration and cross-fertilization: Identifying intersecting ideas and promoting creative thinking across groups, especially regarding current practices.
- Future knowledge management: Anticipating how Web 2.0 and other emerging information and knowledge management techniques could be used to produce more efficient, higher-quality, and increased numbers of LCI datasets as well as how such datasets link to databases, and other distribution mechanisms. Such techniques will need to respect quality and other requirements of more conventionally provided datasets

All of these discussions maintained a clear user perspective with regard to their needs for data and ensuring the credibility of the data. Efforts were made to define users within various organizations for purposes of tailoring the global guidance principles as appropriate.

Summary Results

The following section provides a high-level overview of the workshop findings. These summary results only begin to capture the breadth of discussion and careful deliberation that took place on each topic. Likewise, alternative views, where objectively supportable, are incorporated in the document in a number of ways, but due to length constraints this article is based only on consensus recommendations.

Speaking the Same Language

In addition to providing guidance on technical and operational aspects of datasets and databases, we discovered that differences remain in terminology usage and inconsistencies in principles definitions such as completeness, exchangeability, and transparency. Part of this situation is caused by the evolution of LCA in different regions and cultures, part by language, and part by ambiguity in existing definitions. Thus, one of the workshop's initial exercises was to develop a glossary of terminology and a dictionary of principles to provide a consistent basis of reference for participants. Although not intended as a general reference, the glossary may find use externally. Where possible, the definitions were based on existing ISO standards language.

Current Practice

Much time and effort was spent assessing the current state-of-practice regarding developing datasets, incorporating them into databases, and then managing those databases. From an operational standpoint, recognition that the target audience of the document is database managers (or database management teams) serves to position them as central actors in the data supply chain. This is not to say that other actors will not benefit from these global guidance principles. Far from it: data providers, study commissioners, reviewers, and ultimate users all will find useful insights and recommendations in the document.

Providing high-quality, unit process–level datasets begins with targeted data sourcing and a data collection plan created with the end result firmly in mind, which will result in datasets that are consistent, complete, and exchangeable. A dataset is a collection of input and output data that are related to the same reference process; the process can be a unit process or an aggregated process.

Once raw data are collected according to the plan, the unit process dataset is created by defining specific mathematical relationships between the raw data and various flows associated with the dataset and a defined reference flow. Data developers are provided with guidance on identifying and selecting raw data and on defining the appropriate relationships, as well as supportive information to be included to describe both the decision rules and the nature of the relationships. In some unit process datasets, these relationships are defined parametrically so that changes can be made internally to the dataset while it resides in a database.

There are good reasons to provide datasets on a unit process level. First, doing so provides maximum transparency, allowing the users of the database to understand which ones are used in the LCI of a given

reference flow and how these unit processes are linked. Second, providing datasets on a unit process level makes the database flexible and adaptable in the sense that specific unit processes in an LCI can be adapted or replaced to better reflect the situation to be assessed. Third, providing datasets on a unit process level can improve the interpretation of life cycle studies because the high resolution of unit process–based assessments allows a user to identify the key unit processes through sensitivity analysis by varying methodological and other assumptions as well as parameters, inputs, and outputs.

Although these benefits of providing unit process data argue for their preference when conducting an LCA, they do not imply that good documentation and review are unnecessary.

There also are good reasons to aggregate datasets. First of all, it is considered convenient to work with aggregated process datasets (cradle-to-gate, cradle-to-grave) in a number of LCA software systems and in simplified tools to reduce calculation time and memory size, when answering questions typically addressed by LCA. Furthermore, from a user perspective, it can be beneficial to work with aggregated or pre-connected unit process datasets if the user does not have the technical or engineering know-how to model a complex process chain. Finally, the aggregation of datasets may be required for reasons of confidentiality. Confidentiality may be ensured by different levels of aggregation (e.g., by establishing an industry average, by aggregating some selected unit process datasets along the supply chain, or by aggregating unit process datasets with selected inputs being followed up to the cradle). Consistent with the criteria presented above, an aggregated, reviewed dataset with comprehensive documentation can be an appropriate choice.

For the first time, these global guidance principles show the various aggregation possibilities in a graphical and self-evident way. We recommend that independent verifications be carried out for the unit process dataset and for the product system model used to generate aggregated process datasets.

The documentation of aggregated process datasets is highly important. We strongly recommend that sufficient information be provided and that such information is as transparent as possible. The provision of the unit process datasets used in the product system of an aggregated process dataset is preferable. When there is sufficient basis not to provide the information at the unit process level, we strongly recommend that other information be included in the aggregated process dataset, for example, information about key drivers of the overall environmental impacts, data sources used, assumptions, and key process operational figures.

Data documentation and review are key elements of the global guidance principles. The primary target audience for the global guidance principles are database managers and operators who have the role and responsibility to decide not only what the datasets themselves must include but also what additional information is required and what would be considered recommended or necessary in terms of validation and review prior to data being stored in a database. In order to accomplish these functions, we strongly recommend that the database management team issues a written protocol. Additionally, because datasets need to be both accurate depictions of reality and compliant with the requirements of the database they reside in, validation and review are considered to be critical. These global guidance principles document describes a number of ways in which validation, as an internal "quality-check" process or mechanism, and review, as a more formal and often external procedure, should take place. In particular, these global guidance principles recommends that before a dataset is included in an LCI database, it should undergo a defined validation process to ensure it meets the database protocol.

An LCI database is an organized collection of ISO 14040- and 14044-compliant LCI datasets that sufficiently conform to a set of criteria, including consistent methodology, validation or review, interchangeable format, documentation, and nomenclature, and that allow for interconnection of individual datasets. LCI databases store LCI datasets, allowing for their creation, addition, maintenance, and search. LCI databases are managed by a responsible management team, which enables identifying and tracing the responsibilities of the database creation, content, maintenance, and updating.

In contrast, an LCI dataset library contains datasets that do not sufficiently meet the above criteria, and care must be taken when using them in a life cycle model. If the aspects above apply but the LCI database is limited regarding covered impact categories (e.g., it covers only carbon footprint information) or has a specific focus for certain applications or schemes, the recommendation is to flag this limitation clearly in the documentation as inconsistent with the inclusive nature of LCI datasets.

Moving Beyond Current Practice

Some workshop participants identified a need for additional data and data management to allow LCA databases to provide more comprehensive answers and to answer more comprehensive questions, such as spatially differentiated models, developments over time, and issues related to social and economic impacts.

Another aspect addressed was the filling of data gaps with data estimations from non-process–based approaches.

The workshop participants analysed the different additional data sources, such as geospatial data, data from national environmentally extended economic input–output tables (IOTs) and environmental accounts, data on social indicators, and data on costs. In general, they found that all of these data sources could be used in a complementary way to existing raw data in the development of unit process datasets for some purposes, if the technological specificity and methodological differences are fully taken into account and documented.

Current trends in information technology are expected to shape users' expectations regarding data, software functionality, and interoperability in ways that will alter the scope of what can be done with LCA data. It is important to anticipate these trends along with market drivers in order to be better prepared to properly manage the development of life cycle information with a need to maintain quality. Increased potential for data mobility would allow data from various sources to more easily find its way into LCA databases, and then into a wide range of new applications. Such enhancements can potentially bring significant progress toward sustainable consumption and production.

There are new ways to access the information in LCA databases, which do not change the way data are generated or stored but which do change how users retrieve the data. While not a radical departure from the status quo, the infusion of new technologies into existing database applications is occurring now and will continue into the near future. In the longer term, current trends in information technology may lead to avenues for database management that are radically different from the way we approach it today.

Global coordination among LCI dataset developers and LCA database managers has been identified, together with capacity building and data mining, as components of priority roadmaps to move towards a world with interlinked databases and overall accessibility to credible data. Capacity building is particularly relevant in emerging economies and developing countries where LCA databases have yet to be established. Therefore, it is a goal to convert these global guidance principles document into training material. Strengthening of existing and the development of new regional and national life cycle networks is likewise important.

Synthèse

Lignes directrices mondiales sur les bases de données d'analyse du cycle de vie (ACV)

Alors que les produits et services deviennent de plus en plus diversifiés sur le plan géographique, tant pour l'approvisionnement en ressources, la production et les opérations d'assemblage, que pour l'utilisation ou l'élimination en fin de vie, le besoin pour les utilisateurs de l'ACV d'obtenir des données qui mesurent de manière pertinente et systématique les consommations de ressources et les aspects environnementaux de ces activités n'a jamais été aussi important. L'utilisation d'un fondement scientifique solide pour la gestion des produits par l'industrie et pour le développement de politiques publiques basées sur la pensée cycle de vie contribue au développement d'une société et d'une économie plus durables. Depuis vingt ans, des bases de données ont été développées, entretenues et mises à jour par différents fournisseurs de bases de données générales et sectorielles et par des regroupements industriels. Le principe à la base du développement de directives globales est l'existence actuelle d'un consensus sur la majorité des bonnes pratiques concernant la collecte de données, leur modélisation, agrégation et insertion dans des bases de données. Ce groupe de travail avait donc pour objectif de s'entendre sur les aspects pour lesquels il n'y avait pas encore consensus.

Contexte

Au début du mois de février 2011, 48 participants de 23 pays se sont réunis dans le village de Shonan, situé au sud-est de Tokyo, pour participer à l'Atelier d'orientation sur les bases de données d'analyse du cycle de vie (ACV). Cet atelier de Pellston (communément appelé 'atelier de lignes directrices de Shonan') avait pour objectif le développement de bonnes pratiques pour la création, la gestion et la dissémination des bases de données permettant la réalisation d'analyses du cycle de vie (ACV) de produits et de services dans un contexte international.

Le format de Pellston, mis en place par la Société de Toxicologie et Chimie de l'Environnement (SETAC) dans les années 70 et utilisé depuis dans environ 50 ateliers à travers le monde, cherche à obtenir un consensus au sein d'un groupe de différents experts. De strictes règles de fonctionnement concernant le déroulement de l'atelier et les interventions des participants ont été imposées pour permettre un forum ouvert, honnête, objectif et fondé sur la participation des individus en leur nom (plutôt que comme représentants des différents organismes où ils œuvrent normalement). Les résultats de l'atelier, présentés dans ce rapport, reflètent uniquement l'opinion des participants.

Cet atelier visait à établir une série de bonnes pratiques permettant :

- un meilleur échange de données et l'interconnexion des bases de données dans le monde ;
- d'accroître la crédibilité des données existantes, de générer davantage de données et d'améliorer leur accessibilité ;
- de servir de complément aux initiatives existantes aux niveaux national ou régional, en particulier celles des pays en développement et celles où des indications plus normatives ont été déjà développées.

Approche

Pour assurer la validité des résultats de cet atelier de lignes directrices mondiales, les participants ont été choisis sur la base de leur expertise technique, de leur origine géographique et de leur position dans la 'chaîne d'approvisionnement des données'. La liste finale des participants était constituée d'un mélange équilibré de fournisseurs de données, de prestataires d'études (principalement des consultants et des associations d'industriels), d'utilisateurs de bases de données, d'organisations intergouvernementales (OIG), de gouvernements, d'industries, d'organisations non gouvernementales (ONG) et d'universitaires. Lors de cet atelier, l'accent a été mis sur le développement et l'accès aux ensembles de données au sein des bases de données, l'Organisation Internationale de Normalisation (ISO) ayant déjà développé un ensemble de normes sur la méthodologie et la réalisation des ACV.

Les participants ont été répartis en six groupes thématiques, fondés sur huit accords établis par différents acteurs impliqués dans les missions tenues à travers le monde au cours des 18 mois précédents. Des informations publiées antérieurement ont été mises à disposition pour consultation pendant l'atelier et utilisées pour la préparation de documents de réflexion propres à chaque thématique. Les six thématiques étaient les suivantes :

- Développement de données pour des processus élémentaires : Le rôle de ce groupe est de définir une méthode de collecte de données pour des processus élémentaires garantissant un certain niveau de qualité et une documentation adéquate et de déterminer les exigences de modélisation pour la conversion des données brutes en ensembles de données pour des processus élémentaires, tout en collaborant avec le groupe de vérification des données et documentation sur les questions de vérification et de transparence.
- Développement de données pour des processus agrégés : Le rôle de ce groupe est de définir et de valider les procédures et exigences permettant la combinaison des données de différents processus élémentaires en un ensemble de données décrivant un seul processus agrégé

et de préciser les exigences relatives aux informations additionnelles à fournir aux utilisateurs de ces ensembles de données agrégées, tout en collaborant avec le groupe de vérification des données et documentation sur les questions de pertinence et de transparence.
- Vérification des données et documentation : Analyse détaillée des exigences et des procé-

dures pour la vérification des ensembles de données avant leur intégration dans les bases de données, des rôles et responsabilités des gestionnaires de bases de données et description de la documentation nécessaire pour la caractérisation des données brutes et complémentaires (métadonnées), en collaboration avec les groupes de développement de données.
- Approches ACV adaptatives : Exigences sur les données et sur d'autres aspects de l'ACV nécessaires à l'utilisation de méthodologies non conventionnelles, tels que les techniques basées sur les tableaux nationaux d'entrées-sorties supplémentés d'aspects environnementaux, l'ACV temporelle-dynamique, la régionalisation de l'ACV et les méthodes hybrides.
- Intégration et «fécondation réciproque» : Identifier les idées communes et promouvoir l'échange créatif entre les différents groupes, en particulier sur ce qui concerne les pratiques actuelles.
- Gestion des connaissances pour l'avenir : Entrevoir comment le Web 2.0 et les autres techniques émergentes de gestion de l'information et des connaissances pourraient être utilisées pour créer plus efficacement un plus grand nombre d'ensembles de données ICV de meilleure qualité, ainsi que pour améliorer le lien entre ensembles et bases de données, et les autres mécanismes de distribution. Ces techniques devront respecter la qualité et les autres conditions exigées aux ensembles de données obtenus de façon conventionnelle.

Toutes ces discussions ont été abordées depuis la perspective des utilisateurs, en tenant compte de leurs besoins en termes de données, tout en s'assurant de la crédibilité des ces données. Des efforts ont été déployés afin d'identifier les utilisateurs présents au sein de diverses organisations et d'adapter les recommandations à leurs besoins.

Résumé des résultats

Cette section donne un aperçu général des résultats de l'atelier. Ce court résumé ne fait que survoler chacun des sujets et ne couvre pas toute l'ampleur des discussions et des délibérations qui ont eu lieu sur chaque thématique. Certains points de vue alternatifs ont été incorporés de diverses façons dans le document, lorsqu'ils apparaissaient objectivement justifiables. Mais en raison de contraintes de longueur, ce document synthèse est uniquement basé sur les consensus établis.

Parler le même langage

En plus de fournir des conseils sur les aspects techniques et opérationnels des ensembles et bases de données, l'atelier a permis de découvrir que des divergences subsistent dans l'utilisation de la terminologie, ainsi que des incohérences dans les définitions de certains principes tels que 'l'exhaustivité', 'l'interchangeabilité' et 'la transparence'. Cette situation s'explique en partie par l'évolution de l'ACV dans différentes régions et cultures, mais aussi par des différences de langue et par l'ambiguïté présente dans les définitions existantes. Ainsi, l'un des premiers exercices a été d'élaborer un glossaire de la terminologie et un dictionnaire des différents principes afin de fournir une base de référence cohérente pour les participants. Bien que l'objectif n'était pas de construire une référence générale, le glossaire pourrait éventuellement trouver une certaine utilité à l'extérieur de ce groupe de participants. Lorsque cela était possible, les définitions ont été fondées sur les concepts des normes ISO.

Pratique actuelle

Beaucoup de temps et d'efforts ont été dédiés à évaluer l'état actuel des pratiques concernant le développement des ensembles de données, leur intégration dans des bases de données et leur gestion. Du point de vue opérationnel, il a été reconnu que le public cible de ce document est constitué de gestionnaires de bases de données, ce qui a entraîné leur positionnement comme acteur central dans la chaîne d'approvisionnement de données. Cela ne veut pas dire que les autres acteurs ne bénéficieront pas eux aussi des résultats de ces lignes directrices mondiales. Au contraire, les fournisseurs de données, les mandataires d'étude, les évaluateurs et les utilisateurs, trouveront des renseignements et des recommandations utiles dans ce document.

Afin d'obtenir des ensembles de données pour des processus élémentaires de bonne qualité, cohérents, exhaustifs et interchangeables, il faut dans un premier temps bien identifier les sources de données, puis élaborer un plan de collecte de données en ayant en tête une idée claire du résultat final. Un ensemble de données est une série de données d'entrée et de sortie toutes liées au même processus de référence, qu'il soit unitaire ou agrégé.

Une fois que les données brutes sont collectées en respectant le plan de collecte, l'ensemble de données pour le processus élémentaire visé est créé en utilisant les relations mathématiques définissant le lien entre les données brutes et les différents flux associés et un flux de référence donné. Des règles utiles pour l'identification et la sélection des données brutes et pour la définition de relations mathématiques appropriées ont été identifiées pour les développeurs de données, tout comme une description de l'information de support à inclure afin de bien expliquer les décisions prises et les relations utilisées. Pour les ensembles de données de certains processus élémentaires, ces relations sont définies par des équations paramétriques, de sorte que des changements peuvent être apportés à l'ensemble de données, alors même qu'il fait partie d'une base de données.

Il existe de bonnes raisons de préférer les bases de données constituées de processus élémentaires. Tout d'abord, elles fournissent un maximum de transparence, permettant aux utilisateurs de comprendre quels processus sont utilisés dans le calcul d'inventaire d'un certain flux de référence et comment ces différents processus sont liés entre eux. Ensuite, l'utilisation de processus élémentaires rend la banque de données plus flexible et adaptable (n'importe quel processus élémentaire d'un ICV peut être adapté ou remplacé afin de mieux refléter la situation réelle). Finalement, l'utilisation de données définies pour des processus élémentaires améliore l'interprétation des études d'analyse du cycle de vie en permettant à l'utilisateur d'identifier les processus élémentaires clés par des analyses de sensibilité sur les hypothèses, la méthodologie ou autres, ainsi que sur des paramètres spécifiques ou des entrants ou sortants. Malgré ces arguments en faveur de l'utilisation de données définies pour des processus élémentaires lors de la réalisation d'ACV, il est tout de même important d'avoir une bonne documentation et un processus de révision.

Il existe par ailleurs de bonnes raisons pour rassembler et agréger des ensembles de données. Tout d'abord, il est plus pratique de travailler avec des ensembles de données agrégés ('du berceau à la barrière' ou 'du berceau au tombeau') dans un certain nombre de logiciels ACV et dans certains outils simplifiés, car cela permet de réduire le temps de calcul et la taille de la mémoire nécessaire. De plus, il peut être avantageux pour l'utilisateur de travailler avec des données agrégées ou avec des ensembles de données de processus élémentaires pré-connectés s'il ne dispose pas des connaissances techniques ou du savoir-faire nécessaires pour modéliser une chaîne de processus complexe. Finalement, l'agrégation des ensembles de données peut être requise pour des raisons de confidentialité. La confidentialité peut être assurée par différents niveaux d'agrégation (par exemple, en établissant une moyenne de l'industrie, en agrégeant certains processus élémentaires d'une même chaîne d'approvisionnement, ou en agrégeant des ensembles de données de processus élémentaires avec d'autres entrées sélectionnées et objet d'un suivi d'origine). Pour les cas présentés précédemment, un ensemble de données agrégées, révisé et présenté avec une documentation complète, peut constituer un choix approprié.

Pour la première fois, ces lignes directrices mondiales montrent les différentes possibilités d'agrégation d'une manière graphique et claire. Nous recommandons que des vérifications indépendantes soient effectuées sur les ensembles de données des processus élémentaires et sur le modèle de système de production utilisé pour rassembler et agréger les données.

Documenter le processus d'agrégation des données est fondamental. Aussi, nous recommandons fortement qu'une quantité suffisante d'information soit fournie de la façon la plus transparente possible. La mise à disposition des ensembles de données de chacun des processus élémentaires utilisés dans le système de production pour le calcul d'un ensemble de données agrégées est préférable. Si des raisons valables empêchent la mise à disposition des données des processus élémentaires, il est vivement recommandé que d'autres informations soient fournies avec l'ensemble de données agrégées, comme par exemple, des informations relatives aux principaux aspects environnementaux, aux sources de données utilisées, aux hypothèses et aux paramètres clés.

La documentation et la révision des données sont des éléments clés des lignes directrices mondiales. Les cibles principales de ces recommandations, soit les gestionnaires et opérateurs de bases de données, ont pour rôle et responsabilité de décider non seulement de la composition de ces ensembles de données, mais aussi de déterminer quelles informations supplémentaires sont nécessaires et quels processus de validation et de révision des données sont recommandés avant leur intégration à la base de données. Afin d'accomplir ces fonctions, nous recommandons fortement que l'équipe de gestion de la base de données développe un protocole écrit. Comme les ensembles de données doivent être à la fois des représentations aussi précises que possible de la réalité et conformes aux exigences de la base de données à laquelle ils seront intégrés, l'étape de validation et de révision est considérée comme critique dans le processus. Le document de lignes directrices mondiales décrit un certain nombre de modalités encadrant la validation, définie comme processus ou mécanisme interne de contrôle de qualité, et la révision, définie comme procédure plus formelle et souvent externe. Particulièrement, ces lignes directrices globales recommandent qu'un ensemble de données soit soumis à un processus défini de validation avant d'être inclus dans une base de données afin de s'assurer qu'il réponde au protocole spécifique de la base de données en question.

Une base de données ICV est un ensemble organisé de données ICV conformes aux normes ISO 14040 et 14 044 et répondant à des critères spécifiques, tels qu'une méthode de traitement cohérente, un processus de validation ou de révision, un format interchangeable, une documentation, une nomenclature et la possibilité d'interconnexion entre les ensembles de données. Les bases de données ICV stockent des ensembles de données ICV, permettant leur création, leur assemblage, leur entretien et leur recherche. Les bases de données ICV sont gérées par une équipe de gestion responsable, ce qui permet l'identification et la traçabilité de la création, du contenu, de la maintenance et de la mise à jour des bases de données.

En revanche, une bibliothèque d'ensembles de données ICV contient des ensembles de données qui ne répondent pas nécessairement aux critères mentionnés précédemment. Il faut donc prendre des précautions lors de leur utilisation dans une analyse du cycle de vie. Si les aspects précédents s'appliquent, mais que la base de données ICV est limitée à des catégories d'impacts spécifiques (par exemple, elle ne couvre que les informations relatives à l'empreinte carbone) ou qu'elle met l'accent sur certaines applications ou certains systèmes particuliers, alors il est recommandé d'identifier clairement cette limitation dans la documentation comme étant incompatible avec le caractère inclusif des ensembles de données ICV.

Au-delà des pratiques actuelles

Certains participants de l'atelier ont identifié le besoin d'inclure des données supplémentaires et de nouveaux modes de gestion des données afin de permettre à des bases de données ACV de fournir des réponses plus complètes à certaines questions relatives, par exemple, à la régionalisation, à l'évolution dans le temps ou aux impacts sociaux et économiques. Un autre aspect abordé lors de l'atelier a été l'utilisation d'estimations non basées sur des procédés pour contrer les lacunes causées par le manque de données.

Les participants à l'atelier ont analysé les différentes sources de données supplémentaires, tel que les données géospatiales, les données issues des tableaux nationaux d'entrées-sorties supplémentés d'aspects environnementaux, les données sur les indicateurs sociaux et les données sur les coûts. Le constat général a été que toutes ces sources de données pourraient être utilisées d'une façon complémentaire aux données brutes pour le développement d'ensembles de données pour des processus élémentaires, si la spécificité technologique et les différences méthodologiques sont pleinement prises en compte et documentées.

Les tendances actuelles en technologies de l'information vont probablement modifier les attentes des utilisateurs concernant les types de données, la fonctionnalité du logiciel et son interopérabilité d'une manière telle que la portée de ce qui peut être fait avec des données d'ACV va changer. Il est important de prévoir ces tendances, tout comme les exigences du marché, afin d'être mieux préparés à gérer correctement le développement d'informations relatives au cycle de vie, tout en maintenant son niveau de qualité. L'accroissement du potentiel de mobilité des données permettrait à des données provenant de diverses sources de rejoindre plus facilement les bases de données des ACV, puis un éventail de nouvelles applications. De tels perfectionnements peuvent potentiellement aboutir à des progrès significatifs en matière de consommation et de production durables.

Il existe de nouvelles façons d'accéder à l'information des bases de données d'ACV, sans modifier la façon dont les données sont générées ou stockées, mais en changeant la façon dont les utilisateurs récupèrent ces données. Bien que n'étant pas en rupture radicale avec le statu quo, l'utilisation des nouvelles technologies dans des applications de bases de données existantes est un fait d'actualité et se poursuivra dans un futur proche. À plus long terme, les tendances actuelles en matière de technologie de l'information peuvent conduire à des méthodes de gestion des bases de données radicalement différentes de celles d'aujourd'hui.

Les mécanismes de coordination entre développeurs d'ensembles de données ICV et gestionnaires de bases de données ACV, de même que le développement des capacités et l'exploitation des données, ont été identifiés comme des composants prioritaires à mettre en place en vue d'un monde pourvu de bases de données interconnectées et d'une accessibilité générale à des données crédibles. Le développement des capacités est particulièrement important pour les économies émergentes et les pays en développement où les bases de données ACV n'ont été pas encore établies. En conséquence, un des objectifs de ce document de lignes directrices mondiales est de devenir un outil de formation. Renforcer et développer les réseaux nationaux et régionaux du cycle de vie est aussi très important.

Resumen Ejecutivo

Principios de una Guía Global para Bases de Datos de Análisis de Ciclo de Vida (ACV)

A medida que los productos y servicios se han vuelto geográficamente diversos en cuanto al origen de sus materias primas, su fabricación u operaciones de ensamblaje, su uso y su disposición final, se ha ido agudizando también la necesidad de los usuarios de ACV por obtener datos que midan de forma más precisa y consistente los consumos de recursos y los aspectos ambientales asociados a esas actividades. Disponer de una base científica sólida para la 'gestión y tutela de producto' *[en ingles: product stewardship]* por parte de las empresas e industrias, y la elaboración de políticas publicas basadas en el enfoque de ciclo de vida, contribuye en última instancia a mejorar la sostenibilidad de los productos y de las actividades económicas de la sociedad. Durante las últimas dos décadas, diferentes proveedores de bases de datos: académicos e investigadores, proveedores del sector industrial y grupos internos de la misma industria han desarrollado mantenido y actualizado diferentes bases de datos. La base fundamental para el desarrollo de los principios de una guía global es el convencimiento que existe un acuerdo general respecto a una parte importante de los aspectos relacionados a las prácticas recomendadas para la recolección de datos, modelación, agregación y su posterior inserción en bases de datos. De esta manera, el taller del cual surgieron estos principios de una guía global se centró en buscar consensos en los aspectos donde aún no había acuerdos.

Antecedentes

A inicios de febrero del 2011, cuarenta y ocho participantes de 23 países se juntaron en la aldea de Shonan, al sureste de Tokio, para la realización del "Taller sobre los Principios de una Guía Global para Bases de Datos de Análisis de Ciclo de Vida". Éste taller Pellston (informalmente conocido como el "Taller de Shonan sobre los Principios de una Guía") tuvo como objetivo desarrollar principios para crear, manejar y divulgar conjuntos de datos con el fin de apoyar el ACV de productos y servicios producidos a nivel global. El formato Pellston, establecido por la Sociedad de Toxicología y Química Ambiental (SETAC) en los años 70 y usado hasta ahora en unos 50 talleres alrededor del mundo, se orienta hacia la obtención de un consenso entre un grupo diverso de expertos. Las estrictas reglas de conducción del taller y de la participación de los asistentes, permitieron un foro abierto, honesto, objetivo e individual (más que organizacional). Los resultados del taller presentados en este documento reflejan los puntos de vista y opiniones de los participantes.

La visión del taller fue crear los principios de una guía global que cumpliría lo siguiente:

- Servir como base para mejorar las interconexiones y los atributos de intercambiabilidad de las bases de datos en todo el mundo.
- Incrementar la credibilidad de los datos existentes de ACV, generar más datos y mejorar la accesibilidad a los datos, en general.
- Complementar otras iniciativas relacionadas con datos a nivel nacional o regional, particularmente aquellas de países en vías de desarrollo o donde se hayan desarrollado previamente guías normativas.

Enfoque

Para asegurar la validez de estos principios de una guía global, los participantes del taller fueron seleccionados por su especialización y experiencia técnica, así como también por su representatividad a nivel geográfico y su ubicación sectorial dentro de la "cadena de suministro de datos". La composición final de participantes incluyó por un lado, proveedores de datos y de estudios (básicamente consultores y asociaciones industriales) y del otro, usuarios de datos y bases de datos, incluyendo a organizaciones intergubernamentales, gobiernos, industrias, organizaciones no gubernamentales (ONGs) y académicos. Se hizo énfasis en el desarrollo y acceso a conjuntos de datos al interior de las bases de datos, dado que ya existe un conjunto de estándares de la Organización Internacional para la Estandarización (ISO) sobre la utilización de la metodología y la conducción de ACV.

Los participantes fueron organizados en seis líneas temáticas, definidas en base a las respuestas de las 'partes interesadas e involucradas' *[en ingles: stakeholders]* identificadas a lo largo de ocho consultas llevadas a cabo en todo el mundo durante los 18 meses anteriores al taller. Se prepararon artículos temáticos para cada área y la información previamente publicada fue extraída y colocada en una base de datos para la preparación de dichos artículos y para su consulta durante el taller. Los tópicos y objetivos de los grupos de trabajo incluyeron lo siguiente:

- Desarrollo de datos por proceso unitario: definición de un enfoque y mecanismo de recolección de datos que resulte en conjuntos de datos por proceso unitario, con los atributos de calidad deseada y de documentación adecuada; especificación de los requerimientos para la modelación de datos necesaria para transformar en forma precisa 'datos en bruto', en conjuntos de datos por proceso unitario; y colaboración con el grupo de revisión y documentación, a fin de abordar los asuntos asociados a la verificación y transparencia.

- Desarrollo de datos de procesos agregados: definición y validación de procedimientos y requerimientos para combinar datos de proceso unitario en conjuntos de datos de multiprocesos; especificación de los requerimientos de información adicional que debe ser proporcionada con tales conjuntos de datos a los usuarios, con el objetivo de poder determinar la idoneidad de los datos y colaborar con el grupo de revisión y documentación para abordar los asuntos de verificación y transparencia.

- Revisión de datos y documentación: análisis detallado de requerimientos y procedimientos para la revisión de conjuntos de datos, antes de su integración en las bases de datos, roles de gestión general y responsabilidades de los administradores de bases de datos, y descripción de la documentación necesaria de los datos primarios y características complementarias (meta datos). Este último punto debe ser realizado en conjunto con los grupos de trabajo sobre el desarrollo de conjunto de datos por proceso unitario y procesos agregados.

- Enfoques adaptativos de inventario de ciclos de vida (ICV): incluye el tema de demanda de datos, los avances en las interrogantes acerca de los

ICVs y su relación con metodologías no convencionales, tales como técnicas basadas en matrices insumo-producto, el ICV dinámico, el ICV espacialmente explícito y métodos híbridos.

- Integración y fertilización transversal: identificación de ideas transversales y promoción del pensamiento creativo a través de los grupos establecidos, especialmente con respecto a las prácticas actuales.

- Gestión futura del conocimiento: anticipación de cómo el Web 2.0 y otras técnicas emergentes de gestión de la información y del conocimiento podrían ser utilizadas para producir de forma más eficiente y con mayor calidad, un mayor número de conjuntos de datos de ICV, y además sobre cómo éstos conjuntos de datos se integran a bases de datos y a otros mecanismos de distribución. Estas técnicas deberán respetar la calidad y demás requisitos de los conjuntos de datos proporcionados convencionalmente.

Todas estas discusiones se mantuvieron principalmente bajo un enfoque del usuario con respecto a sus necesidades de datos y asegurando la credibilidad de los datos. Se hicieron esfuerzos para definir los usuarios dentro de varias organizaciones, con el propósito de adaptar estos principios de guía apropiadamente.

Resumen de Resultados

La siguiente parte proporciona una visión general de alto nivel de los resultados del taller. Este resumen de resultados puede únicamente capturar una pequeña parte de la exhaustiva discusión y cuidadosa deliberación que ocurrió sobre cada línea temática. Asimismo, las opiniones diferentes, en la medida que hayan sido objetivamente defendibles, fueron incorporadas al documento de varias maneras; sin embargo, debido a las restricciones de espacio, este resumen se basa únicamente en recomendaciones consensuadas.

Hablando el Mismo Idioma

Además de proporcionar unos principios guía de aspectos técnicos y operacionales sobre conjuntos de datos y bases de datos, se identificó que las diferencias en el uso de la terminología persisten y que hay inconsistencias en las definiciones de principios tales como la completitud, intercambiabilidad y transparencia. Parte de esta situación es causada por la forma en que evolucionó el ACV en diversas regiones y culturas, también por diferencias de idioma y en parte por la ambigüedad de las definiciones previamente existentes. Así, uno de los ejercicios iniciales fue desarrollar un glosario de terminología y un diccionario de principios para proporcionar a los participantes una base de referencia consistente. Aunque el objetivo del glosario no era servir de referencia general, éste puede ser usado externamente de manera amplia. En lo posible, las definiciones fueron basadas en los estándares ISO existentes.

Práctica Actual

Se ha desaprovechado mucho tiempo y esfuerzo en evaluar el estado actual de la práctica en cuanto al desarrollo de conjuntos de datos, su incorporación en bases de datos y la gestión de dichas bases de datos. Desde un punto de vista operativo, el reconocimiento de que el público objetivo del documento son los administradores de base de datos (o equipos de gestión de bases de datos) fue de utilidad para posicionarlos como actores centrales en la cadena de suministro de datos. Esto no quiere decir que otros actores como los proveedores de datos, los encargados de estudios, los revisores y los usuarios finales no se beneficiarán de estos principios de una guía global, sino al contrario. Los otros actores también encontrarán recomendaciones útiles en el documento.

Proporcionar conjuntos de datos de alta calidad a nivel de proceso unitario, comienza con un aprovisionamiento de datos muy específicos y un plan de recolección de datos creado con un resultado final en mente, lo que dará lugar a conjuntos de datos consistentes, completos e intercambiables. Un conjunto de datos es una colección de datos de entrada y de salida que se relacionan con el mismo proceso de referencia; el proceso puede ser un proceso unitario o un proceso agregado.

De acuerdo al plan, primero se recolectan los datos en bruto; luego se crea el conjunto de datos por proceso unitario definiendo relaciones matemáticas específicas entre los datos en bruto y los diferentes flujos asociados al conjunto de datos y un flujo de referencia definido. A los desarrolladores de datos se les proporciona una guía para la identificación y selección de datos en bruto y para la definición de las relaciones apropiadas, así como información de apoyo que debe ser incluida para describir tanto las reglas de decisión así como la naturaleza de las relaciones. En algunos conjuntos de datos por proceso unitario, estas relaciones se definen en base a parámetros para poder realizar cambios internos al conjunto de datos mientras esté resida en una base de datos.

Hay buenas razones para suministrar conjuntos de datos a nivel de proceso unitario. Primero, al hacerlo se provee de máxima transparencia, permitiendo a los usuarios de la base de datos entender que conjuntos de datos se están utilizando en el ICV de un flujo de referencia dado, y cómo estos procesos unitarios se vinculan entre sí. En segundo lugar, el suministro de conjuntos de datos a nivel de proceso unitario permite una flexibilidad y adaptabilidad de la base de datos en el sentido de que los procesos unitarios específicos en un ICV pueden luego ser adaptados o reemplazados para reflejar mejor la situación a ser evaluada. En tercer lugar, el suministro de conjuntos de datos a nivel de proceso unitario puede mejorar la interpretación de los estudios del ciclo de vida. La alta resolución de las evaluaciones basadas en procesos unitarios permite que el usuario pueda identificar los procesos unitarios claves por medio de un análisis de sensibilidad variando metodológicas y otros supuestos así como los parámetros, las entradas y las salidas. Aunque estas ventajas de proveer datos a nivel de proceso unitario promueven su utilización, no se debe descuidar la documentación y la revisión, que siguen siendo igual de importantes.

También hay buenas razones para consolidar conjuntos de datos. En primer lugar, en varios sistemas de software de ACV y en herramientas simplificadas, con el objetivo de dar respuesta a preguntas típicamente tratadas por un ACV, se considera conveniente trabajar con conjuntos de datos de procesos agregados ("de la cuna a la puerta", "de la cuna a la tumba") para reducir el tiempo de cálculo y el tamaño de la memoria requerida para almacenar los datos. Además, desde una perspectiva de usuario, puede ser beneficioso trabajar con conjuntos de datos de procesos agregados o de procesos unitarios pre-conectados, si el usuario no tiene conocimientos técnicos o de ingeniería para modelar una cadena de proceso compleja. Finalmente, la agregación de conjuntos de datos puede requerirse por razones de confidencialidad. La confidencialidad se puede asegurar a través de diferentes niveles de agregación (por ejemplo: estableciendo un promedio industrial, agregando algunos conjuntos de datos seleccionados por proceso unitario a lo largo de la cadena de suministro, o agregando conjuntos de datos por proceso unitario con entradas seleccionadas desde la cuna). Para los casos anteriormente presentados, un conjunto de datos agregado y revisado con una documentación completa puede ser una opción apropiada.

Por primera vez, estos principios de una guía global muestran las diversas posibilidades de agregación de una manera gráfica y evidente. Por otro lado se recomiendan verificaciones independientes a) para el conjunto de datos por proceso unitario y b) para el modelo del sistema de producto usado para generar los conjuntos de datos de procesos agregados.

La documentación de conjuntos de datos de procesos agregados es muy importante. Se recomienda de manera especial que se proporcione información suficiente y que tal información sea tan transparente como sea posible. Es preferible contar con conjuntos de datos por proceso unitario usados en el sistema del producto a tener solo los conjuntos de datos de procesos agregados. De haber una razón para no proporcionar la información en el nivel del proceso unitario, se recomienda fuertemente que otro tipo de información esté incluida en el conjunto de datos de proceso agregado, por ejemplo, información acerca de los determinantes generales de los impactos ambientales, de las fuentes de datos usadas, de los supuestos, y de los números operacionales del proceso clave.

La documentación y la revisión de los datos son elementos claves de los principios de una guía global. Los administradores y operadores de bases de datos son el principal publico de estos principios, ellos tienen el rol y la responsabilidad de decidir no sólo lo que deben incluir los conjuntos de datos sino también la información adicional requerida, recomendada, o considerada como necesaria para los fines de validación y revisión antes de que los datos sean almacenados en una base de datos.

Con el objetivo de cumplir con su rol, se recomienda fuertemente que el equipo de gestión de la base de datos establezca un protocolo escrito. Debido a la necesidad adicional de que los conjuntos de datos sean descripciones exactas de la realidad y que cumplan con los requisitos de la base de datos en la que se encuentran, los procesos de validación y revisión se consideran esenciales. El documento de principios de una guía global describe las diferentes formas bajo las cuales debería ocurrir la validación -como un proceso o mecanismo interno de verificación de la calidad- y la revisión -como un procedimiento más formal y frecuentemente externo. Antes de que un conjunto de datos se incluya en una base de datos de ICV, los principios de una guía global particularmente recomiendan que este conjunto de datos pase por un proceso de validación definido, para asegurar de que cumple efectivamente con el protocolo de la base de datos.

Una base de datos de ICV es una colección organizada de conjuntos de datos de ICV que cumple con el sistema de criterios establecidos por los estándares ISO 14040 y 14044, y que incluyen: una metodología consistente, validación o revisión, un formato intercambiable, documentación y nomenclatura y que permiten la interconexión de conjuntos de datos individuales. Las bases de datos de ICV almacenan conjuntos de datos de ICV permitiendo su creación, adición, mantenimiento, y búsqueda. Las bases de datos de ICV son manejadas por un equipo de gestión responsable que permite la identificación y trazabilidad de las responsabilidades en lo referente a la creación de base de datos, su contenido, mantenimiento y actualización.

En cambio, una biblioteca de conjuntos de datos de ICV contiene conjuntos de datos que no cumplen totalmente los criterios antes mencionados y por tanto deben tomarse con precaución si se utilizan en modelos de ciclo de vida. Si una base de datos de ICV cumple con los criterios anteriores, pero es limitada con respecto a las categorías de impacto cubiertas (ejemplo: si cubre sólo información para el cálculo de la huella de carbono) o si tiene un foco específico para ciertas aplicaciones o esquemas, se recomienda alertar al usuario acerca de esta limitación en la documentación y resaltarla como inconsistente con los principios de inclusión de los conjuntos de datos ICV.

Más Allá de las Prácticas Actuales

Algunos participantes del taller identificaron una necesidad de datos adicionales y de gestión de datos, para permitir que las bases de datos de ICV proporcionen respuestas más exhaustivas y respondan a preguntas más amplias, tales como modelos diferenciados espaciales, desarrollos en el tiempo y temas relacionados con impactos sociales y económicos. Otro aspecto que fue tratado es la posibilidad de completar los vacíos de datos con datos estimados provenientes de enfoques no basados en procesos.

Los participantes del taller analizaron las diversas fuentes de datos adicionales, tales como datos geoespaciales, datos de matrices insumo-producto de cuentas económicas nacionales ambientalmente extendidas y de las cuentas ambientales, y datos sobre indicadores sociales y sobre costos. En general, se encontró que para ciertos propósitos, si la especificidad tecnológica y las diferencias metodológicas se toman en cuenta y se documentan exhaustivamente, todas estas fuentes de datos podrían ser utilizadas complementariamente a los datos en bruto existentes en el desarrollo de conjuntos de datos por proceso unitario.

Se espera que las tendencias actuales en las tecnologías de la información influyan en las expectativas de los usuarios con respecto a los datos, la funcionalidad de los programas informáticos y a su interoperabilidad, de maneras que alterarán el alcance de todo lo qué se puede hacer con los datos de ICV. Es importante anticipar estas tendencias a la par de los determinantes del mercado con el objetivo de estar mejor preparado en cuanto al manejo correcto del desarrollo de información de ciclo de vida a la vez que se mantiene su calidad. El potencial creciente de 'movilidad' de los datos permitirá que los datos de varias fuentes puedan integrarse con mayor facilidad en bases de datos de ICV y consecuentemente insertarse en una amplia gama de nuevas aplicaciones. Potencialmente, tales mejoras pueden traer un progreso significativo hacia el consumo y producción sostenibles.

Las nuevas formas de acceso a la información en las bases de datos de ICV no cambian la manera en que se generan o almacenan los datos, pero sí el modo cómo los usuarios recuperan los datos. Sin representar aún un cambio radical del *status quo*, la aparición de nuevas tecnologías en las aplicaciones de bases de datos existentes está ya ocurriendo y continuará en el futuro cercano. A largo plazo, las tendencias actuales en las tecnologías de la información pueden llevar a nuevas corrientes en la gestión de bases de datos que pueden ser radicalmente distintas a la forma en que las vemos actualmente.

Se ha identificado como elementos prioritarios de una hoja de ruta, una coordinación global entre desarrolladores de conjuntos de datos de ICV y de administradores de bases de datos, así como el desarrollo de sus capacidades y una búsqueda intensa de datos –minería de datos-para avanzar hacia un mundo con bases de datos interconectadas y una accesibilidad total a datos confiables. La construcción de capacidades es particularmente relevante para las economías emergentes y los países en desarrollo donde las bases de datos de ACV tienen todavía que ser desarrolladas. Por esta razón, el propósito es convertir este documento de principios de una guía global en un material de capacitación. Fortalecer las redes de "ciclo de vida" existentes a nivel nacional y regional, así como desarrollar nuevas, es asimismo muy importante.

Sumário Executivo

Princípios de Guia Global para Bases de Dados para Avaliação do Ciclo de Vida

Na medida em que os recursos, manufatura e montagem, uso e descarte final de produtos e serviços tornou-se geograficamente mais diversa, tornou-se mais aguda a necessidade dos usuários da ACV de obtenção de dados que meçam mais precisa e consistentemente o consumo de recursos e os aspectos ambientais daquelas atividades. A disponibilização de uma base científica correta para o gerenciamento do produto nos negócios e na indústria e para políticas governamentais baseadas no ciclo de vida, em última análise contribui para o avanço para a sustentabilidade de produtos e das atividades econômicas da sociedade. Durante as duas últimas décadas, bases de dados foram desenvolvidas, mantidas e atualizadas por diferentes provedores gerais de bases de dados, por acadêmicos e pesquisadores, por provedores de bases de dados setoriais industrias e por grupos internos das indústrias. A base fundamental para o desenvolvimento de um guia global é a crença de que existe concordância sobre práticas recomendadas para coleta de dados, modelagem, agregação e inserção em bases de dados para uma larga porcentagem de aspectos a serem enviados. Assim, a oficina da qual resultou este guia global focou na obtenção de consenso nos aspectos para os quais não havia acordo anterior.

Contexto

No início de fevereiro de 2011, reuniram-se em Shonan Village, sudeste de Tóquio, Japão quarenta e oito participantes de 23 países para a oficina sobre Princípios de Guia Global para Bases de Dados para Avaliação do Ciclo de Vida, uma oficina Pellston (informalmente conhecida como a "Oficina Shonan de Princípios de Guia") para desenvolver princípios para a criação, gerenciamento e disseminação de conjuntos de dados com a finalidade de apoio a avaliações de ciclo de vida (ACVs) de produtos e serviços produzidos globalmente. O formato Pellstonk estabelecido pela Society of Environmental Toxicology and Chemistry (SETA) nos 1970s e usado desde então em cerca de 50 oficinas ao redor do mundo, busca um modelo de consenso entre um grupo diversificado de especialistas. Regras básicas estritas na condução da oficina e a atuação dos participantes conduziu para um fórum aberto, honesto, objetivo e individual (mais do que institucional). Os resultados da oficina apresentados neste relatório refletem apenas os pontos de vista dos participantes.

A visão para a oficina foi a de criar um guia que pudesse atingir o seguinte:

- servir de base para promover a intercambialidade e as interligações de bases de dados mundiais;
- aumentar a credibilidade dos dados de ACV existentes, gerar mais dados e aumentar a acessibilidade geral aos dados;
- complementar outras iniciativas relacionadas a dados, em nível nacional ou regional, particularmente aquelas em países em desenvolvimento e onde tenham sido desenvolvidas mais guias perspectivos.

Abordagem

Para garantir a validade deste guia os participantes da oficina foram selecionados por sua competência técnica, bem como por sua representação geográfica e por sua perspectiva na "cadeia de suprimento de dados". O conjunto final dos participantes consistiu de um balanço de provedores de dados e de estudos (principalmente consultores e associações industriais) além de usuários de dados e de bases de dados, incluindo organizações intergovernamentais (OIGs), governo, indústria, organizações não governamentais (ONGs) e academia. Aqui, a ênfase foi no desenvolvimento e acesso a conjuntos de dados dentro de bases de dados, uma vez que já existe um conjunto de normas da Organização Internacional para Normalização (ISO) sobre metodologia e execução de ACVs.

Os participantes foram organizados em seis áreas temáticas com base nas respostas a uma série de oito compromissos de partes interessadas conduzido em torno do mundo durante os 18 meses anteriores. Foram preparados documentos com questões para cada área e a informação previamente publicada foi colocada em uma base de dados para uso no preparo destes documentos e para consulta durante a oficina. Os tópicos para cada grupo, além dos objetivos de cada um incluem o seguinte:

- Desenvolvimento de dados de processos elementar: definir um modelo e um mecanismo de coleta de dados que resulte em conjuntos de dados de processo elementar com os atributos de qualidade desejados e adequada documentação, especificando os requisitos de modelagem de dados para transformar com precisão os dados brutos em bases de dados de inventário do ciclo de vida (ICV) e colaborar com o grupo de revisão e documentação para atingir as questões de verificação e de transparência.
- Desenvolvimento de dados de processos agregados: definir e validar procedimentos e requisitos para a combinação de dados de processo elementar em bases de dados de multi-processo, especificando os requisitos para informação adicional a ser fornecida, para os usuários, com tais conjuntos de dados para permitir a determinação de sua ade quação e colaborar com o grupo de revisão e documentação para atingir as questões de verificação e de transparência.
- Revisão de dados e documentação: prover análise detalhada e requisitos e procedimentos para a revisão dos conjuntos de dados antes de sua aceitação pelas bases de dados, regras de gerenciamento global e descrição, junto com os grupos de trabalho de desenvolvimento de conjuntos de dados, sobre as características da documentação necessária para os dados primários e suplementares (metadados).
- Modelos de ACV adaptativas: estabelecer aspectos e demandas de dados sobre questões de ACV acessíveis por metodologias não-convencionais , tais como técnicas ambientalmente estendidas baseadas em tabelas de entradas-saídas, ACV dinâmica-temporal, ACV explícita espacialmente e métodos híbridos.
- Integração de fertilização cruzada: identificar ideias interceptantes e promover reflexões criativas entre os grupos, especialmente com relação às práticas correntes.
- Gestão do conhecimento futuro: antecipar como a Web 2.0 e outras informações emergentes e técnicas de gestão do conhecimento poderiam ser usadas para produzir conjuntos de dados de ICV mais eficientes e de maior qualidade, bem como tais conjuntos de dados se ligam às bases de dados bem como aos ou-

tros mecanismos de distribuição. Tais técnicas deverão atender aos requisitos de qualidade e outros requisitos existentes em conjuntos de dados mais convencionais.

Todas estas discussões mantiveram uma clara perspectiva do usuário com vistas às suas necessidades de dados e a garantia da credibilidade dos dados. Foram feitos esforços para definir usuários dentro de várias organizações para efeito personalização apropriada das diretrizes.

Resumo dos resultados

A seção que se segue fornece uma visão global dos resultados da oficina. Este resumo dos resultados apenas começa a capturar a extensão da discussão e da cuidadosa deliberação tomada em cada tópico. Além disso, pontos de vista alternativos foram objetivamente suportáveis e incorporados no documento em varias formas; porém, devido a restrições de espaço, este artigo se baseia apenas nas recomendações consensuais.

Falando o mesmo idioma

Além de fornecer diretrizes técnicas e operacionais de conjuntos de dados e de bases de dados, nós descobrimos que existem diferenças na terminologia usada e inconsistências nas definições de princípios, tais como completeza, intercambialidade e transparência. Parte desta situação é causada pela evolução da ACV em diferentes regiões e culturas, parte pelo idioma e parte pela ambiguidade nas definições existentes. Assim, um dos exercícios iniciais da oficina consistiu em desenvolver um glossário de terminologia e um dicionário de princípios para fornecer uma base de referencia consistente para os participantes. Embora sem a intenção de ser um referencia geral, o glossário pode encontrar uso externamente. Quando possível, as definições foram baseadas na linguagem das normas ISO existentes.

Prática corrente

Foram dedicados muito tempo e esforços na busca do estado da prática atual relativamente ao desenvolvimento de conjuntos de dados, à sua incorporação em bases de dados e ao gerenciamento dessas bases de dados. Do ponto de vista operacional, o reconhecimento de que o público alvo do documento são os gestores de bases de dados (equipes de gerenciamento de bases de dados) serve para posiciona-los como atores centrais na cadeia de suprimento de dados. Isto não significa dizer que outros atores não se beneficiarão deste guia global. Longe disso: fornecedores de dados, comissionadores, revisores e usuários finais vão encontrar recomendações e sugestões úteis no documento.

A provisão de conjuntos de dados de alta qualidade em nível de processo elementar começa com a identificação de fontes de dados e um plano de coleta de dados criado foco no resultado final, o que resultará em conjuntos de dados consistentes, completos e intercambiáveis. Um conjunto de dados é uma coletânea de dados de entrada e de saída, os quais estão relacionados ao mesmo processo de referência; o processo pode ser um processo elementar ou um processo agregado.

Uma vez coletados os dados brutos de acordo com o plano, o conjunto de dados do processo elementar é criado pela definição de relações matemáticas específicas entre os dados brutos os vários fluxos associados com o conjunto de dados e um fluxo de referência definido. Os desenvolvedores de dados recebem diretrizes para a identificação e seleção dos dados brutos e para a definição das relações apropriadas, bem como sobre a informação de suporte a ser incluída para descrever as regras de decisão e a natureza das relações. Em alguns conjuntos de dados de processo elementar estas relações são definidas para metricamente de forma que possam ser feitas mudanças internas do conjunto de dados, quando ele estiver dentro da base de dados.

Existem boas razões para fornecer conjuntos de dados em nível de processo elementar. Primeiro, este procedimento fornece transparência máxima, permitindo aos usuários da base de dados o entendimento quais são usados no ICV de um dado fluxo de referencia e como estes processos elementares estão interligados. Segundo, o fornecimento de conjuntos de dados em nível de processo elementar torna a base de dados flexível e adaptável no sentido em que processos elementares específicos em um ICV possam ser adaptados ou substituídos para refletir melhor a situação a ser avaliada. Terceiro, o fornecimento de dados em nível de processo elementar pode aprimorar os estudos de ciclo de vida pois a alta resolução de avaliações baseadas em processo elementar permite ao usuário a identificação dos

processos elementares chave por meio de análise de sensitividade por variação metodológica e outras hipóteses, bem como parâmetros, entradas e saídas. Embora estas vantagens do fornecimento de dados do processo elementar indiquem a sua preferência na condução de uma ACV, elas não implicam em que boa documentação e revisão sejam desnecessárias.

Existem também boas razões para agregar conjuntos de dados. Antes de tudo, é considerado conveniente trabalhar com conjuntos de dados de processos agregados (berço-ao-portão, berço-ao-túmulo) em vários sistemas de software de ACV e em ferramentas simplificadas para reduzir o tempo de cálculo e o tamanhão da memória, quando respondendo perguntas tipicamente endereçadas pela ACV. Além disso, da perspectiva do usuário, pode ser benéfico trabalhar com conjuntos de dados de processo elementar agregados ou pré-conectados se o usuário não conhecimento técnico ou de engenharia para modelar uma cadeia de processo complexa. Finalmente, a agregação dos conjuntos de dados pode requerer razões de confidencialidade. A confidencialidade pode ser assegurada por meio de diferentes níveis de agregação (por exemplo, pelo estabelecimento de uma média da indústrias, pela agregação de alguns conjuntos de dados de processos elementares selecionados ao longo da cadeia de suprimento, ou pela agregação de conjuntos de dados de processo elementar com entradas selecionadas seguidas até o berço). Consistentemente com os critérios apresentados acima, um conjunto de dados agregado e revisado, com documentação abrangente, pode ser um escolha apropriada.

Pela primeira vez, estes princípios de guias globais mostram as várias possibilidades de agregação de uma forma gráfica e auto-explicativa. Recomendamos que sejam conduzidas verificações independentes do conjunto do dados de processo elementar e do modelo do sistema de produto usado para gerar os conjuntos de dados de processo agregado.

A documentação dos conjuntos de dados de processo agregado é muito importante. Recomendamos firmemente que seja fornecida informação suficiente e que tal informação seja tão transparente quanto possível. É preferível fornecer os conjuntos de dados de processo elementar usado no sistema de produto de um conjunto de dados de processo agregado. Quando não existe base suficiente para fornecer a informação no nível de processo elementar, recomendamos firmemente que outra informação seja incluída no conjunto de dados de processo agregado, como por exemplo, informação sobre elementos chave dos impactos ambientais globais, fontes de dados usadas, hipóteses e valores chave do processo operacional.

A documentação dos dados e a revisão são elementos chave dos princípios de guia global. O público alvo primário do princípios de guia global são os gestores e operadores de bases de dados que têm o papel e a responsabilidade de decidir, não apenas o que os conjuntos de dados em si devem incluir, mas também que informação adicional é requerida e o que seria considerado recomendável ou necessário em termos de validação e revisão antes dos dados serem armazenados na base de dados. Com o objetivo de executar estas funções, recomendamos firmemente que a equipe de gerenciamento da base de dados faça um protocolo escrito. Adicionalmente, pelo fato dos conjuntos de dados terem que ser

um modelo preciso da realidade e terem que atender os requisitos da base de dados na qual serão armazenados, a validação e a revisão são consideradas críticas. O documento de guias globais descreve varias formas pelas quais a validação – como um processo ou mecanismo interno de "verificação de qualidade" – e a revisão – como um procedimento mais formal e muitas vezes externos – podem ser conduzidas. Em particular este guia global recomenda que, antes do conjunto de dados seja incluído em uma base de dados de ICV, ele deva ser submetido a um processo de validação definido para assegurar que ele atenda o protocolo da base de dados.

Uma base de dados de ICV é uma coletânea organizada de conjuntos de dados de ICV coerentes com as ISO 14040 e 14044 que atende um conjunto de critérios, incluindo metodologia consistente, validação ou revisão, formato intercambiável, documentação e nomenclatura e que possibilita a interconexão de conjuntos de dados individuais. As bases de dados de ICV armazenam conjuntos de dados de ICV, permitindo sua criação, adição, manutenção e pesquisa. As bases de dados de ICV são gerenciadas por uma equipe de gerenciamento responsável, a qual possibilita identificar e rastrear as responsabilidades sobre a criação da base de dados, seu conteúdo, manutenção e atualização.

Em contraste, uma biblioteca de conjuntos de dados contem conjuntos de dados que não atendem suficientemente os critérios acima e deve-se tomar cuidado quando do seu uso em um modelo de ciclo de vida. Se os aspectos acima se aplicam mas a base de dados de ICV é limitada em relação às categorias de impacto cobertas (por exemplo: ela cobre apenas informação sobre a pegada de carbono) ou tem foco específico para certas aplicações ou esquemas, a recomendação é ressaltar claramente essa limitação na documentação como inconsistente com a natureza inclusiva dos conjuntos de dados de ICV.

Movendo além da Prática Corrente

Alguns participantes da oficina identificaram a necessidade de dados adicionais e de gerenciamento de dados para possibilitar que bases de dados de ACV forneçam respostas mais abrangentes e respondam questões mais abrangentes tais como modelos espacialmente diferenciados, desenvolvimentos ao longo do tempo e questões relacionadas a impactos sociais e econômicos. Outro aspecto apontado foi o preenchimento de falhas de dados com estimativas de dados de modelos não baseados em processo.

Os participantes da oficina analisaram as diferentes fontes adicionais de dados tais como dados geoespaciais, dados de tabelas de entradas e saídas econômicas nacionais e contabilidade ambiental, dados sobre indicadores sociais e dados sobre custos. De forma geral eles concluíram que todas estas fontes de dados podem ser usadas de forma complementar aos dados brutos existentes no desenvolvimento de conjuntos de dados de processo elementar com os mesmos objetivos, desde que as diferenças tecnológicas e metodológicas forem integralmente levadas em consideração e documentadas.

Espera-se que tendências correntes em tecnologia da informação moldem as expectativas dos usuários em relação aos dados, à funcionalidade dos softwares e à interoperacionalidade nas formas que irão alterar o escopo do que pode ser feito com dados de ACV. É importante antecipar estas tendências junto com os condutores do mercado afim de estar mais bem preparado para gerenciar apropriadamente o desenvolvimento da informação sobre ciclo de vida com a necessidade de manter a qualidade. O potencial aumento da mobilidade dos dados poderia possibilitar que dados de varias fontes possam encontrar mais facilmente seus caminhos nas bases de dados de ACV e dai em um largo espectro de novas aplicações. Tais melhorias podem potencialmente trazer progresso significativo na direção do consumo e produção sustentáveis.

Existem novos caminhos para acessar a informação nas bases de dados de ACV, os quais não modificam a forma como os dados são gerados ou armazenados, mas modificam a forma como os usuários recuperam os dados. Ainda que sem diferença radical do status quo, a introdução de novas tecnologias nas aplicações das b ases de dados existentes está ocorrendo atualmente e continuará ocorrendo no futuro próximo. A longo prazo, tendências correntes na tecnologia da informação pode levar a avenidas para o gerenciamento de bases de dados que são radicalmente diferentes da forma que temos hoje.

Uma coordenação global entre os desenvolvedores de conjuntos de dados e gerenciadores de bases de dados de ACV tem sido identificada, em conjunto com capacidade de construção e garimpagem de dados, como componentes de roteiros prioritários para caminha na direção de um mundo com bases de dados interligadas e acessibilidade global a dados confiáveis. A capacidade de construção é particularmente relevante em economias emergentes e países em desenvolvimento, onde as bases de dados ainda não foram estabelecidas. Portanto, é uma meta converter este documento guia em material de treinamento. O fortalecimento das existentes e o desenvolvimento de novas redes regionais e nacionais é também importante.

执行概要
全球生命周期评价数据库指导原则

随着产品和服务在资源开采、生产、组装、使用和最终废弃过程中呈现出越来越多的地域性差异,LCA数据库用户越来越迫切地需要获得准确并规范描述这些过程中资源消耗和环境影响的数据。这些数据可以为工商业界的产品管理以及为政府部门的基于生命周期的政策提供一个健全的科学基础,并将最终有助于推动产品和社会经济活动的可持续发展。

在过去的二十多年里,不同的通用数据库提供商、学术界和研究人员、行业数据库提供者和企业内部工作组一直在开展数据库的建立、维护和更新工作。鉴于在数据收集、建模、汇总计算以及添加到数据库等环节已经在很多方面形成了一致的操作建议,本次研讨会以及编著的全球指导原则特别专注于在之前没有达成一致的方面形成共识。

用,其目的是促成不同背景的专家达成共识。遵循严格的研讨会组织原则和与会者行为准则,研讨会力图成为一个开放、诚实、客观和个人化(而非代表其组织)的论坛。因此,呈现在本报告中的研讨会结果仅代表与会者的观点。

本次研讨会及其编写的全球指导原则旨在:

- 为增强全球范围内LCA数据集和数据库的可交换性和互连性提供基础;

- 增强已有LCA数据的可信度,促进数据库的扩展,并从整体上强化数据的可得性;

- 与各个国家或地区的LCA数据库工作相互补充,尤其是在发展中国家和已经立了许多规范性指南的地区。

背景

2011年二月初在日本东京东南部的湘南国际村,48位来自23个国家的代表参加了《全球生命周期评价数据库指导原则》研讨会(非正式称为"湘南指导原则研讨会")。会议研讨了生命周期评价(LCA)数据库的创建、管理和传播原则,以支持对全球化生产的产品和服务进行LCA研究。研讨会采用了Pellston研讨会的形式,这是国际环境毒理学与化学学会(SETAC)在二十世纪70年代建立的会议形式,已被全球范围的50多个研讨会广泛使

方法

为了保证本指导原则的有效性,在挑选研讨会的与会者时,考虑了他们的技术专长、地域代表性和他们在"数据供应链"上的位置,并力图在数据提供者和数据用户之间达到平衡,前者主要是咨询机构和行业协会,后者包括政府间组织(IGOs)、政府、行业、非政府组织(NGOs)和学术界。由于国际标准化组织(ISO)已经制订了有关LCA方法学和案例研究的标准,本全球指导原则的重点是LCA数据库中数据集的开发与使用。

在研讨会之前的18个月中,在全球范围内举行了八次利益相关方会议。根据这些会议的反馈,本次研讨会的与会者被分为6个主题工作组,并在会议前分别准备了议题文件。此外,LCA数据库领域的主要文献被收集和整理为一个文献库,以便在研讨会准备和进行期间参阅。各个工作组的主题及目标如下:

- "单元过程数据开发"工作组:定义一个收集数据的方法和机制,用以产生具有所需数据质量和充分文档记录的单元过程数据集;详细说明数据建模的要求,以准确地将原始数据转化为单元过程清单数据集;与数据审核和记录工作组合作处理有关数据审核与透明性的问题。

- "汇总过程数据开发"工作组:定义和验证将单元过程数据组合为多过程汇总数据集的步骤与要求;明确这些数据集需要提供的额外信息,以便用户决定数据集的适用性;与数据审核和记录工作组合作处理有关数据审核与透明性的问题。

- "数据审核与记录"工作组:详细分析以下的步骤与要求,包括数据集进入数据库之前的审核、数据库管理者的角色和职责,并与两个数据开发工作组协作,确定原始数据和补充信息(元数据)的描述方式。

- "LCA方法的演变与适应性"工作组:阐述非常规LCA方法的数据要求及其可处理的LCA问题,例如环境扩展的投入产出表方法、时间动态的LCA方法、空间定域化的LCA方法、LCA混合方法等。

- "整合与交流"工作组:辨别工作组之间交叉的想法、促进不同组之间的创新思想,特别是有关当前LCA做法的创新。

- "未来知识管理"工作组:预测Web 2.0和其他新兴的信息和知识管理技术如何用于开发更高效、更高质量、更多数量的LCI数据集,以及这些数据集如何链接到数据库和其他分发传播机制。与传统的数据集开发一样,采用这些信息技术也仍应遵循数据质量及其它要求。

所有这些讨论都试图从LCA数据用户的角度考虑他们对数据的需求,并确保数据的可信度。讨论过程中对LCA数据用户进行了划分,以使本全球指导原则更适用于各种用户的需要。

结果摘要

以下章节是对研讨会结果的总体概述,这只是对各主题讨论范围和深入思考的初略概括。对于不同的观点,在客观条件允许的情况下,已以各种方式被纳入全文中,但由于长度的限制,本执行概要仅包含取得一致性共识的建议。

使用相同的语言

本全球指导原则除了在有关数据集和数据库的技术与操作方面提供了指导，我们还发现在术语使用上存在着差异、在数据库原则上（如完整性、可交换性和透明性）存在着不一致。造成这种状况的部分原因是由于LCA在不同地区、文化和语言背景下演化发展所形成的差异，而定义本身的模糊性也是部分的原因。因此，研讨会最初的活动之一就是制定了一个术语表和一套基本原则，为与会者提供了一致的参考依据。虽然并未打算作为通用的参考依据，但术语表在研讨会之外应该也可以使用。在可能的情况下，术语定义是基于现有的ISO标准的。

目前的建议做法

在研讨会以及筹备阶段，花费了很多的时间和精力评估当前在开发数据集、纳入数据库和管理数据库中的典型做法。从操作的角度来看，本全球指导原则非常适合作为数据供应链中核心角色的数据库管理者（或数据库管理团队）使用，但这并不是说其他的人员不能从中得到益处。事实上，数据提供者、研究的委托方、审核者和最终的数据库用户都会在全球指导原则中发现有用的见解和建议。

数据集是一个过程的输入和输出数据的集合（这个过程可以是单元过程或汇总过程），这些输入输出数据都基于同一个基准流。提供高质量的、单元过程级的数据集，应该从制订有针对性的数据源和数据收集计划开始，以保证数据集的一致性、完整性和可交换性。

一旦按计划收集了原始数据，通过具体的数学计算关系，可以将原始数据转换为基于相同基准流的输入输出流数据，从而得到单元过程数据集。单元过程数据开发者可以在本全球指导原则中找到如何识别和选择原始数据、如何定义适当的数学计算关系、应该包含的支持信息（如选择的规则和数学关系属性）等内容。在一些单元过程数据集中，数学计算关系可以被定义为参数化形式，使得数据集可以从内部被调整改变。

提供单元过程水平的数据集很有必要。首先，这样做可以提供最大限度的透明度，允许数据库的用户掌握在一个LCI和给定的基准流中，究竟使用了哪些单元过程以及这些过程是如何连结在一起的。其次，这样做使得数据库更有灵活性和适应性，因为一个LCI中的某些单元过程可以被修改或替换，以便更好地反映待评价的系统。第三，提供单元过程数据集可以改进生命周期解释，因为通过对单元过程的详尽评价，可以允许用户对方法和假设进行敏感性检查，以及对参数、输入和输出数据进行敏感度分析，从而确定关键单元过程。当然，在LCA研究中提供的单元过程数据集还需要充分的文档记录和仔细的数据审核。

提供汇总数据集也有很好的理由。首先，在典型LCA案例研究中采用汇总过程数据集（从摇篮到大门，或从摇篮到坟墓）更方便，在各种LCA软件系统和简化的工具中都可以减少计算时间和内存占用。此外，从用户的角度来说，如果用户不具备相关的工程和技术知识，不知道该如何模拟一个复杂的过程链时，采用汇总的或预先连结好的单元过程数据集也是非常有益的。最后，出于保密的原因也需要汇总过程数据集。保密性可以通过不同层次的汇总来实现（如，建立行业平均数据集、在供应链上选择并汇总部分单元过程数据集、或选择并汇总部分输入的上游数据）。为与数据库的基本原则保持一致，一个审核过的汇总过程应该有完整的文档记录。

本指导原则第一次以一种图形化的、直观的方式显示了各种汇总的可能性。我们建议对用于产生汇总过程数据集的单元过程数据集和产品系统模型进行独立的审核。

汇总过程的文档记录是极其重要的。我们强烈建议应该提供足够的信息并且这些信息应该尽可能的透明。一个汇总过程数据集最好能提供在其产品系统中使用的单元过程数据集。当有足够的理由不提供单元过程的信息时，我们强烈建议其他的信息应该包括在汇总过程数据集中，比如，造成总体环境影响的主要因素、使用的数据来源、假设和关键过程的操作数据。

数据文档记录和审核是本指导原则的关键组成部分。数据库管理者和经营者是本全球指导原则的主要目标读者，他们的任务是决定数据集必须包含的内容以及必要的额外信息，另外在数据集被放入数据库之前的审核和检查中，应考虑哪些建议或必要的因素。为了实现这些目标，我们强烈建议数据库管理团队发布一个书面的数据库工作指南。另外，因为数据集既需要描述实际发生的情况，又需要符合所在数据库的要求，因此数据集的检查与审核是至关重要的。本全球指导原则描述了若干检查（内部质量检查的程序和机制）和审核（更为正式的、通常是外部的检查程序）的方法，并建议在一个数据集进入LCI数据库之前，应该进行预定的检查程序以确保其满足数据库的要求。

一个LCI数据库（LCI database）是一些符合ISO14040和14044标准的LCI数据集的集合，这些数据集充分满足一系列准则，包括一致的方法学、检查和审核、可交换的格式、文档记录和命名法，并允许数据集的互连。LCI数据库存储LCI数据集，允许数据集的创建、添加、维护和搜索。LCI数据库应由一个可靠的管理团队管理，他们应有能力识别和追踪数据库的创建、内容、维护和更新。

相比之下，LCI数据集的集合（LCI dataset library）包含的数据集并不完全满足以上准则，在一个生命周期模型中使用时必须慎重。即使满足相关准则，但数据集仅包含有限的环境影响类型（例如只涵盖碳足迹信息）或仅针对某个具体的应用，建议在文档记录中明确地标记出这些局限性，作为与普通LCI数据集包容性不一致的说明。

超越当前的做法

一些研讨会的与会者指出，除基本的LCA清单数据外，还存在着多种附加的数据和数据管理需求，以便允许LCA数据库提供更全面的信息以及回答更广泛的问题，例如，空间差异化模型、跨时间的开发以及与社会和经济影响有关的问题，另外还涉及通过非基于过程（non-process–based）的方法对数据进行估计，以填补数据的空缺。

研讨会的与会者分析了其他的数据来源，如地理空间数据、基于国家经济投入产出表（IOT）扩展的环境信息和环境会计、社会指标数据以及成本数据。总体而言，如果充分考虑并记录了技术的特异性和方法的差异，所有这些数据来源都可以成为单元过程数据集的原始数据的补充，并应用于特定的分析目的。

当前信息技术的发展趋势有可能影响用户对于数据、软件功能和互操作性方式的期望，这将改变LCA数据的使用范围。预测这些发展趋势以及市场需求并为此进行准备是很重要的，以便在保证质量的同时更好地管理生命周期信息。数据传播潜力的增加将会允许各种来源的数据更容易地进入LCA数据库，并进入更广泛的应用领域。这种增强的潜力有可能为可持续消费与生产带来显著的推动作用。

新的访问LCA数据库中信息的方法，不用改变数据产生或存储的方式，但会改变用户重获数据的方式。虽然不会使现状发生彻底的飞跃，但新技术正在与现有的数据库应用发生融合，并将在不远的将来持续进行。从长远来看，信息技术目前的趋势可能会导致新的数据库管理途径，这与我们今天的做法是截然不同的。

Prologue

A "green economy" is one that results in increased human well-being and social equity, while significantly reducing environmental risks and ecological scarcities (UNEP 2011). Two of the United Nations Environment Programme's thematic priorities support the transition to a green economy: resource efficiency, and sustainable consumption and production. Initiatives with governments and all civil society groups to create new and revise existing public policies, and to improve application of policy tools support the themes of sustainable consumption and production.

Resource efficiency seeks to tie together efficient use of economic resources with minimization of the potential environmental impacts of resource use, including materials, energy, water, land, and emissions associated with the consumption and production of goods and services over their full life cycles. Efficient use of economic resources is addressed by attempting to produce more well-being with less resource consumption. Overall, resource efficiency enhances the means to meet human needs while respecting the ecological carrying capacity of the earth.

The working definition of sustainable consumption was adopted during the Oslo Symposium in 1994 (Norwegian Ministry of the Environment 1994):

"The use of services and related products which respond to basic needs and bring a better quality of life while minimising the use of production natural resources and toxic materials as well as emissions of waste and pollutants over the life cycle of the service or product so as not to jeopardise the needs of future generations".

Both resource efficiency and sustainable consumption and production refer to life cycle thinking as a means of expanding the traditional focus from the production site and manufacturing processes to incorporate activities over a product's entire life cycle, that is, from the extraction of resources, through the manufacture and use of the product, to the final processing of the disposed product. As expressed by Klaus Töpfer, former UNEP Executive Director, there is a strong need to inform production and consumption decisions based on life cycle thinking and assessment tools:

"Consumers are increasingly interested in the world behind the product they buy. Life cycle thinking implies that everyone in the whole chain of a product's life cycle has a responsibility and a role to play, taking into account all the relevant external effects. The impacts of all life cycle stages need to be considered comprehensively when taking informed decisions on production and consumption patterns, policies and management strategies" (De Leeuw 2005).

This statement is relevant for governments, enterprises, and citizens.

UNEP has identified the topic of green claims in the marketplace as an emerging issue. Hence, we must create a global knowledge base and build capacity worldwide for developing product sustainability information to enable institutional and individual consumers to make informed consumption choices. Today, organizations and countries must understand their sustainability performance in the form of national, corporate, and product environmental footprints. For instance, Unilever (2011) states on their website: "Understanding life cycle impacts is crucial to delivering our new target of reducing our overall environmental impacts across our value chain while doubling the size of our business".

Sustainability has been identified as an emerging megatrend. "Over the past 10 years, environmental issues have steadily encroached on businesses' capacity to create value for customers, shareholders, and other stakeholders. Globalized workforces and supply chains have created environmental pressures and attendant business liabilities. These forces are magnified by escalating public and governmental concern about climate change, industrial pollution, food safety, and natural resource depletion, among other issues. Consumers in many countries are seeking out sustainable products and services or leaning on companies to improve the sustainability of traditional ones. Governments are interceding with unprecedented levels of new regulation. Further fuelling this megatrend, thousands of companies are placing strategic bets on innovation in energy efficiency, renewable power, resource productivity, and pollution control. What this all adds up to is that managers can no longer afford to ignore sustainability as a central factor in their companies' long-term competitiveness" (Lubin and Esty 2010).

To put sustainability into practice and hence allow future generations to be able to meet their own needs, society must put in place strategies and supporting programs to encourage the following listed actions:

1) Develop greener products, services, and business models.
2) Purchase greener products and services (civil society and public purchasers).
3) Implement laws and regulations that foster the development and purchase of greener products, services, and business models.
4) Use incentives that do not create unexpected environmental impacts, for example, by solving one environmental problem while generating other, often unexpected, problems.

5) Create products that reduce impact on one hand and create value and add benefits to society by enhancing human well-being and social equity on the other hand.

These programs must encourage the use of fundamental sustainable consumption strategies: New concept development, physical optimization, optimized materials use, production techniques, and distribution systems can reduce impact during the use stage and optimize end-of-life management systems.

Many approaches to environmental protection continue to be based on end-of-pipe solutions, focused on a single medium (air, water, soil), a single stage in the product's life cycle (production, use, disposal), or a single issue (e.g., individual chemical limits). These strategies do not always lead to an overall reduction in environmental impacts.

Consequentially, one of the rapidly evolving landscapes in business and in policy-making today is being able to adapt from managing our environmental impacts by focusing on single site and/or issue, to expanding the focus to include a full understanding of the impacts of products over their entire life cycle. Many stories and advertisements exist which speak to how green a product might be. However, all products have environmental impacts. Life cycle thinking implies the understanding that materials are extracted from the earth, converted into process materials, combined with other materials to make parts, assembled into a finished product, shipped to customers who use the products and then the products are disposed of in some fashion. Along that value chain, energy is used, waste generated, other natural resources used, etc.

Life cycle thinking seeks to develop a fuller and more complete understanding of the consumption of energy and materials, and the resulting release of emissions associated with the extraction, processing, manufacturing, use and end of life management of materials and products. Without this thought paradigm, governments, businesses and civil society are often shooting in the dark (so to speak) as to what strategies, actions, policy instruments, and/or incentives are needed to direct society on the journey towards greener products and services. Without an understanding of where along a product life cycle lie the greatest opportunities for environmental impact reductions (e.g., in the use phase, or the mining activity), changes may be made which will create unexpected impacts elsewhere in the product's life cycle. That means there may be a shift of the burden to other phases in the life cycle; to other regions of the world; and to other impact cate-

gories such as from contributing to climate change by burning fossil fuels in the use phase, mostly in developed countries, to impacts on nutrient flows, increased use of pesticides, water and land use, and ultimately biodiversity loss due to intensified agriculture, often in developing countries, as described by UNEP (2009) for the case of biofuels.

Life cycle assessment (LCA) evaluates environmental performance throughout the sequence of activities executed in creating a product or performing a service. Extraction and consumption of resources (including energy), as well as releases to air, water, and soil, are quantified through all stages along the life cycle of products and services. Their potential contribution to environmental impact categories is then assessed. These categories include climate change, human and eco-toxicity, ionizing radiation, and resource base deterioration (e.g., water, non-renewable primary energy resources, land). According to the ISO 14040 series, LCA is structured in four phases (Figure 0.1).

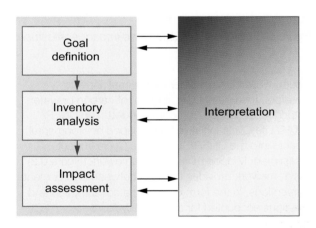

Figure 0.1: Phases of life cycle assessment (reprinted with permission from UNEP 2002)

Other life cycle approaches cover carbon and water footprints only. Carbon footprint is a measure of the direct and indirect greenhouse gas (GHG) emissions associated with all activities in the product's life cycle. Such a footprint can be calculated by performing an LCA that concentrates on GHG emissions. Water footprint is a measure of the impacts of the direct and indirect water use and consumption associated with all activities in the product's life cycle. This measure is especially relevant for water-intensive processes and at locations where water scarcity is a serious problem.

It should be emphasized that carbon footprint and water footprint consider only one environmental

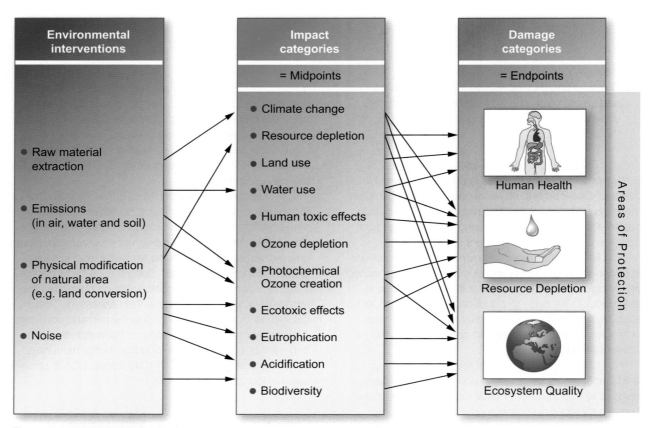

Environmental interventions	Impact categories	Damage categories

Figure 0.2: UNEP/SETAC Life Cycle Impact Assessment Midpoint-Damage Framework (based on Jolliet et al. 2004)

aspect, while LCA considers additional aspects. Therefore, the use of LCA, and not of carbon or water footprint approaches, is recommended. The UNEP/SETAC Life Cycle Initiative has grouped environmental impacts into the UNEP/SETAC Life Cycle Impact Assessment Midpoint-Damage Framework (Figure 0.2). This framework provides the links between environmental interventions, in the form of resource consumption and emissions accounted for in the life cycle inventory (LCI) analysis, and different impact categories, such as climate change, water use, and eutrophication, and final damage categories, in the form of human health, ecosystem quality, and resource depletion as areas of protection.

Considerable efforts are underway to build global knowledge and capacity for understanding, developing, and promoting more sustainable products and services. One key effort is to increase the availability of foundational data on energy, materials, land, and water consumption, and on related emissions into water, air, and soil, so that we have comprehensive information on materials and products over their life cycle. This comprehensive information is obtained by the use of LCA. As the technical basis for the practice of LCA has become more standardized and as more decisions are supported with this methodology, the demand for high-quality documented, transparent, and independently

reviewed data has increased tremendously. Applications of carbon and water footprinting also can be supported by these LCA data because LCA data include all environmental emissions and consumption.

When we talk about LCA data, the main focus is on LCI data, although characterization factors associated with life cycle impact assessment methods are often included in LCA databases. Since the early 1990s, LCA databases have proliferated in response to the growing demand for life cycle information, mostly from Northeast Asia, North America, and Western Europe.

In a global economy, however, products and services are sourced from many countries. A coordinated global effort to define and produce high-quality LCA data is required if LCA practice is to advance in the most resource-efficient manner. Further, a similar effort on data interchange is required to allow for the maximum exchange of information among LCA practitioners. Only with widespread availability of LCA information will society be able to make efficient and effective decisions on policies and design options that will allow future generations to meet their own needs and aspirations.

The life cycle management (LCM) framework for the environmental sustainability of products (Figure 0.3) describes a scheme where strategies to achieve sustainability form the basis of the overall vision, which is

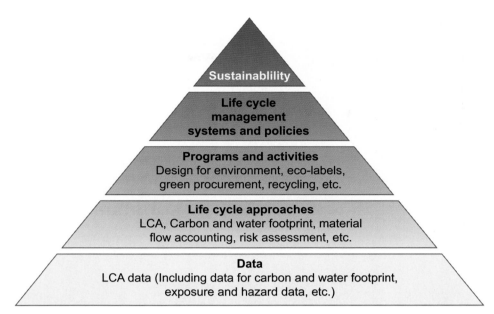

Figure 0.3: Life cycle management framework for the environmental sustainability of products

supported by LCM systems and policies. These strategies are achieved through implementation and execution of programs and activities like design for environment, eco-labels, green procurement, and recycling. Success is achieved when the vision of a green economy results in the reality of sustainable consumption and production patterns through resource efficiency. All these systems, programs, and activities are made operational by tools such as LCA and other life cycle approaches, which

need appropriate data, most easily provided by reliable databases. Access to credible information on the potential life cycle environmental impacts of products is especially crucial when we attempt to communicate the preferable environmental characteristics of a product, and hence make green claims to influence institutional and individual consumers to purchase products while considering their environmental footprints.

References

De Leeuw B. 2005. The world behind the product. J Industrial Ecol. 9(1–2):7–10.

Lubin DA, Esty D. May 2010. The sustainability imperative. Harvard Business Review, The Magazine.

Jolliet O, Müller-Wenk R, Bare J, Brent A, Goedkoop M, Heijungs R, Itsubo N, Peña C, Pennington D, Potting J, Rebitzer G, Stewart M, Udo de Haes H, Weidema B. 2004. The LCIA midpoint-damage framework of the UNEP/SETAC Life Cycle Initiative. Int J LCA. 9(6):394–404.

Norwegian Ministry of the Environment. 1994. Oslo Roundtable on Sustainable Production and Consumption. [cited 2011 Feb 1]. Available from: http://www.iisd.ca/consume/oslo004.html.

Unilever. 2011. Lifecycle assessment. [cited 2011 Feb 1]. Available from http://www.unilever.com/sustainability/environment/manufacturing/assessment/?WT.LHNAV=Lifecycle_assessment.

[UNEP] United Nations Environment Programme. 2002. Evaluation of environmental impacts in life cycle assessment. Meeting report. [cited 2011 Feb 1]. Available from: http://lcinitiative.unep.fr/default.asp?site=lcinit&page_id=F511DC47-8407-41E9-AB5D-6493413088FB.

[UNEP] United Nations Environment Programme. 2009. Towards sustainable production and use of resources: Assessing biofuels: A report of the International Resource Panel. [cited 2011 Feb 1]. Available from: http://www.unep.org/publications/contents/pub_details_search.asp?ID=4082.

[UNEP] United Nations Environment Programme. 2011. Towards a green economy: Pathways to sustainable development and poverty eradication: A synthesis for policy makers. [cited 2011 Feb 1]. Available from: http://www.unep.org/greeneconomy/GreenEconomyReport/tabid/29846/Default.aspx.

The Context for Global Guidance Principles for Life Cycle Inventories

Guido Sonnemann
Bruce Vigon
Martin Baitz
Rolf Frischknecht
Stephan Krinke
Nydia Suppen
Bo Weidema
Marc-Andree Wolf

CHAPTER

1

Guidance principles are needed to provide direction to users on selecting data that meet their needs, regardless of where an activity in a life cycle inventory (LCI) occurs. In addition, data developers and database managers need guidance on how to create datasets and operate databases, respectively, in order to provide exchangeable and fully documented datasets to users. Globally harmonized guidance will support an efficient allocation of resources, to ensure reliability and quality of data.

Since 2007, discussions about producing a manual on developing countries' LCI data for energy systems have indicated that a global guidance document would need to address a number of contentious issues about how to develop a life cycle assessment (LCA) database. Diverging comments covered both technical topics, such as goal, scope, modelling, quality, review, and documentation, as well as visionary questions like which technologies and management structure work best and should be used to govern and further develop LCA databases in the future, which was seen as a business opportunity. It became clear that guidance principles were needed in particular to support LCA database development in emerging economies and developing countries, where data developers and database managers should have a reference document on which to rely.

A process was set up under the auspices of the United Nations Environment Programme/Society of Environmental Toxicology and Chemistry (UNEP/SETAC) Life Cycle Initiative with the following vision:

- to provide global guidance on the establishment and maintenance of LCA databases, as the basis for future improved dataset consistency and interlinkages of databases worldwide;
- to facilitate additional data generation (including data specific to certain applications such as carbon and water footprint creation) and to enhance overall data accessibility;
- to increase the credibility of existing LCA data through the provision of guidance on the usability or fitness of data for various purposes; and
- to support a sound scientific basis for product stewardship in business and industry, for life cycle–based policies in governments, and ultimately, to help advance the sustainability of products.

This process will complement other ongoing initiatives. For example, developers of databases should consult this global guidance principles document in concert with development of their database protocol, to ensure consistency with more detailed directions contained in guidance documents at the regional or national

level. It is further hoped that regional and national database efforts themselves will coordinate around the global guidance in order to best support database users. It is expected that the process will contribute to setting a foundation for designing, developing, and marketing greener products, materials, and technologies (Figure 1.1).

1.1 Glossary of Terminology

The glossary of terminology in Annex 1 has been created to provide a common vocabulary for people around the world to use when they talk about LCA data and databases. The glossary uses the International Organization for Standardization (ISO) termin-ology, as far as it is available, and provides additional explanation or modification to these definitions if necessary. Overall, an "equivalency approach" is applied for bridging to the terms used in reference documents that refer to similar terms (such as "life cycle inventory", "life cycle result", "life cycle dataset" and "agregated process dataset") that however are not part of the glossary. In general, one term is being identified as "preferred" in order to have a globally accepted reference. Only a few new terms and abbreviations are added to those found in existing documents. General terms that are defined in any dictionary (such as "assumption") are not part of the glossary.

1.2 Overall Principles for Global Guidance

The following overall principles for global guidance for LCA databases were identified[1]:

- Accessibility ensures that a product, device, service, or environment is as widely available as possible.
- Accountability ensures that the responsible party understands and accepts the consequences of an action or agreed activity (used synonymously with concepts such as responsibility, answerability, and liability).
- Accuracy ensures that reported resource consumption and emissions are not consistently greater than or less than actual consumption and emissions for a defined LCI process. The overall aim is to achieve sufficient accuracy to enable users to make decisions with reasonable assurance as to the reliability of the reported information (WBCSD and WRI 2004).
- Completeness ensures that the inventory report

---

[1] Unless specifically referenced, principle definitions were created by the workshop participants or were obtained from standard dictionaries.

Figure 1.1: Setting a foundation for a life cycle–informed future

covers all product life cycle emissions and extractions within the specified boundaries (including temporal), and stating clearly any life cycle stages or significant environmental impacts that have been excluded and justify these exclusions (WBCSD and WRI 2004).

- Consistency ensures the non-contradictory use of methodologies, models, data, and assumptions to allow for meaningful comparisons of an LCI (or its component datasets) over time (derived from WBCSD and WRI 2004).
- Exchangeability and compatibility ensure that datasets from the same or different databases can be used together in LCAs or in different application contexts without loss.
- Materiality ensures that data or information supplied is relevant and significant to a user's need that is not trivial or superfluous.
- Practicality ensures that an action is achievable and does not necessitate a disproportionate amount of resources (relative to the benefit) to accomplish.
- Quality assurance ensures through a systematic process that data meet specified requirements.
- Relevance ensures that LCI data serve the decision-making needs of all identified users in terms of technological reach and detail, geographical

reach and detail, system modelling options, and environmental indicators covered (derived from WBCSD and WRI 2004).
- Reproducibility ensures that datasets are able to be developed independently from raw data for validation, review, and update purposes by fully documenting relevant data and information used in their creation. These principles are either goals or requirements to which the global guidance is expected to adhere. They are relevant for all aspects related to LCA databases being addressed throughout the document.
- Transparency ensures open, comprehensive, and understandable presentation of information (ISO 2006a, 2006b)[2].

1.3 Context for the Creation of the Global Guidance Principles

The global guidance principles derive from a definition of the audience, from the nature and conduct of the workshop, from the foundations of existing guidance, and from the concept that the principles are supportable without requiring absolute consensus. The subsections

---

[2] See Chapters 3 and 4 for additional specifics on how this principle is reflected in recommended practices.

of this topic address the audience for the guidance, the approach used in arriving at the guidance, and suggestions on implementation.

1.3.1 Audiences for the Global Guidance Principles

The primary target audience for these global guidance principles is database managers. These individuals or organizations have been identified as holding key positions in organizing and controlling the flow of information between data providers and users. As described in the following sections, database managers' actions are essential to provide users with datasets that are of suitable quality and sufficiently documented to be confidently used for an intended application. These managers also are an important link in receiving feedback from users about their experiences, and then either acting on that feedback within their management scope, or communicating to upstream providers what improvements or enhancements would increase a database user's ability to effectively access and apply LCI datasets from the database.

Within the larger group of database managers, those in emerging economies and developing countries are a particularly relevant audience. It is they who will be prime movers in setting up national-level databases where none currently exist or are only now starting up, and they can implement this guidance as a way to organize these efforts. Depending on the local arrangements, they are essential linkages with government or industrial entities that will support the efforts, either monetarily or with data.

The identification of database managers as the target audience does not mean to imply that other audiences within the data supply and use chain will not benefit from these guidance principles. While this guidance provides a range of specific benefits to other actors, one of the major ones is an understanding of their roles in the data chain and what expectations they should have from database managers regarding data development, review, and use. It is expected that those actors in a data supply role, dataset developers, will especially appreciate the clarity this guidance brings on the requirements and expectations of data submitted for assembly of data sets, particularly on the recommended associated documentation.

On the user side, the need for understanding of the use and limitations associated with data from databases is a long-standing issue for LCA. The guidance brings a new level of clarity here as well by defining and consistently applying terminology, as well as promoting certain practices in creating and communicating information about datasets and supporting a determination of fitness for purpose.

1.3.2 Workshop Development and Context

The first element of the global guidance development process was to organize and conduct an expert workshop. The workshop was built on the SETAC Pellston model[3]. This format is based on an intensive week-long workshop that brought together 48 knowledgeable individuals from 23 countries, including emerging and developed economies. These participants were experts in commissioning and performing LCAs, developing datasets, managing databases, providing LCA software, and developing guidance and policy on LCA. The results of the workshop presented in this report reflect only the views of these participants. Collectively, these individuals had balanced affiliations among business, academia, government, and nongovernmental organizations (NGOs), although each was participating on the basis of their own knowledge. Strict ground rules were agreed as a condition of participation. A 12-person steering committee was integral to the organization and participant selection, itself being constituted as a balanced body across sectors.

The primary basis for development of global guidance is the belief that agreement on recommended practices for data collection, modelling, aggregation, and insertion in databases exists for a large percentage of the aspects to be addressed. Thus, the workshop focused on integration of those aspects and getting additional consensus on aspects where prior agreement was not achieved. The individuals were assigned to one of several work groups, each of which focused on an aspect of LCA data, with the resulting product being one of the chapters in this guidance document. One work group created and assessed future scenarios in order that the LCA community might be proactive rather than reactive in responding to potential developments.

1.3.3 Developing Recommendations that Build on Existing Guidance

The starting points for identification and consideration of the body of recommended practices were the previously issued guidance documents at the national or regional level, along with supplemental information contained in various scientific publications (see Bibliography in Annex 4). The process consisted of two steps: 1) examination of the previously published guidance documentation on a particular topic (limited to those aspects on data and databases) with assessment of whether the various guidance commentaries in those documents are conflicting or not, and 2) summarizing or extracting the national or regional guidance to incorporate into this global guidance. Details or additional specifics from the

---

[3] See the Foreword by SETAC for additional description of the history and structure of SETAC Pellston workshops.

national or regional guidance may be incorporated by citation of one or more of the reference documents.

Another basis for building on existing guidance exists where there is not currently agreed practice, but the existing national or regional guidance provides a starting point for discussion. Rather than creating the global guidance only from expert discussion, the body of experts, according to the workshop process principles and rules, assign levels of support for a practice. These levels are stated by consistently applying terminology of "strongly recommended", "recommended", and "suggested or advisable", working within the consensus-building process of the workshop. Terminology such as "shall" or "should", normally associated with a standard-setting process, is avoided where possible. If such wording is used within a section of text, the reader should consider such use as equivalent to use of the term recommendations with the corresponding level of support; for example, "shall" is equivalent to "strongly recommended." For some aspects, the experts may not have been able to formulate a clear recommendation. In these cases, either no supportable single recommendation is made or various alternatives are presented with no specific recommendation.

1.3.4 Supportable, but Not Consensus Guidance

Not all of the global guidance needs to be based on an achieved consensus. Recommendations for global data for LCA and database practices are based on a consensus-building process, objectively and practically supportable evidence, and goals of promoting consistency and exchangeability. However, as long as minority views are supportable (i.e., based on facts, an underlying basis of argumentation in science, or demonstrated practical application) and are not based on opinion or commercial interests, they are included in this guidance principles document, but they are not given the prominence of more highly recommended approaches.

1.4 Data Flow Maps

Understanding data flow as well as the roles of all the actors involved, from raw data providers to LCI data users, is important because data move from raw state to and through datasets and databases.

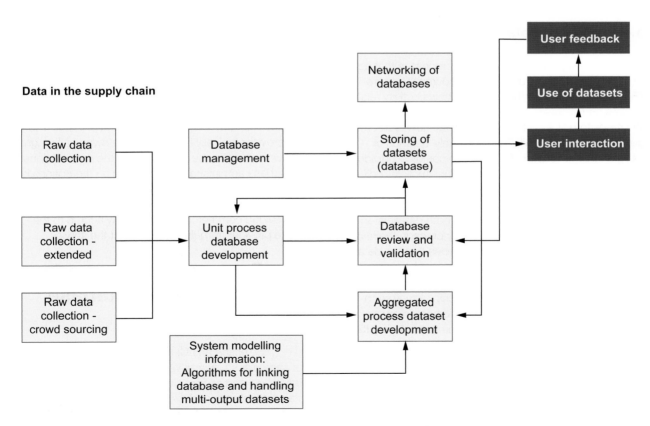

Figure 1.2: Flow of data from raw data through to LCI data user with feedback loops

**Roles of actors
in the data supply chain**

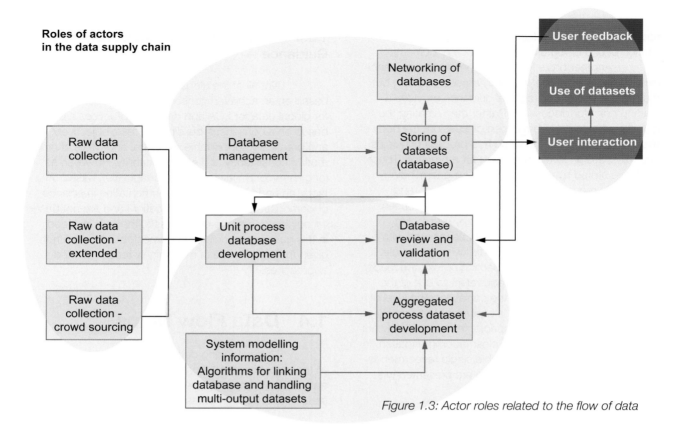

Figure 1.3: Actor roles related to the flow of data

1.4.1 Flow of Data

Relationships exist among processes that act on data as they flow from raw data sources to users (Figure 1.2). Note that the diagram shows activity related to data and datasets and does not indicate whether the repository at a particular point in the flow is discrete (separate) or integrated. The most likely instance of integration is where an LCI database contains individual datasets. The diagram also shows, for simplicity, only one place for review, which is as datasets are admitted to a database. Other review or validation points may also be possible, and recommended, on both datasets and raw data. In particular, validation may precede the review when the database manager determines that the dataset conforms to the database protocol, which prevents the need for a second review loop.

Finally, the flow after the receipt and application of data by users is illustrated by commentary or feedback on the data to the review process. Again, this is only one instance of possible data feedback. Alternative feedback loops go to the original data provider, the dataset developer, or the database manager, depending on the nature of the feedback and the rules for providing such feedback.

1.4.2 Flow of Roles and Responsibilities

There are several actors involved in the flow of data from raw data providers to final LCI data users (Figure 1.3). The same person or organization may have several roles at the same time; for example, the database administrator can also be the data provider. The data provider typically is also the data owner, although this ownership may be transferred to the commissioner or database administrator, depending on the options in the national intellectual property rights legislation. When services (data provision, review, and database services) are provided commercially, liability may accrue to the service provider from the purchaser of the service.

1.5 Factors that Determine Data Needs and Database Requirements

Selecting an LCI dataset or database for use in a particular study requires an understanding of the study's goal and scope, clear communication about the data's consistency and exchangeability so the potential user can determine its applicability, and the implications of the user's choice of modelling approach.

1.5.1 Study Goal and Scope: Different Application Contexts

Clearly, when approached from the view of performing an LCI, the selection process for use of datasets or the development of primary data is greatly influenced by the study goal and scope. From the perspective of data development, inclusion in a database, or communication of database content to prospective users, the influences of the goal and scope are narrower.

For example, a unit process or aggregated process dataset that has limited process boundaries, obsolescent technology coverage, or some other constraint could be following all accepted and recommended practices and therefore in principle could be included in a database. The goal and scope dependency here centres on clear and transparent communication of this potential application limitation to data users.

Thus, the question is whether a set of global guidelines on clear communication of data characteristics suffices or whether additional explicit indications of allowable or unallowable applications are wanted or needed. A related question is whether or not, regardless of specific quality aspects and study-specific goal and scope, user assurance of the stated quality, external and independent of the developer or producer, should be considered for externally published or used datasets in an LCI database.

More specifically put, is it possible to define what characteristics are necessary in an LCI database in order to ensure that either the database inherently contains consistent and exchangeable datasets, or the information communicated to users ensures their ability to judge such consistency and applicability for themselves?

1.5.2 Relationship with Modelling Approach

In general, questions to place the guiding principles in a particular decision context or modelling approach or to recommend correctness of a study methodology are not applicable for this guidance document. In the past decade, two different approaches to LCA, and particularly to LCI modelling, have been distinguished.

1) Attributional approach (also called "accounting" or "descriptive approach"):

- The attributional approach attempts to provide information on what portion of global burdens can be associated with a product (and its life cycle).
- In theory, if one were to conduct attributional LCAs of all final products, one would end up

with the total observed environmental burdens worldwide.
- The systems analysed ideally contain processes that are actually directly linked by (physical, energy, and service) flows to the unit process that supplies the functional unit or reference flow.

2) Consequential approach (also called "change-oriented approach"):

- The consequential approach attempts to provide information on the environmental burdens that occur, directly or indirectly, as a consequence of a decision (usually represented by changes in demand for a product).
- In theory, the systems analysed in these LCAs are made up only of processes that are actually affected by the decision, that is, that change their output due to a signal they receive from a cause-and-effect chain whose origin is a particular decision.

Both approaches are associated with different objectives, and hence aim to provide different information to the end user of the LCA studies. Figure 1.4 shows the conceptual representation of the attributional and consequential approaches. The circle in both diagrams represents total environmental burdens at any given point. On the left diagram, representing the attributional approach, a share of the total burdens is imputed (represented by the delineated wedge), using normative rules, to a given product system. The right diagram, representing the consequential approach, reflects how the total environmental burdens change as a result of a decision that is of interest (represented by the shaded region). Additional description of these two approaches as well as of a third, emerging approach is provided in Chapter 3.

The starting point for development of these global guidance principles derives from the data and database implications, once the appropriate modelling approach has been decided or once it has been determined that an impact assessment phase of an LCA is needed.

1.6 Database User, Dataset Provider, and Database Manager Perspectives

The development and management of LCI datasets and databases requires interaction among users, providers, and managers if these data are to have such necessary characteristics as accountability, transparency, security, and quality.

1.6.1 Perspectives on Responsible LCI Database Management

In the 1990s, the first independent LCI databases emerged and the use of LCA grew. Widespread professional use of LCA increased, and a market developed for high-quality and credible LCA studies. For the past two decades, databases have been developed, maintained, and updated by different general database providers, by industry-sector database providers, and by industry-internal groups with a high level of professionalism.

Responsible database management to support this marketplace implies additional procedures and processes for LCI databases beyond those applied to general data libraries. Some important ones are these:

1) Responsibility and accountability: Data provision from an LCI database implies a continuing responsibility for the provided information. We recommend that a providing organization designate an individual to address issues with data in the database in case of any future problem with customer communication. Otherwise, responsible use of the LCI data will not be endorsed.

2) Technical and methodological support: Being responsible for customer inquiries about data means being able to respond quickly. Therefore, technical and methodological support in a reasonable amount of time is recommended.

3) Routines for consistent maintenance and updating: Standard routines for consistent maintenance and updating are recommended to guide the user through an update and to prevent mistakes and errors in an update procedure.

4) Conforming documentation: Suitable documentation conforming to the guidance principles is recommended to provide a basis for use of the database and to avoid misleading the customer (accountability).

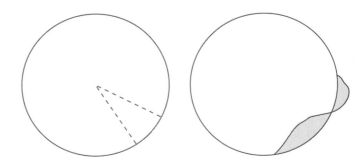

Figure 1.4: Conceptual differences between attributional and consequential approaches (Weidema 2003)

5) Balance between continuity and innovation (frequent, but only relevant updates): There is no position on the absolute frequency of updates. As a responsible practice, the frequency of updates should not harm or significantly slow down the application of the database contents in the user application. For the sake of efficiency, the frequency of updates should be judged against the relevancy and significance of the changes.

6) Appropriate level of transparency: Database providers are recommended to offer datasets with the level of transparency requested by the user, while respecting the confidentiality requirements of datasets that contain classified content. Conformance to these transparency responsibilities should be in accord with the principles in this guidance document.

7) Secure storage: It is strongly recommended that suitable measures be undertaken to prevent unintended loss or accidental distribution of data content.

8) Harmonization of new approaches and datasets with existing approaches and datasets: If databases are to be expanded, it is recommended that existing databases be harmonized with newly provided content. We recommend that database operators (managers) take all necessary measures to facilitate such harmonization.

9) Commonly available interfaces for data exchange: In order to communicate and exchange data, the database contents should be suitable for exchange via standard interfaces into other LCA software or systems. However, contents need first be harmonized to avoid misunderstanding, misinterpretations, and unintended inconsistencies.

A promising prospect, from a dataset provider's perspective, would be to have any LCA data from any source be compatible with any other data from any other source (or at least to have the data be exchangeable from one source repository to another), based on globally harmonized guidance for the development of LCI datasets. This exchangeability would help to ensure global compatibility and consistency of different content, irrespective of its source. In order to implement such guidance, database managers would have to adopt these guidance principles and conform any content, either existing or new.

1.6.2 A User Definition and Perspective

In the context of this guidance, a user is a person or organization responsible for building an LCA model from one or more unit process datasets or aggregated process datasets taken from one or more databases. The user may combine data from existing databases with those from their own investigations. The user is responsible for presenting and interpreting the LCA results and the resulting recommendations within a decision process. The user is not necessarily the decision maker. In that sense, users can be found within industry, government, consultancy and academia, whereas decision makers are primarily located in industry and governments.

Within industry, there are small- and medium-sized companies, as well as large, multinational companies. Some companies' financial and personnel resources are too limited to allow them to perform detailed LCA studies, or they simply may choose not to acquire the necessary expertise themselves. In such instances, the company commissions the LCA study, which is then carried out by an external consultant. The consultant (considered the user in this guidance) then defines the requests and demands on LCI data, and the company's contribution to the definition is limited, interpreted by the consultant from the company's expression of need or statement of purpose.

Other companies, because of their interests and greater financial capability, have internal staff and funds to perform LCAs based on their own work and in many instances with their own LCA software and LCI databases. In this case, the needs are to have comprehensive and consistent LCI data to match internally owned and externally sourced operations.

Governments may base laws and regulations on LCA. They must rely on LCI data provided by LCA databases and data providers, which in many instances by law or directive are required to comply with stringent requirements regarding verifiability, traceability, and third-party verification, which may supersede the guidance provided in this document. This level of requirements is typically needed in public consultations of laws and regulations.

Furthermore, public research institutes and academic institutions rely on high-quality LCI data

provided by LCA databases to make sure that they steer their research projects in a sustainable direction. For a new generation of engineers, chemists, architects, and economists, these data are also helping to create a deeper understanding of how to develop and market greener products and services.

For all these groups, the following requirements for LCI data can be listed:

- high-quality, regularly updated, reviewed data that offer a maximum of information and transparency about the underlying processes;
- support from the data provider or database manager in terms of information about updates and quality improvements of the LCI data;
- reliable and sound information about technical background and operational conditions of the LCI data that likely are not included in the database but that could be needed within a decision context, especially when the decision involves operations the company does not own or control (this information is directly linked to the decisions to be taken, e.g., energy efficiency of a specific plant, production capacities, and plant size); and
- reliable support for LCI metadata, such as process operating conditions, which are not available in the database but necessarily are needed within a decision context and therefore must be produced and delivered to the user in an appropriate manner corresponding to the timeline within the decision context.

Another user consideration is provision of LCI information for processes, technologies, and materials where no LCI data previously existed or which were not in an accessible form. Especially for new (non-commercial) processes, technologies, and materials, often only limited LCI data are available. Here it is important for the user needing such information to get sufficiently consistent and complete LCI data within a reasonable time and with a reasonable effort in terms of cost and personnel resources. Providing this information when requested helps to alleviate gaps and deficiencies in the LCA model and to derive sound and reliable decisions from the LCA results. We recommend as much transparency as possible for such datasets, but the key aspect in this specific context may be timeliness. Therefore, science and consultancy are invited to offer dataset developers' and database managers' solutions for this challenge.

When industry provides datasets to be used publicly or make public claims based on the data, then they need to be as transparent as possible. This transparency could mean that mechanisms such as aggregation, supplemental information provision, and data review and external verification are used only when it is essential to protect confidential information, and then only to the extent necessary.

1.6.3 Perspectives on Provision of Guidance

Two overall perspectives on provision of global guidance can be described:

1) One perspective supports the idea that it is sufficient to provide users with guidance on understanding the consequences or limitations of datasets and the use of such datasets from databases so that users are able to decide for themselves which datasets meet their needs. Providing this type of guidance for users does not necessarily lead to more consistency of datasets within a single database or to more exchangeability of data among databases. Establishing specific documentation requirements for data providers, and communication requirements for presenting this documentation on datasets to users, does serve to enhance the user's ability to confidently acquire LCI data.
2) An alternative perspective is that direct guidance to database developers or data providers is needed so that recommended practices are known and can be adopted over time as information in databases is revised or created. Conditions for admittance of datasets to databases should be well defined, objectively stated, and known to providers. From this perspective, market forces are in play as users state their needs and un-

derstand what is recommended for consistency and applicability of datasets. This clarity supports a broad demand for higher-quality datasets from the user community so that providers can choose to modify their offerings accordingly.

Creating guidance around either one of these perspectives necessitates that a range of actors along the data supply chain interact.

1.7 Structure of the Global Guidance Principles Report

This global guidance document comprises a prologue, eight chapters, and supporting annexes (see Figure 1.5 for the conceptual and organizational relationships among the chapters). Examples and references are provided to assist the reader in understanding the guidance principles and to allow a more in-depth exploration and evaluation of specific elements of practices that relate to data and databases. Chapters 2 and 3 address data-related aspects of current LCI practice, including formulation and execution of a data collection plan, modelling of data, validation of data and datasets, and dataset review. Chapter 3 gives a stepwise process for aggregation, including the important step of ensuring consistency and completeness of any datasets being used in the aggregation. Chapter 4 then takes up the definition of an LCI database; procedures and recommendations for database construction, documentation, and management;

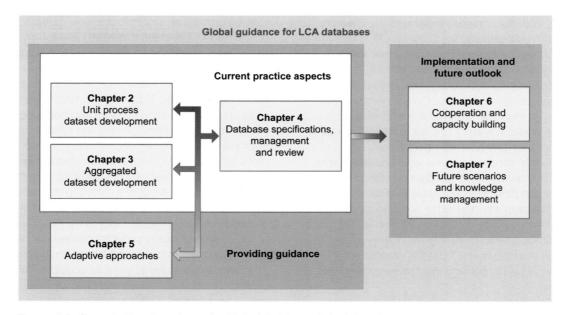

Figure 1.5: Organizational roadmap for Global Guidance Principles document

database user interactions; and potential aspects of networking across databases.

Life cycle assessments should use the most appropriate datasets and modelling approaches (as discussed in Chapters 2 through 4) to meet the specific goal and scope required to satisfactorily answer the questions posed[4]. Current LCI databases are often sufficient to provide the required information to meet many consumer, industry, and government objectives. However, additional details on the current data as well as supplemental data sources will likely be needed to provide satisfactory answers to emerging questions in the fields of LCA and sustainability. The continuing evolution in consumer preferences, and market and industry imperatives and public policy, forces continuous development and improvement of datasets and methodologies for LCA to meet these needs. This development and improvement includes adapting and extending data collection and modelling methods. In this vein, Chapter 5 then moves beyond current practice in some ways to extend data availability through non-process–based alternative sources and to enhance the range of questions addressable by increasing spatial and temporal resolution or creating hybrid solutions with combinations of conventional and alternative data.

Chapters 6 and 7 move from actually providing guidance to thinking about implementation and the future. Chapter 6 addresses needs, especially in developing countries, for capacity building in various aspects of data collection, processing, management, and database creation. Further, the notion is explored of networking among databases, which could be at the technology or human level. Chapter 7 then takes this a step further and develops a set of scenarios of possible future states for the purpose of beginning to highlight how the LCA community might actively help shape the future and accommodate technology developments while at the same time maintaining a quality and user-support focus. Chapter 8 summarizes key messages and the recommendations of the workshop participants.

1.8   References

[ISO] International Organization for Standardization. 2006a. ISO 14040. Environmental management — Life cycle assessment — Principles and framework. [cited 2011 Feb 1]. Available from: http://www.iso.org/iso/iso_catalogue/catalogue_tc/catalogue_detail.htm?csnumber=37456.

[ISO] International Organization for Standardization. 2006b. ISO 14044. Environmental management — Life cycle assessment — Requirement and guidelines. [cited 2011 Feb 1]. Available from: http://www.iso.org/iso/iso_catalogue/catalogue_tc/catalogue_detail.htm?csnumber=38498.

[WBCSD and WRI] World Business Council for Sustainable Development and World Resource Institute. 2004. The greenhouse gas (GHG) protocol: A corporate accounting and reporting standard. Revised edition. ISBN 1-56973-568-9. 113 p.

Weidema BP. 2003. Market information in life cycle assessment. Copenhagen: Danish Enviromental Protection Agency. (Enviromental Project no.863)

---

[4] ISO also indicates that the data quality requirements "shall be specified to enable the goal and scope of the LCA to be met" (ISO 2006b).

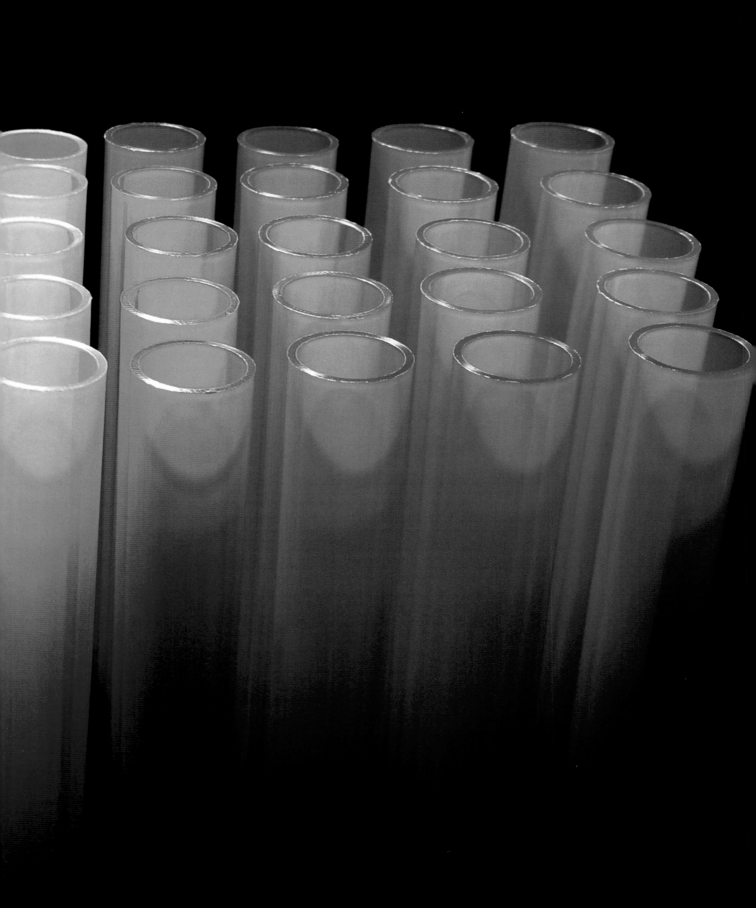

Development of Unit Process Datasets

Hongtao Wang
Andreas Ciroth
Pierre Gerber
Charles Mbowha
Thumrongrut Mungcharoen
Abdelhadi Sahnoune
Kiyotaka Tahara
Ladji Tikana
Nydia Suppen (liaison)

CHAPTER

Key Messages

• Data collection for life cycle inventory (LCI) represents a type of "know-how" that has been developed since the early days of LCA. Conducting raw data collection properly can be cumbersome and is often underestimated. This chapter addresses it in a structured way.

• This chapter provides a new definition of "unit process dataset", which is created from raw data. Raw data is understood as data that is not yet related to the process for which the dataset is being developed. Dataset modelling is the action that allows us to move from raw data to the unit process dataset.

• The procedure for generating a unit process dataset can be structured using the following steps: goal and scope definition, dataset generation, and validation and documentation in a parallel track.

• Creation of a unit process dataset should be guided by the intended application for this dataset. We recommend keeping the dataset flexible so that it can be used in different applications or under different goal and scope settings of LCA studies and for aggregated datasets with a different goal and scope. One practical consequence of this flexibility is that it can provide multi-product unit process datasets as unallocated datasets. The allocation or system expansion can then be applied according to the goal and scope of a life cycle assessment (LCA) study or aggregated dataset generation.

• Practical considerations to be kept in mind when developing unit process datasets: the credibility of LCA depends critically on the quality of unit process datasets used in the analysis, and development of unit process datasets is time consuming. Development of unit process datasets should be done by individuals or groups familiar with LCA methodology.

Unit process datasets are the basis of every life cycle inventory (LCI) database and the foundation of all life cycle assessment (LCA) applications. This chapter provides guidance for developers and users on how to develop a unit process dataset and how to document the procedures in a structured way.

Unit process datasets are usually distinguished from aggregated process datasets. A unit process dataset is obtained as a result of quantifying inputs and outputs in relation to a quantitative reference flow from a process. These inputs and outputs are generated from mathematical relationships that operate on raw data that have not previously been related to the same reference flow. On the other hand, an aggregated process dataset is obtained from a collection of existing unit process or other aggregated datasets[1]. Chapters 2 and 3 will address the development of these two types of datasets respectively (Figure 2.1).

In this chapter, applicable definitions, principles, and the methodological framework provided by the International Organization for Standardization (ISO) are used as a starting point in developing recommendations for developing unit process datasets. Modifications and extensions are provided when necessary. In this regard, Global Guidance Principles for LCA Databases should be seen as a technical supplement to ISO-LCA standards (ISO 14040:2006; ISO 14044:2006), as earlier guidelines (Weidema et al. 2004) have been, building upon knowledge acquired through current LCA practice.

The development of a unit process dataset is divided into three iterative steps and a parallel track of documentation, which form the sections of this chapter (Figure 2.2).

2.1 Definition of Goal and Scope

Definition of the goal and scope is the first step in developing a unit process dataset. It basically describes what kind of process the dataset intends to represent. Developers are required to define the goal and scope in a similar way as LCI and LCA studies do, to guide the steps needed to develop the dataset and to provide corresponding information for users when they choose datasets for their own LCI or LCA studies. While the principal approach is similar to an LCA study goal and scope, the scale being addressed is smaller for a

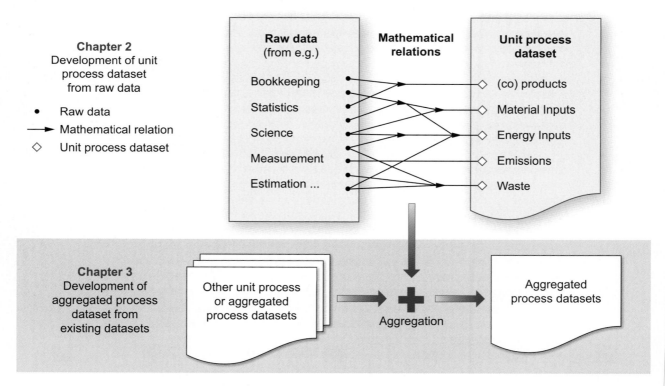

Figure 2.1: Unit process dataset and aggregated process dataset

---

[1] "Unit process" is defined as "smallest element considered in the life cycle inventory analysis" in ISO 14040. Therefore, when so-called "unit process datasets" and "aggregated process datasets" in this database guidance are applied in an LCI analysis, both of them will be unit processes.

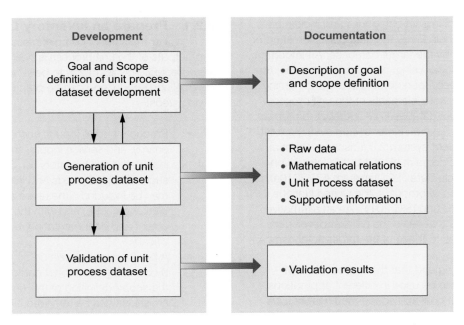

Figure 2.2: Structure of development and documentation of a unit process dataset

unit process dataset. In particular, the developer should consider the following:

- physical delimitation of activities such as principal process type (e.g., from site-specific to industry-average type) and the specific size of the process to be modelled;
- impact categories to be evaluated during the impact assessment;
- technology covered;
- time period covered;
- geographical area covered;
- cut-off rules for data, if any are applied (these rules should provide a rationale for the significance of the various flows of the unit process dataset);
- provision of uncertainty information for inputs and outputs of the process in order to allow for uncertainty analysis;
- targeted databases for the unit process dataset; and
- intended use of the dataset in general (applications, modelling situations including attributional or consequential modelling, comparative assertions).

The developer is also encouraged to assess whether the activity under consideration can be split into smaller units. While splitting the activity might be more demanding in terms of data collection, doing so will provide more flexibility in LCA modelling of various products and processes. However, separate reporting of unit processes should be avoided when such reporting does not add any useful information in an LCA context. This is the case when one unit process always supplies all of its products directly to another specific unit process at the same location, so that the product of the first unit process never appears as a marketable product and cannot be provided by an external supplier. In fact, there will be situations in which boundary expansion is a better approach (Box 2.1).

Box 2.1: Example of Preferred Use of System Boundary Expansion over Allocation

When data for different exchanges represent incongruent system boundaries — for example, when volatile organic compound (VOC) emissions are measured for unit process A separately and for unit processes B+C together, while energy use is measured for unit process A+B together and for unit process C separately — a separate description for each unit process can be obtained only by partitioning the data, separating from the original measurements that part of the energy and emissions that belong to unit process B. In this situation, the uncertainty in the partitioning must be held up against the need for separate data for each unit process, as opposed to providing only one dataset for A+B+C together (Weidema et al. 2004).

When developing the unit process dataset, in alignment with the database management and documentation requirements, it is also important that the developer clearly defines the final intent of the unit process dataset, in terms of impact categories and indicators. This definition will help focus the data collection effort on the flows required by the target database. An important action is the developer using, as much as possible, the common and agreed-upon nomenclature and naming schemes for the various elements of the unit process dataset of the target databases or aggregated process inventories (APIs). Several nomenclature systems exist, such as the ecoinvent system 2.0 (Frischknecht et al. 2007) and 3.0 (Weidema et al. 2011), the International Reference Life Cycle Data (ILCD) system (EC 2010a), or for the classification of products, the United Nations (UN) classifications (CPC and ISIC 2011). As an alternative, mapping schemas that relate the dataset developer's own nomenclatures to those of the target database can be used[2].

We recommend that the dataset be kept flexible so that it can be used in different applications and under different goal and scope "settings" of LCA studies and for aggregated datasets with a different goal and scope. As a result, we recommend that multi-product unit process datasets be provided as unallocated datasets. The allocation or system expansion can then be applied according to the goal and scope of an LCA study or aggregated dataset generation.

2.2 Generation of Unit Process Dataset

This section describes how to generate a unit process dataset from raw data and how to document the procedures. Using the general guidance and data collection sheets in ISO 14040 and ISO 14044 as the starting point, this section proposes the following steps:

Step 1: Prepare an inventory list of inputs and outputs.
Step 2: Define the mathematical relationships.
Step 3: Collect the raw data needed.
Step 4: Perform calculations.
Step 5: Provide other supportive information.

The developer also should document relevant data and information for validation, review, and update purposes, and for dataset "end users" (i.e., practitioners who create LCA models with the respective datasets), including these:

- mathematical relationships;
- raw data;
- unit process dataset; and
- supportive information.

2.2.1 Prepare an Inventory List

For the sake of completeness, a list of inputs and outputs of the unit process is needed before data are collected. This list needs to be in accordance with the goal and scope, and can be prepared using the following steps:

- Products and all inputs, such as materials, energy, and service inputs, should always be included in the inventory list. Special inputs, such as capital goods and infrastructure, also may be included if these are aligned with the goal and scope, and with the database management and documentation requirements specifically.
- A list of emissions can be preliminarily prepared by checking the impact categories targeted in the scope definition of this unit process. Then, emissions can be removed if they are not relevant to this unit process.
- It is also helpful to check the inventory list of existing datasets with the same technology and practice for differences that might indicate omissions or extraneous data, as well as review related literature outside of that prepared for LCA, and consult subject area experts. As part of the documentation process, describe the search space in accordance with the principles of systematic review and meta-analysis. Include in the documentation process a listing and justification of omissions within the context of the goal and scope and in accordance with ISO completeness guidance; the treatment of missing data and data gaps should result in:

  - a "non-zero" data value that is explained;
  - a "zero" data value if explained; or
  - a calculated value based on the reported values from unit processes employing similar technology.

For the sake of consistency at the database level, developers also should check the rules for the targeted databases, such as rules about nomenclature and conventions or measurement of special inventory data.

At the end of this step, the inventory list should be complete, and it can then be used to obtain values for the flows. It can be modified, for example, when the scope definition is changed. It will be documented in the unit process dataset as part of the dataset generation steps described below.

---

[2] For example, as they are used and publicly available in the openLCA format converter, http://openlca.org/Converter.8.0.html

2.2.2 Define the Mathematical Relationships

Before the data collection begins, mathematical relationships must be defined so that the necessary raw data can be identified. To clarify, the inventory items to be quantified may not be the items for which process data are collected; the mathematical relationships define how the inventory items of interest can be derived from the raw data. It may be necessary to derive a second set of mathematical relationships that one might use to parameterize the dataset (those relationships that link process production to process consumption). This second set of relationships will be defined during data collection and should be checked and refined as part of this step. Further, the data necessary for parameterization should be collected, processed, and subjected to data quality checks just as the raw process data are. For the same inventory list, different mathematical relationships can be proposed for each inventory item. During the definition of the mathematical relationships, the most correct or resource-efficient relationship may often depend on raw data availability, but data quality also should be considered.

Data availability can be influenced by the type of inventory data (e.g., product, material, energy, emissions) and by the desired or required representativeness as defined in the goal and scope:

- For product, by-product, material, and energy use, or for waste to be treated, if bookkeeping or statistical data are available for the unit process, the mathematical relationships based on total amount of occurrence are preferred. Theoretical calculations also are common, such as stoichiometric calculations or mass, element, or energy balance calculations.
- For emissions, theoretical calculations are sometimes used. Emission factors are also widely used, such as in national greenhouse gas (GHG) inventories (Eggleston et al. 2006). Mathematical relationships based on on-site measurement may be preferred, if the value of measurement, (e.g., the concentration of the emission) can be properly transformed and related to the reference flow of the unit process.
- For the producer-specific unit process dataset, bookkeeping data normally are available for products and material or energy inputs, so the mathematical relationship based on total amount consumed or produced is always preferred.
- For the average unit process dataset, data availability depends largely on what is required by the goal and scope.

The choice of mathematical relationships affects the data quality of the unit process dataset to be generated. These mathematical relationships and their effect on the data should be evaluated during the validation step in Section 2.3.

Sometimes, aggregation also can be adopted as an optional routine to generate an inventory dataset, especially when the dataset to be generated is an average type. Developers should consider the possibility of breaking the unit process into several categories, generating unit processes for each category, and then aggregating these according to their market shares. This possibility may be preferable to generating a single unit process, as prescribed by the definition in the goal and scope, for which poor raw data may exist. In this case, a reasonable choice is needed of categories of key influential factors, such as differing technologies, production practices, or plant or processing line capacities. (More guidance for aggregation can be found in Chapter 3.)

For example, to obtain an industry average dataset based on different combustion processes for coal-fired power generation, different data source and mathematical relations can be considered:

- using total material inputs (e.g., coal use) and total yield of electricity from industry statistics;
- using such data from sampling coal-fired power plants and averaging them; or
- classifying all coal-fired power plants into different categories (e.g., large, medium, and small capacity), sampling in each category to obtain three unit process datasets, and aggregating three datasets with their market shares.

At the end of this step, for each data item in the inventory list, one or a series of mathematical relationships should have been defined. These mathematical relationships and the rationale for selection should be documented for validation, review, and update purposes. Some LCA data formats and databases already support developers by providing for documentation of mathematical relationships for such purposes, for example, in ILCD format (ILCD 2010), EcoSpold01 format (Hedemann and König 2007), and EcoSpold02 format (EcoSpold 2011). Unfortunately, EcoSpold01 format does not support this capability. Other available LCA software, with their associated data formats, also support documentation of such mathematical relationships.

2.2.3 Raw Data Collection

This section provides guidance to the user on the process of data collection, including not only methods of data collection, but also suggestions on which data collection methods to apply in which situations, how to deal with missing data, and insights into the documentation that is required.

Data collection is the process of gathering data for a specific purpose[3]. "Raw data" are data that have not been set in relation to the quantitative reference of the unit process dataset. Data gathering needs should be supported by the unit process dataset's mathematical relationships and by the goal and scope.

The following options for data collection exist, as data collection procedures or sources[4]:

1) Primary data can include
   - interviews,
   - questionnaires or surveys,
   - bookkeeping or enterprise resource planning (ERP) system,
   - data collection tools (online, offline), and
   - on-site measurements.
2) Secondary data can include
   - interviews,
   - statistics, and
   - literature.
3) Data generation can include
   - calculations (e.g., missing emission factors from input data) and
   - estimates.

For each unit process dataset, a combination of these options usually is applied. Also, several techniques may be used in a sequence (e.g., based on on-site measurements of other parameters, calculations can be used to fill data gaps). Data collection provides the data needed to complete a unit process dataset, but it also covers data needed for quality assurance (benchmarks, comparisons, or other similar data), and data needed to describe the process (metadata, temperature and pressure of a vaporizer, size, or other descriptive process data). It is closely linked to the process modelling (the application of the mathematical relationships), where process modelling tells what data are needed and data collection is the process of locating the needed data. These activities may overlap, especially when data collection involves the calculation of missing data.

Data collection also supports validation by collecting and comparing data from other sources with the raw data and inventory data. Validation results may lead to the conclusion that the existing data are insufficient or that further data are needed.

2.2.3.1 Data Collection Guidance

This section provides suggestions and detailed discussion of the mechanics of soliciting data from sources and references. Before starting data collection, the data collector or team should make sure that the goal and scope and any mathematical relationships are clear, in order to avoid doing too much or forgetting to contact relevant data sources or collect raw data. There are various ways to obtain useful data.

---

[3] Extension of a definition "Data collection is the process of gathering data." Economic Commission for Europe of the United Nations (UNECE), "Glossary of Terms on Statistical Data Editing", Conference of European Statisticians Methodological material, Geneva, 2000, found at http://stats.oecd.org/glossary/detail.asp?ID=534
[4] See also the data collection guidance in Section 2,2,3,15

- Interviews: Compile a complete list of flows that must be considered. Address knowledgeable people in factories. Do your homework beforehand, which is to say, be familiar with the process, product, and terminology, and pre-calculate a reference process as a benchmark. Prepare a simple introduction of how the data will be used. Explain and clarify sensitive issues. Gain the support of top-level management, and talk to production line and engineering staff.
- Questionnaires and surveys: Prepare a quality check of the questionnaire, and include built-in quality checks to uncover misunderstandings. Make the questionnaire clear and as short as possible, and use the language of the addressees. Perform statistical analysis for quality checks. Make sure that results are representative (e.g., definition of sample, size of sample). Surveys are similar to questionnaires but will include sampling of a process in addition to collection or extraction of data from process information.
- Data collection tools (online, offline, software-driven questionnaires): While having similar issues as questionnaires and surveys, these tools offer much better possibilities for automated consistency and completeness checks.
- Measurements on site: Sampling time and sampling method (equipment, specific methodology) need to be selected according to goal and scope.
- Statistics: Be aware of statistical artefacts (e.g., only larger companies are shown in the European Pollutant Release and Transfer Register [E-PRTR, http://prtr.ec.europa.eu/] statistics).
- Calculations (e.g., missing emission factors from input data): Document the calculation formulas[5].
- Estimates: Provide a reason for providing only estimates, or a motivation for the estimate[6].
- Proxy unit process: In some cases, a particularly useful data source is an existing similar (proxy) unit process, for example, a related technology or the same technology for another region or another time period. The unit process data for the proxy may be able to be used directly (e.g., use the same emission factor). However, care should be taken and such direct use of data should be done only in cases where 1) one can reasonably assume that the values indeed would be the same or very similar, 2) the flow is not environmentally relevant, or 3) no other data sources are available ("better than nothing" principle). Or if sufficient documentation is available for the existing unit process, one may be

able to find the original calculation method to quantify a given input or output, and hence one can target data collection to the parameters that are significant in the calculation of these flows. For any uses of the proxy unit process data, one's actions must be made transparent through documentation about the borrowing of data that may not be directly applicable to the unit process being modelled.

If allocations are needed during data collection, they should be documented. A desire to avoid allocations may be a reason to enlarge the process size (system expansion).

2.2.3.2 Selecting among Data Collection Procedures

There is a general ranking of data collection methods: measurements > calculations > estimations (of the same quality)[7]. Estimates should be avoided, and if they cannot be avoided, they should be backed by measurements or by calculations, which then can be used as plausibility checks. The use of estimation to fill data gaps is useful even if the specific missing data cannot be measured, but other data are available and can then be used by relation to a common operation.

2.2.3.3 Specific Topics in Data Collection

The data collector should be aware of impacts on the utility of the collected information for the end user and the ability for an expeditious review; of how to fill in blank, unknown, or other missing values; of the need to match the data collected to the period of interest for the unit process.

It is good practice to use a group approach to organize the work in data collection, where data owners and data collectors collaborate. As an example, trade associations often are good groups to task with data collection because they will have expertise in the process and the environmental, regulatory, economic, and societal drivers. It may be necessary to supplement the trade association's expertise with LCA expertise so that all of the critical proficiencies are present within the data collection group:

- persons proficient in product technology, process, and manufacturing data;
- persons proficient in environment, energy technology, process, and data; and
- persons proficient in LCA.

---

[5] Calculation appears twice: once in data collection, where calculations are based on raw data, and once in modeling, where the mathematical relations for the dataset are specified.

[6] Estimates are understood here as results of an approximate judgment or opinion regarding the worth, amount, size, weight, etc., of something (http://dictionary.reference.com/browse/estimate); estimates may be obtained by calculation, therefore calculation and estimates overlap; however, calculations can also be used in precise, non-approximated measurements, and estimates can also be performed without calculation.

[7] Data collection is always also a selection of the best quality data; if several suitable candidates for a dataset exist, their quality can be assessed by looking at the technology, time, and geography they represent, and by the way the data have been obtained. Technology, time, and geography will not perfectly fit for the dataset that has to be collected or modelled. There are trade-offs between better data collection methods and better-fitting technology, time, or geography. If the quality concerning technology, time, and geography is comparable, then the ranking mentioned above holds.

In addition to being the most efficient means of data collection, there is a secondary benefit of using groups such as trade associations for data collection: the potential for education of or exposure to their membership to how LCAs are conducted and the benefits of performing an LCA (AIST–JEMAI 2008).

It is good practice to distinguish missing values from zero. "When the data is not clear, it should be entered as '?'[8] which should be distinguished from the entry '0' when clearly not used or emitted" (AIST–JEMAI 2008).[9]

This is also recommended by ISO 14044, 4.2.3.6.3:

"The treatment of missing data shall be documented. For each unit process and for each reporting location where missing data are identified, the treatment of the missing data and data gaps should result in

- a "non-zero" data value that is explained,
- a "zero" data value if explained, or
- a calculated value based on the reported values from unit processes employing similar technology".

The sampling period must reflect the desired temporal averaging of the process. For example, a single day's sampling should not be used to represent the annual average operations of a process without adequate documentation of the representativeness of the sampling data. Seasonal changes should be taken into account.

2.2.3.4 Dealing with Closed Loops in the Investigated Process

There is no general practice on how to deal with closed loops in processes. Closed loops exist where materials that have left the process boundary are reclaimed and reintroduced as part or all of the raw materials. Common examples include recycled steel into steelmaking and recycled aluminium back into aluminium sheet. Clearly, items that originated from or are released to outside the process boundary need to be included in the data collection. Conversely, materials that are recycled internally, within the process boundary, do not need to be tabulated. The materials that are recycled internally will be reflected in process inputs and outputs. (see, e.g., AIST–JEMAI 2008).

At the end of this step, all raw data should be ready for calculation. All raw data and the rationale supporting the choice of data sources should be documented for validation, review, and update purposes.

2.2.4 Calculation

When both mathematical relationships and raw data are ready, raw data are fed into the mathematical relationships to produce the unit process dataset. In general, this can be summarized as:

f (raw data) → unit process dataset.

The result of the calculations is the intended unit process dataset, without documentation. It will be fully documented for the users in the next step.

2.2.5 Other Supportive Information

In addition to the unit process dataset *per se*, supportive documentation should be provided for validation, review, and update purposes, as well as for the users. Such documentation could include justification for selecting mathematical relationships and raw data, information for allocation and consequential modelling purposes, and suggestions to the users.

2.2.5.1 Allocation

In case of multi-output products, supportive information needs to be provided to allow for allocation, for example, heating values, content or concentration, and prices.

2.2.5.2 Consequential Analysis

In order for consequential analysis to be performed in an automated manner, the technology must be classified according to a specific nomenclature so that the technology's level of development becomes machine interpretable just as the geographical and temporal representativeness can be machine interpreted. Likewise, the specification of numerical annual production volumes is essential for linking of datasets into production or consumption mixes.

2.2.5.3 Suggestions to the Users

This section is intended to help the developer prepare guidance for the user of the unit process dataset and to highlight key information for the recommended use of the unit process dataset, similar to an executive summary, of which the practitioner should be aware when using the unit process dataset.

The developer should indicate the domain of relevance of the unit process dataset. This often is best done by informing the user about characteristics of the unit process dataset as discussed in the following bullet items (the dataset developer also should discuss the types of LCA for which the unit process dataset is not applicable, to the best of their knowledge).

---

[8] An interesting technical point is that often data formats and databases do not allow entering a non-number as "?" in a value field.

[9] Missing values can always be "found" by data collection methods, see ecoinvent report No. 1 (ecoinvent data v2.0, 2007); there is, however, an impact on the quality of the process dataset.

- Scope: In general terms, a unit process dataset should be used only within an LCA where the scope of the study is consistent with the scope of the dataset (e.g., coverage of the same flows, and of similar temporal and geographic boundaries.). The developer shall thus list technologies and practices, geographic areas, industry sub-sectors, and periods of time in which the unit process dataset is expected to be relevant. In doing so, the developer may consider highlighting the most significant flows in the dataset, and may highlight where using the unit process dataset would have significant impact on the results of the LCA. Any applied cut-off rules should be clearly explained so the user can appreciate implications at the LCA level. The specific life cycle impact assessment (LCIA) methods consistent with or considered during the modelling of the unit process dataset also should be mentioned.

Example 1: This unit process dataset is for Chinese coal-fired power generation, which is dominated by pulverized coal-fired boilers. It cannot be used for circulating fluidized bed (CFB) boiler, nor combined heat and power (CHP).

Example 2: This unit process dataset addresses global warming, ozone depletion, acidification, and eutrophication according to the CML method 1992, but most heavy metals are missing. So human toxicity and ecotoxicity impact assessments are not supported by this dataset.

- Certainty level: The unit process dataset comes with a level of uncertainty and shall not be used in LCAs that seek a greater level of precision. The unit process dataset user shall thus be made aware of uncertainty issues and any other specific validation problems (see further discussion of validation in Section 2.3).
- Allocation rules: If the unit process dataset has multiple outputs, the developer should indicate the type of allocation technique the inventory data can support, for example, economic allocation, content-based allocation, or avoiding allocation through system expansion or substitution.

The developer may consider preparing a standard text box that summarizes the main unit process dataset elements (Box 2.2).

2.3 Validation

This section describes how to validate a unit process dataset and how to document the results. ISO

14040 specifies "completeness check, sensitivity check, consistency check, and any other validation" for LCI and LCA studies. In this section, where applicable, such validation methods are adapted for the development of a unit process dataset.

Validation is understood as the procedure of ascertaining that the developed unit process dataset represents the "real" process dataset well, by comparing the behaviour of the developed process to that of the real one (see also the glossary). In order to validate a unit process dataset, some key control steps need to be applied. Most of these steps are elements of the quality control process during collection of data on the unit process, which is an important part of the data collection phase. The following approaches can be applied in a less intensive manner than they would be applied in validating a full LCA:

- identifying significant issues,
- completeness check,
- sensitivity check,
- uncertainty assessment, and
- consistency check.

By applying these checks in parallel with data collection, the dataset's accuracy, completeness, and precision can be improved. This improvement can limit the number of full iterations needed to achieve the required or desired quality of the final results.

Drawing on these steps, the following can be checked in parallel or at the end of data collection and modelling:

- Does the unit process inventory include all relevant product, waste, and elementary flows that would be expected based on the input of processed materials, based on the nature of transformations that occur in the process, and/or based on experience gained with similar processes? When doing so, make sure to reflect the required technological, geographical, and temporal representativeness.

- Are the amounts of the individual flows and of the chemical elements, energy, and parts in the input and output in expected proportion to each other? Often, stoichiometric or other systematic relationships can help to check whether measured data are plausible. Performing chemical element and energy balances, as well as cost balances between the input and the output of a unit process (and also LCI result) are key checks not only for improving data completeness but also for identifying errors.
- Have the results been compared with data of the same or similar processes or systems from other sources to identify possible problems? However, this comparison is useful only if the other sources are of high quality and especially of high degree of completeness. Completeness of a dataset can be assumed only when it includes all flows that are found in a similar process from another source.
- Have the findings been checked and any observed discrepancies in the inventory data been clearly explained, either qualitatively or quantitatively? This step can be accomplished by consulting additional data sources or technical experts for the analysed process. They may also help to improve the data, at least qualitatively.
- Finally, are the findings reported in the dataset quality criteria? The dataset documentation must appropriately describe the process and the achieved accuracy, precision, and completeness, as well as any limitations (Frischknecht et al. 2007; EC 2010b, p 205–206).

Figure 2.3: Sensitivity vs. uncertainty analysis matrix. (reprinted with permission from Heijungs 1996, Journal of Cleaner Production)

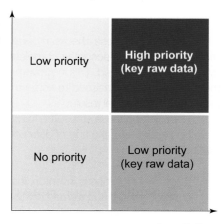

2.3.1 Completeness Check

Similar to the ISO definition for completeness of LCAs, a completeness check at the unit process dataset level is the process of verifying whether information from that dataset is sufficient to reach conclusions that are in accordance with the goal and scope definition of the unit process dataset.

In reality, however, even for simple products, all economic activities performed anywhere on the globe are somehow part of the system. However, the number of processes that contribute to the system in a quantitatively relevant degree is typically rather limited. For this reason, the theoretical problem has little relevance in practice. In practice, all non-reference product flows, waste flows, and elementary flows that are quantitatively irrelevant can be ignored; they can be "cut-off" (Frischknecht et al. 2007, p 10; EC 2010b, p 99), However, care must be taken not to cut off more flows and related impacts than are acceptable to still meet the goal and scope, and that the datasets used to model a system meet the required completeness.

A checklist can help to verify that the data comprising the unit process dataset are consistent with the system boundaries and representative of the specified product or technology e.g., accounting for a certain percent of all raw materials and environmental releases, in a specified unit. (The precise amount is specified in goal and scope.) The result of this effort will be to indicate that the unit process dataset is complete and reflective of the stated goals and scope.

If deficiencies are noted, additional efforts are required to fill the gaps (additional data collection or changes in the modelling). In some cases, data may not be available to fill the data gaps; under these circumstances, the differences in the data should be reported in documentation (USEPA 2006).

2.3.2 Plausibility Check

Plausibility can be defined as something that is apparently reasonable. For unit process development, the "something" is the mathematical relationships of the process, the values, and the metadata. Plausibility is part of the overall quality criteria. Its aim is to ensure that the unit process dataset results and the raw data are reasonable and, therefore, acceptable.

Based on the dataset developer's previous experience and existing knowledge, if unusual or surprising deviations from expected or normal results are observed, such deviation should be examined for relevance. The following approaches are applied for plausibility checks:

- balance checks (e.g., mass or energy);
- data checks (by inspecting level and magnitude of values);

- results comparison from alternative data sources or mathematical relationships;
- processes and literature data comparison, also by calculating LCIA results from the process;
- expert information exchange; and
- statistical tools used to identify outliers, for example, box and whisker plots.

Not all of these checks can always be applied, and some checks are very difficult to apply to some data (e.g., agriculture). However, it is not necessary to apply all of them within one plausibility check.

2.3.3 Sensitivity and Uncertainty

The main goal of sensitivity analysis is to gain insight into which raw data inputs and assumptions are critical to each output flow in the unit process dataset.

The process involves various ways of changing raw data input values or model parameters to determine the effect on the output value.

Uncertainty of raw data input to the unit process can be categorized into two types: the natural variability of the data and the uncertainty in the data. Both may have quite an impact on the accuracy of the flows (Huijbregts et al. 2001; Eggleston 2006).

Similar to their application at the life cycle level (Heijungs 1996, Maurice et al. 2000), sensitivity and uncertainty analyses can also be used to assess the reliability of each flow of the unit process dataset derived from raw data and mathematical relationships. It aims at improving the unit process dataset as a whole to meet the requirements stated in the goal and scope definition. Key raw data with high sensitivity or high uncertainty (Figure 2.3) should be the focus (high data-quality requirements) during the data collection phase. The influence

Table 2.1: Major Consistency Issues for Unit Process Data Development
(adapted from EU 2010a, p 52–53, 299–300)

CONSISTENCY ISSUE	RECOMMENDATIONS
Basic consistency	Basic consistency in such items as nomenclature and terminology should be ensured. Nomenclature can support data consistency by using the same elementary flows and units of measurement.
Methods, assumptions, and data	All methods and assumptions shall be applied in a sufficiently consistent manner, regarding accuracy, precision, and completeness, in line with the goals and scope definition at the unit process level. All data for the elements of the unit process goal and scope definition shall be addressed consistently and checked for consistency with set requirements. This is a general requirement of ISO 14044. Methodological issues of relevance are extrapolations, completeness and precision of the data, and assumptions. (ISO 14044, 2006)
Unit process modelling	Relevant unit process modelling choices such inventory analysis, assumptions made when collecting and modelling the data, selection of secondary data, extrapolations and use scenario analysis techniques shall be applied in a way that ensures consistency.
Defining functions and reference flows	Consistency is crucial when defining the functions and reference flows. Consider the representativeness of measures of temporal, geographical, and technological completeness, and precision.
Data formatting	Specify the same data format using standard or the same nomenclature as requested by users. Link to database requirements.
Inconsistencies	Any inconsistencies considered to be insignificant should be documented and communicated. Evaluate the relevancy and significance of the inconsistencies.
Trade-off of completeness and uncertainty	Data that are not fully but sufficiently consistent according to goal and scope can be used to fill any remaining data gaps as a last resort in unit process assessment. The use of the data must be justified on an individual basis. There is a trade-off between completeness and uncertainty of the provided information; both relate to data quality.

Table 2.2: Examples of Data Inconsistency (USEPA 2006, p 56–58)

CATEGORY	EXAMPLE OF INCONSISTENCY
Data source	Some unit process data can be based on literature or on measured data.
Data accuracy and integrity	Data can be developed using a detailed process flow diagram or using limited process information for a process that is not described or analyzed in detail. Data accuracy and integrity are important if data consistency is to be assured.
Data age	Data can be 30 years old or one year old.
Technological representativeness	The unit process can be based on a bench-scale laboratory model or on a full-scale production plant operation.
Temporal representativeness	Data can be based on a recently developed technology or it can be based on a technology mix, including recently built and older plants.
Geographical representativeness	Data can be from technology employed under local, regional, or international environmental standards. These alternatives can provide different data.
Goal, scope, models and assumptions	Unit process dataset modelling and assumptions will depend on the skill of the modeller in terms of rigor, scientific approach, and methodology.

of raw data uncertainty for key issues (in the LCI application) can be checked by allowing the raw data and modelling parameters to vary within the limits given by the uncertainty estimates while modelling the unit process and comparing the results (Heijungs 1996; Maurice et al. 2000). Obviously, the determination of key issues benefits from the insight provided by impact assessment results, hence LCIA is important in the sensitivity and uncertainty analysis of the inventory data.

The review of the raw data quality and the sensitivity analysis results, and acting to improve the quality of key raw data, should lead to a substantial increase in confidence in the unit process dataset. This represents good practice (Maurice et al. 2000).

There are two principal ways to perform the sensitivity and uncertainty analyses:

1) qualitative method, using expert judgement, and
2) quantitative method, using spreadsheet programs, linear programming, nonlinear programming for sensitivity analysis, for example, and using Pedigree matrix or Monte Carlo simulation, for uncertainty analysis.

In most cases, the qualitative method is used. However, the quantitative method may be needed for complicated unit processes.

2.3.4 Consistency Check

For unit process datasets, a consistency check is the process of verifying that the assumptions, methods, and data are uniformly applied throughout the data collection and data processing activities and that the developed process is in accordance with the goal and scope definition. A number of checks for internal consistency may be performed on a dataset and supporting data and methods (Table 2.1).

The methodological approach and viewpoints must be very clear so that independent data collection activities can yield similar data. A formal checklist can be developed to communicate the results of the consistency check (Table 2.2) Expanding upon the goal and scope of the unit process dataset, some inconsistency may be acceptable. If any inconsistency is detected, its role in the overall consistency evaluation should be documented.

2.4 References

[AIST–JEMAI] National Institute of Advanced Industrial Science and Technology–Japan Environmental Management Association for Industry. 2008. JEMAI-LCA Pro manual. Edited by AIST and JEMAI. Section II, Installed data, p 24-134. Tokyo: JEMAI.

[CPC and ISIC] Central Product Classification and International Standard Industrial Classification. 2011. [cited 2011 Feb 1]. Available from: http://unstats.un.org/unsd/cr/registry/regct.asp.

[EC] European Commission – Joint Research Centre – Institute for Environment and Sustainability. 2010a. International Reference Life Cycle Data System (ILCD) handbook - General guide for life cycle assessment - Detailed guidance. EUR 24708 EN. Luxembourg: Publications Office of the European Union. [cited 2011 Feb 1]. Available from: http://lct.jrc.ec.europa.eu/pdf-directory/ILCD-Handbook-General-guide-for-LCA-DETAIL-online-12March2010.pdf.

[EC] European Commission. 2010b. ILCD data documentation format 1. [cited 2011 Feb 1]. Available from: http://lca.jrc.ec.europa.eu/lcainfohub/ilcd/ILCD_Format_SDK.zip

Ecospold. 2011. Ecospold data documentation format 2. [cited 2011 Feb 1]. Available from http://www.ecoinvent.org/ecoinvent-v3/ecospold-v2/.

Eggleston HS, Buendia L, Miwa K, Ngara T, Tanabe K, editors. 2006. IPCC guidelines for national greenhouse gas inventories. Prepared by the National Greenhouse Gas Inventories Programme, Institute for Global Environmental Strategies (IGES), Japan. [cited 2011 Feb 1]. Available from http://www.ipcc-nggip.iges.or.jp/public/2006gl/index.html.

Frischknecht R, Jungbluth N, Althaus H-J, Doka G, Dones R, Heck T, Hellweg S, Hischier R, Nemecek T, Rebitzer G, Spielmann M. 2007. Overview and methodology. ecoinvent report No. 1, v2.0. Dübendorf (CH): Swiss Centre for Life Cycle Inventories.

Hedemann J, König U. 2007. Technical documentation of the ecoinvent database. Final report ecoinvent data v2.0, No. 4. Dübendorf (CH): Swiss Centre for Life Cycle Inventories. (formerly 2003 v1.01).

Heijungs R. 1996. Identification of key issues for further investigation in improving the reliability of life-cycle assessments, in Journal of Cleaner Production, Vol. 4, No. 3-4, pp. 159-166

Huijbregts MAJ, Norris G, Bretz R, Ciroth A, Maurice B, von Bahr B, Weidema B, de Beaufort ASH. 2001. Framework for modelling data uncertainty in life cycle inventories, Int J LCA. 6(3):127-131.

[IPCC] International Panel on Climate Change. 2000. Good practice guidance and uncertainty management in national greenhouse gas inventories, Annex 1: Conceptual basis for uncertainty analysis. [cited 2011 Feb 1]. Available from http://www.ipcc-nggip.iges.or.jp/public/gp/english/.

Maurice B, Frischknecht R, Coehlo-Schwirtz V, Hungerbühler K. 2000. Uncertainty analysis in life cycle inventory. Application to the production of electricity with French coal power plants. J Cleaner Prod. 8(2):95-108. doi:10.1016/S0959-6526(99)00324-8.

[USEPA] United States Environmental Protection Agency. 2006. Life cycle assessment: Principles and practice. EPA/600/R-06/060. Cincinnati (OH).

Weidema BP, Bauer C, Hischier R, Nemecek T, Vadenbo CO, Wernet G. 2011. Overview and methodology. Data quality guideline for the ecoinvent database version 3. Ecoinvent Report 1. St. Gallen (CH): The ecoinvent Centre.

Weidema BP, Cappellaro F, Carlson R, Notten P, Pålsson A-C, Patyk A, Regalini E, Sacchetto F, Scalbi S. 2004. Procedural guideline for collection, treatment, and quality documentation of LCA data. CASCADE Project report. [cited 2011 Feb 1]. Available from: http://www.enea.it/produzione_scientifica/pdf_volumi/V2004_ProceduralLCA.pdf.

Aggregated Data Development

Clare Broadbent
Martha Stevenson
Armando Caldeira-Pires
David Cockburn
Pascal Lesage
Ken Martchek
Olivier Réthoré
Rolf Frischknecht (liaison)

CHAPTER

3

Key Messages

• Although unit process–level data are preferable, there are legitimate reasons to aggregate data. The level of aggregation of the data should be as little as possible, but as much as necessary. In all cases, the motivation for aggregation should be clearly stated and justified.

• All modelling should be as consistent as necessary, and inconsistencies should be reported when relevant. Reporting of inconsistencies should include the modelling approach chosen, the treatment of multi-functional processes, allocation procedures, and other aspects of modelling.

• Transparency should be as high as possible, with sufficient documentation (e.g., unit processes are preferable, but when there is sufficient motivation not to provide unit processes, other information, such as key drivers, should be provided).

• There are multiple modelling approaches; aggregated datasets should be very clear about their use with each approach.

• We recommend using the necessary and relevant technical, engineering, and scientific knowledge when an aggregated dataset is built,

• The use and completeness of appropriate and consistent data and system boundaries should be ensured, depending on the LCA approach being used and the goal and scope of the study (e.g., cradle-to-grave datasets should include use and end-of-life phases).

• The generation of the aggregated datasets should be validated.

• Several allocation approaches exist. The approaches chosen should be justified and clearly described.

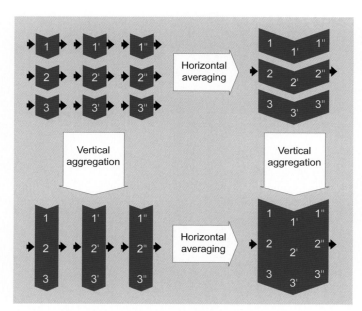

Figure 3.1: Horizontal averaging and vertical aggregation

"Aggregation" refers to the action of combining multiple unit process datasets into a single aggregated process dataset. One can distinguish between two broad types of aggregation (see Figure 3.1). The first, vertical aggregation refers to the combination of unit processes that succeed each other in a product life cycle, connected with intermediary flows. As a result of vertical aggregation, the inputs and outputs of the aggregated process dataset reflect the summation of the combined unit process datasets, which result in a loss of detailed information concerning the linkages between the original unit process datasets[1]. The second broad type is horizontal averaging, where multiple unit processes (or aggregated datasets) supplying a common reference flow are combined in order to produce an averaged dataset.

This section will provide guidance on the various motivations and methods of aggregation with an eye toward maintaining usability, interpretability, and transparency to the highest degree possible.

Individual unit processes (1, 1', 1", etc.) can be combined in the two ways described above, namely horizontal averaging and vertical aggregation (Figure 3.1). The steps necessary to aggregate multiple unit process datasets into a single aggregated process dataset include the following:

- Define the **goal** of the aggregation process.
- Identify the **reference flow** that the aggregated process dataset should supply.
- Define the **system boundaries** of the aggregated process dataset.
- Make explicit the ways the unit process datasets are **linked**.
- Ensure consistency and completeness of datasets being used.
- **Scale** each unit process to the selected reference flow.
- **Sum** the inputs and outputs of the scaled unit process datasets.
- **Document** the aggregation process and **characterize** the resultant aggregated process dataset. Documentation requirements are detailed in Chapter 4, which gives specific requirements for aggregated datasets.

The process above describes aggregation as carried out by a life cycle inventory (LCI) dataset provider or an LCI database provider. This same set of steps can be automated by software tools when calling on unit process or aggregated process datasets from an intrinsically linked database[2]. Because the same steps are followed for both manual and automated aggregation, the results achieved with each approach should be consistent.

3.1 Scope for Aggregation

The calculation of LCIs in the course of life cycle assessment (LCA) studies is an example of aggregation (ISO 2006, section 4.3). Indeed, scaling and aggregating the different unit processes within the system boundaries are necessary steps to calculate the LCI. In the context of LCI databases, aggregation is not a necessary step. Indeed, it is possible to store unit process datasets in databases in their disaggregated form (as unit process datasets as described in Chapter 2), and to let the users of the database aggregate the data in the course of their own LCA studies (as described above).

Multiple ways might be used and combined to aggregate unit process datasets, from basic horizontal averaging to more or less comprehensive vertical aggregation. There are different ways in which unit processes can be aggregated (or averaged; Figure 3.2), both at a company-specific level and also in creating an industry average dataset, and can cover a number of production steps and different life cycle stages. The basis for each of the 12 examples in Figure 3.2 is a cradle-to-grave LCA for PVC pipe. It shows three sites (site A has pro-

---

[1] Please note that it is also possible to further aggregate previously aggregated datasets. The majority of the document will address the aggregation of unit process datasets to aggregated process datasets, but the methods to further aggregate aggregated process datasets into new aggregated process datasets are similar and can be adapted to that context. This will be discussed further in Section 3.3 and Section 3.4.

[2] The term "intrinsically linked" (or "aggregatable") LCI database refers here to databases that are structured in such a way that it is possible for software to automatically create aggregated process datasets. These databases contain datasets for which one process input is linked, directly or through a set of rules contained in an algorithm, to another process output, and treats all multifunctional processes (through allocation or system expansion) such that fully terminated aggregated process datasets have only one reference flow.

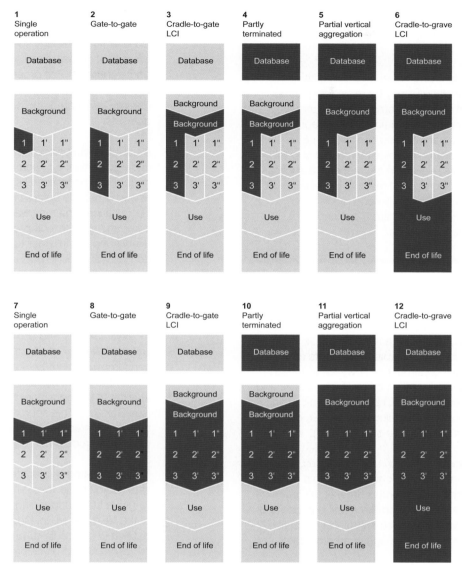

Figure 3.2: Aggregated datasets

cesses 1, 2, and 3; site B has processes 1', 2', and 3'; site C has processes 1", 2", and 3") that all have upstream processes (background) that are needed to make the final product, and these are all connected to the upstream, elementary flows (database). The product is then connected to a use phase and end-of-life phase to complete the cradle-to-grave LCA.

The following are examples of each of the aggregated datasets:

1) plastic extrusion process in plastic pipe manufacture of company A;
2) plastic pipe manufacture of company A;
3) plastic pipe manufacture of company A including feedstock supply and storage;
4) plastic pipes of company A (all inputs and outputs being elementary flows except for the reference product and some upstream process [background]), e.g., the inputs of feedstock, electricity, and natural gas);
5) plastic pipes of company A (all inputs and outputs being elementary flows except for the reference product, i.e., cradle-to-gate LCI);
6) plastic pipes of company A used in a building's sewage system, including end-of-life recycling or disposal (i.e., cradle-to- rave LCI);
7) Asian average plastic extrusion process in plastic pipe manufacture;
8) Asian average plastic pipe manufacture;
9) Asian average plastic pipe manufacture including feedstock supply and storage;
10) Asian average plastic pipes (all inputs and

outputs being elementary flows except for the reference product and, e.g., the inputs of feedstock, electricity, and natural gas);

11) Asian average plastic pipes (all inputs and outputs being elementary flows except for the reference product (i.e., cradle-to-gate LCI); and

12) Asian average plastic pipes used in a building's sewage system including end-of-life recycling or disposal (i.e., cradle-to-grave LCI).

Where single operation unit processes, sharing a common function, have been averaged into a horizontally averaged, aggregated process dataset (a type of aggregation), this can be treated like a unit process and will be referred to as such for the rest of the chapter.

The following types of aggregated datasets can be distinguished:

- Company-specific vs. industry average aggregated process datasets: Depending on whether the aggregation remains purely vertical or mixes up both vertical aggregation and horizontal averaging (respectively referred to as "company-specific" and "industry average" in Figure 3.2).

- Non-terminated vs. partially vs. fully terminated aggregated process datasets: Depending on whether respectively none, some, or all of the aggregated inventories are followed all the way back until only elementary flows cross the system boundaries. Such an aggregated process dataset will be made only of elementary flows if fully terminated, and will stand as a mix of both elementary and non-elementary flows if non- or partially terminated. Some examples of each type of terminated datasets are described below.

- Totally non-terminated aggregated process datasets: A gate-to-gate unit process, whether it is company specific or industry average. It comes as an aggregation of single operation unit processes (discussed in Chapter 2).

- Partially terminated aggregated process datasets:

  - A gate-to-gate unit process that would undergo vertical aggregation with one or more unit processes in its immediate vicinity, whether it is upstream or downstream. For instance, one may want to aggregate a company-specific unit process with one or a few suppliers in order to maintain confidentiality of specific data or information. An example of this is presented as "partial vertical aggregation" in Figure 3.2.

  - Terminate only some inventory items of an aggregated process dataset in order to leave flexibility and some parameterization ability. For instance, the electricity consumption might be the non-terminated part of the inventory, allowing the user to adapt it to the considered geographic zone (see Box 3.1). This approach may be useful to allow different modelling approaches while using a common database.

- Fully terminated aggregated process datasets: Both cradle-to-gate LCIs and cradle-to-grave LCIs, depending on which phases of the life cycle are included within the dataset (e.g., cradle-to-grave must include the use and end-of-life phases).

- The distribution phase (e.g., transport, retailing) may or may not be included in a cradle-to-gate LCI. System boundaries need to be well defined and explicitly stated to understand what is and is not included within the dataset.

3.2 Motivations for Aggregation

There are several goals or motivations for carrying out aggregation as well as types of aggregation that can meet the objectives of aggregation (Table 3.1). The list is not exhaustive, but provides some insight to the types of aggregation that can meet different data supplier needs. For example, if the motivation for aggregation is to protect business-sensitive, competition-sensitive, or proprietary information, it is possible to provide data as a cradle-to-gate, fully terminated dataset (Figure

3.2, numbers 5 and 11). It may also be sufficient to aggregate the unit process with one or a few unit processes adjacent in the supply chain (Figure 3.2, numbers 3 and 9), or to leave key flows non-terminated (Figure 3.2, numbers 4 and 10). If the sensitive data concerns a specific process, it may be possible that gate-to-gate data (Figure 3.2, numbers 2 and 8) is sufficient (hence the word "sometimes" in the corresponding cell of Table 3.1). There is no preference expressed in the order of the motivations, and the user is encouraged to look at the many alternatives to decide which best fits the needs of their LCA project.

Although many of the reasons for aggregation are valid, aggregation necessarily leads to a loss of information and affects transparency, adaptability, and interpretability. For this reason, the following two recommendations are made:

1) In the context of providing datasets via an LCI database, the level of aggregation should be as little as possible, but as large as necessary. We offer some guidance in choosing the lowest level of aggregation that meets a data supplier's needs (Table 3.1).
2) Whenever possible, both the aggregated process datasets and the individual unit process datasets should be made available, hence meeting both the objectives of the aggregation and retaining the advantages of individual unit process datasets.

Documentation of the motivations for aggregation could lead to a better understanding in the market regarding these various approaches.

Keeping the disaggregated, but linked unit process level of resolution in databases has several advantages (focusing on vertical aggregation):

- It provides model transparency, allowing the users of the database to understand which unit processes are used in the life cycle model of a given reference flow, and how these unit processes are linked. Although in itself it is not sufficient, this level of model transparency provides more potential information than any report on an aggregated dataset can, because all supply chains can be explored to any depth.
- It makes the database adaptable, in the sense that anyone can replace specific unit processes in a product system or make changes to a specific unit process in order to better represent the product life cycle that the model is meant to represent. Examples of adaptation include the updating of unit process data for which new data are available, and the regionalisation of unit processes when differences in emission

factors or employed technologies are known. These changes at the unit process level, be they unit processes supplying the reference flow of interest or a unit process many tiers down the supply chain, will change the LCI. These types of adaptations of aggregated process datasets cannot be done by the user, only those who initially aggregated the dataset (and who therefore hold the unit process level models) can make these adaptations. In most cases, it can be cost effective for the user to make these types of adaptations, provided the disaggregated datasets are available, or at least to choose who can carry out the adaptations.

- It can improve the interpretation phase of an LCA. One way disaggregated databases improve interpretation is by increasing the resolution at which one can conduct sensitivity analyses, contribution analyses, or both. For example, one can know not only which material or chemical contributes significantly to a given impact category, but specifically which process in that material's life cycle is the greatest contributor, allowing one to better focus subsequent process improvement activities toward reduction of the burden. Closely related is the increased resolution at which one can conduct sensitivity analyses, because more parameters (e.g., inputs or process conditions) are exposed to the user, more values in product systems can be varied as part of the sensitivity analyses. Another example of improved interpretation resulting from leaving databases disaggregated is the potential to carry out meaningful uncertainty and contribution analyses.
- It puts the unit process datasets and the life cycle model details in the hands of many practitioners, which enables the dataset to be reviewed many times and by different people, hence increasing the possibility that errors will be noticed and reported to the database provider. This type of review is not possible in aggregated datasets.
- Because the scope of the datasets can be more easily determined by the users, there can be less chance of double-counting or leaving out specific activities in LCA models (e.g., transportation between processes).

3.3 LCA Approach-dependent Modelling

In the past decade, two different approaches to LCA and, particularly, LCI modelling, have been dis-

Table 3.1: Motivations for aggregated datasets

GOAL OF AGGREGA-TION	EXPLANATION	GATE-TO-GATE	PARTIAL VERTICAL AGGREGATION
Ensure confidentiality	Datasets may be aggregated in order to protect business-sensitive, competition-sensitive, or proprietary information, including trade secrets, patented processes, process information used to easily derive costs, etc.	Sometimes	Yes
Protect data ownership	Datasets may be aggregated in order to combine processes together to protect ownership of specific datasets.	Sometimes	Yes
Provide computation efficiency	Datasets may be aggregated to increase the speed of calculations. This enables a more time efficient procedure to set up life-cycle systems in ad hoc and on-demand decision support (e.g., LCA-based design tools).	Sometimes	Sometimes
Ensure analysis efficiency	Datasets may be aggregated to the level appropriate for the resolution of analysis desired. For example, a company may have produced individual unit process datasets for each of its dozens of internal processes. While this level of detail may be interesting for the company itself, because it allows them to identify hot spots, it may provide too much information, which hinders effective analysis for an external user.	Yes	Yes
Appropriate relevance	Datasets may be aggregated where the individual unit process datasets built are not relevant outside of the model (i.e., the reference flows of the individual unit process datasets are never used externally in the market, but always associated within the gate-to-gate process, e.g., individual processes within an oil refinery). These unit process datasets are combined and associated with a reference flow that would be relevant to the market and thus meaningful within a database.	Yes	Yes
Preserve data integrity	Datasets may be aggregated in order to ensure a technically correct model. The combination of different unit process datasets to model a more complex system requires knowledge beyond LCA, including technical knowledge of the physical system being modeled (e.g., science, engineering). Providing disaggregated information could lead to incorrect models being developed and used for decision-making in the market.	Yes	Yes
Protect business model	Datasets may be aggregated to create an environment that maintains a constant revenue stream to the database, by ensuring a user community. This is a typical consulting model in which information is exchanged for money.	Sometimes	Sometimes
Increase ease of use	Cradle-to-gate or aggregated LCI dataset results can be treated as simple, monolithic modules in LCA studies. This treatment can simplify understanding for new users of LCA and embed information in upstream processes concerning adequate decisions (e.g., combining, allocating, and substituting the unit processes). This practice should not be seen as mutually exclusive from transparency because there is a growing trend to provide both the individual unit process datasets alongside aggregated cradle-to-gate datasets to databases.	Sometimes	Sometimes
Mask the source of environmental burden	Datasets may be aggregated in order to obscure a process within a system that is a major contributor to environmental damage. While somewhat contrary to the spirit of LCA, it maintains control of process changes internally to the industry but may limit the ability of those working in the public interest (e.g., government or nongovernmental organizations [NGOs]) to develop policy or campaigns to catalyse what they see as necessary changes.	Sometimes	Yes

PARTLY TERMINATED SYSTEM	CRADLE-TO-GATE	CRADLE-TO-GRAVE	NOTE
Yes	Yes	Yes	Any aggregation level that extends beyond an industry's "gate" may be sufficient to meet this goal. If the confidentiality concerns a specific process within an industry, gate-to-gate aggregation may be sufficient.
Yes	Yes	Yes	Most types of aggregation should be sufficient to meet this goal.
Sometimes	Yes	Yes	The computation efficiency discussed here is enabled only by terminated processes. The "gate to gate," "partial vertical aggregation," and "partly terminated system" meet this goal if all non-terminated flows are themselves pre-linked to terminated processes.
Yes	Yes	Yes	All levels of aggregation allow the elimination of unnecessary detail concerning, e.g., plant-level operations.
Yes	Yes	Yes	All levels of aggregation allow the fusion of unit processes that supply goods that are not put on the market but rather are always used by a subsequent unit process. However, this goal can be met without aggregation beyond the aforementioned adjacent processes.
Yes	Yes	Yes	If the unit processes whose quantitative linkages need to be frozen are plant or industry specific, then gate-to-gate aggregation may be sufficient. If they extend beyond the gates of a company or an industry, then the aggregation level needs to be increased.
Yes	Yes	Yes	The best means to meet this goal is to terminate processes. Gate-to-gate and partial vertical aggregation may in some cases allow one to meet this goal, if proprietary data from which one draws revenues are on the level of single operations.
Sometimes	Yes	Yes	Only fully terminated processes can be used as 'monolithic modules' as described here. Note that tools with explicit links between unit process datasets may render this goal moot. The 'gate to gate', 'partial vertical aggregation' and 'partly terminated system' meet this goal if all non-terminated flows are prelinked and write protected.
Yes	Yes	Yes	The level at which sources of environmental burdens are masked is directly proportional to the level of aggregation. If it is desirable to mask industry-specific or company-specific burdens, all aggregation levels beyond gate-to-gate meet the goal. If the burdens from a specific operation within a company or industry is what is to be masked, gate-to-gate aggregation may be sufficient.

tinguished, namely the attributional approach and the consequential approach (see also Chapter 1). Both approaches are theoretically associated with different objectives, and hence aim to provide different information to the end user of the LCA studies.

Different objectives of the two approaches have real repercussions on the models used in the LCA. These differences are usually (but in theory not exclusively) reflected in the LCI phase:

- The attributional approach
  - uses data on actual suppliers or average data and
  - commonly uses allocation as a means to deal with multifunctional processes or systems.
- The consequential approach
  - uses data on actual supplier as long as this supplier is not constrained (i.e., insofar as it can respond to an increase in demand with an equal increase in supply), otherwise uses data representing marginal technology (i.e., suppliers that will actually respond to a change in demand); and
  - uses a system expansion approach to deal with multifunctional processes to expand the analysed system with additional processes.

Although the conceptual differences in goal and in modelling procedures between these two approaches are quite stark, the separation in current LCA practice is not as clear, as shown in the following examples:

- The stated or implicit goal of the study is not reflected in the modelling approach (e.g., attributional approach is used as a means to estimate the consequences of a decision or to generate information meant to influence the decision of other actors).
- The system modelling used contains elements from both approaches (e.g., average data used when determining what processes should be linked to in the system, but system expansion is used to deal with multifunctional processes, as in the PAS 2050 (BSI 2011) or in International Reference Life Cycle Data System (ILCD; EC 2010).

Other approaches also are proposed. For example, the decisional approach (proposed by Frischknecht and Stucki 2010 based on Frischknecht 1998) aims at supporting decisions in companies to improve the environmental profile of their products or their production. The decisional approach links to anticipated future suppliers with which one may establish financial and contractual relations, even if the said sup-

pliers are constrained, and uses long-term marginal market mixes based on official statistics and sectoral forecasts published by the relevant industry associations. The decisional approach does not imply the application of one particular allocation approach.

There are important implications for LCI dataset suppliers and database operators:

- As far as possible, a single modelling approach should be used within a single dataset. In practice, the choice of modelling approach, as well as the choice of particular datasets, can be guided by the *mutatis mutandis* principle (all necessary changes being made). Focusing on the key processes relevant in one modelling approach rather than striving for a pure model helps to optimise between efforts (time and money spent) and accuracy.
- This single approach should be clearly documented, specifying, for example, how processes are linked in general (e.g., average vs. marginal), how these are actually defined (e.g., average based on consumption or production mix; marginal based on simplified approach or necessarily based on forecast data), and what approach is used in dealing with multifunctional processes.

If the datasets chosen to complete the LCI modelling are inconsistent with the chosen LCI modelling approach, the inconsistency and its potential effects on the results should be stated and discussed in the LCI results of the aggregated process datasets.

Relatively small-scale (or marginal) changes or variations in overall production volumes are usually of interest in LCA. For this scale of change, one can make simple and consistent assumptions on the response of different producers in the economy, be they based on the attributional, consequential, or any other approach. It is therefore possible to create databases where linking between unit processes (and other inventory modelling aspects) follow these sets of assumptions. However, when dealing with large-scale market changes to the product system, for example, driving towards significant production volume changes in terms of technology mix or towards novel technology solutions, LCI database information would be insufficient to inform life cycle–based decision-making. Indeed, the systemic changes that would accompany larger-scale changes require *ad hoc* and sometimes more refined information sources and models (this is discussed more in Chapter 5).

To the extent that unit process datasets are application neutral (i.e., unallocated) and minimally aggregated over technology levels and producing regions, it is possible to use them to construct life cycle models that use any of the previously mentioned approaches.

All modelling approaches are different, but we

do not recommend pointing to one approach as the general best approach without looking at the explicit modelling or decision context.

3.4 Modelling Aggregated Process Datasets

The following sections provide suggestions and recommendations for aggregating unit process data into process datasets that are larger in scope.

3.4.1 Goal and Scope

Before performing a data aggregation, one should clearly define and document the goal and scope as follows:

- product (good or service) that the aggregated process dataset will represent (reference flow). In particular, information should be provided on
  - properties and functions of the product;
  - geographical, temporal, and technological validity of the dataset (e.g., steel produced in Europe in 2010 via electric arc furnace); and
  - in the case of horizontally averaged datasets, a clear statement as to whether the average represents a production or a consumption mix for the region.
- motivation for aggregation (see Section 3.2).
- type (horizontal, vertical, engineering-based) and level (e.g., gate-to-gate, partially- or fully-terminated) of aggregation.
- modelling approach and guidelines to be followed in the aggregation (e.g., attributional, consequential, in line with database-specific guidelines) and the types of uses for which the aggregated dataset is suitable.
- intended level of verification or review of the aggregated dataset.
- LCIA requirements to be met and the elementary flows to be included.
- data quality requirements.
- intended audience.

The goal and scope help determine which unit process datasets or aggregated process datasets to include within the modelled system boundary. Particular databases may be designed to address specific categories of user needs and might therefore prescribe the nature of the aggregated process datasets that can be submitted for inclusion.

The goal and scope definition at the aggregated dataset level is generally the same as for the LCA study level except that it may be smaller or larger in scale, depending on the system being studied. In all cases, adequate documentation should be provided.

3.4.2 Horizontal Averaging

Horizontal averaging is the action of aggregating multiple unit process datasets or aggregated process datasets in which each provides the same reference flow in order to create a new process dataset.

Beyond the elements mentioned in the previous section (3.4.1), the following aspects should be considered when applying horizontal averaging:

- Provide information on the nature and source of the datasets that are aggregated.
- Ensure that the boundaries of the averaged datasets are equivalent. For example, averaging gate-to-gate unit process datasets with cradle-to-gate aggregated process datasets is not appropriate.
- Provide information on the representativeness of the averaged dataset (e.g., the percentage of the total production volumes represented by the aggregated unit processes).
- For production mixes, there is a preference for production-volume weighted averages.
- If providing consumption mixes, then specify how the consumption mix was determined and the principal producing regions that are supplying the consumption mix.

3.4.3 Technical-based Aggregation

Technical- or engineering-based aggregation refers to vertical aggregation of unit processes that are directly linked within a single facility or process train.

In such cases, the decision of which processes to be linked (e.g., average or marginal) and how allocation should be considered in joint production processes are not of relevance.

For this approach, it is of utmost importance that technical, scientific, or engineering knowledge is directly involved while constructing the model. This knowledge becomes more and more important with increasing complexity of the modelled system. Examples of complex systems include a crude oil refinery, a steel production site, and agricultural cultivation. For these complex systems, technical and economic knowledge are most appropriate to ensure proper linking of processes. Salient features of the topics discussed in the workshop were these:

- Engineering processes often define the way in which unit processes need to be linked. There are defined links between each manufacturing process, which need to be maintained. These links are often complex, and the processes may have re-circulating loops that further complicate the nature of the system definition. It is desirable for these aggregated, gate-to-gate datasets to be developed by those with the relevant industry knowledge and provided as unallocated datasets with documentation on the process flow diagram and main contributing factors (processes or inputs, etc.).
- The outcome of this process is necessarily a non-terminated process. If terminating any of the flows, one is doing life cycle modelling for which some knowledge beyond the sector- or facility-specific technical knowledge is required. One should refer to the next section for this type of modelling.
- In the case of multifunctional processes, technical and engineering knowledge can be very relevant. This is true for combined production for datasets that can be further subdivided. For true joint production, LCA modelling knowledge is required, and technical and engineering knowledge is no longer sufficient (see Section 3.4.4). The result of vertical aggregation based on engineering principals can be a multifunctional process dataset.

3.4.4 Vertical Aggregation Based On Life Cycle Modelling Principles

The previous section dealt with vertical aggregation that could be done using strictly technical and engineering expertise for a specific facility, sector, or technology. Once one starts building aggregated process datasets that include processes from the background (i.e., when one starts connecting inputs and outputs from the gate-to-gate facility with unit processes that can produce or absorb these flows), then knowledge on life cycle modelling is required. This is true especially because there are many ways to model (partially or fully terminated) product life cycles (see Figure 3.2).

This section deals specifically with choosing the unit processes that one links together to construct a model, and the approaches for dealing with multifunctional processes. Further considerations are included below in Section 3.4.5.

3.4.4.1 Modelling: Linking between Different Products

Vertical aggregation involves combining unit process datasets (or aggregated process datasets) together linked by a flow. How the processes that are linked are chosen depends on which modelling approach is chosen (Section 3.3). We distinguish between three general cases. Consider, however, that the different modelling approaches (Section 3.3) may dictate rules that govern when and how one should deviate from the general rules.

First, specific supplier data may be required for certain situations, but more often current practice is to include this type of data within an LCA study, rather than compiling it into an aggregated process dataset in a database. Increasing market demand for traceability through supply chains and supply chain reporting, together with evolving and increasingly more sophisticated data handling capability, may lead to developments in this area. One can base linking rules on current or future contractual arrangements irrespective of eventual constraints (Frischknecht and Stucki 2010).

Linking to supplier-specific datasets can be relevant in all types of modelling approaches. In the consequential approach, however, linking to a specific supplier is acceptable only if it can be assumed that this supplier will actually meet the modelled demand with an increase in production. If it is a constrained supplier, that is, if the supplier is unable to supply the increased amount without reducing the amount supplied to other customers, then it is by definition not an affected process and should not be included in the model.

Second, linking to average datasets of global or regional market mixes can prove useful to a wide range of users where the good or output is freely traded at such a geographic level, to provide data when more specific data are otherwise lacking, or the impact of using average data is liable to be insignificant, particularly for elements of background systems.

Market mixes with more tightly defined geographic scope may be required for goods where local markets exist. The technological scope will need to be more specific where users may desire to distinguish between different technologies producing the same good (e.g., certified electricity, certified agricultural products). More tightly defined mixes may allow greater discrimination in subsequent analysis and interpretation.

The user should be aware of the differences and trade-offs between using Production vs. Consumption mixes. Consumption mixes provide ease of use for end users of the aggregated process dataset. If a dataset purports to be a consumption mix, this approach should have been followed consistently in the modelling of the aggregated process dataset.

Production mixes provide flexibility for users who can combine these to produce a required consumption mix. Production mixes themselves should have been compiled using inputs with appropriate consumption mix. In LCI databases, we recommend linkage between consumption mixes when available and distinctly different from production mixes.

Third, in linking to actual or average suppliers, one implicitly assumes that a demand of one unit is automatically met by a supply of one unit (full elasticity). Linking to marginal production does not make this assumption, but instead looks at the consequences of the additional demand. In trying to determine the consequences of a decision, one may want to link only to the technologies that are ultimately affected by a demand for a specific product. It is ultimately impossible to know with precision what processes are affected, because the cause-and-effect chain includes modelled market mechanisms that are impossible to verify empirically. Several approaches exist, including referring to forecast data (Weidema 2003), Computable General Equilibrium models (Dandres 2011), and simplified approaches based on general knowledge on market trends and technology levels.

In the consequential approach, one should avoid linking to constrained processes. The correct approach is to determine and link with the unit process dataset or aggregated process dataset that will change production volume in response to an increase in demand for the output in question. The marginal dataset can be determined by considering the economics of the relevant market (Box 3.2). Weidema (2003), Ekvall and Weidema (2004), and the European Commission (2010), for example, provide current practice in applying this approach.

allow that the rules may be relaxed where the preferred data are unobtainable and the contribution from the process is insignificant or may be reasonably approximated by an available proxy dataset.

Where a specific supplier cannot be identified or determined for a particular good or service, one would choose a dataset representing the relevant consumption market mix, and the choice should be well documented. For example, use a regional average dataset for a particular material that is used in the production of the product in question.

Because the differences in modelling described above deal with how unit processes are connected to each other and not with how individual unit process datasets are modelled, the same set of unit process datasets could be used to produce many different types of life cycle models (and hence aggregated process datasets). To do so, one could create various parallel databases, all relying on the same unit process datasets, but where the linking rules differ. An alternative is to model life cycles using parameterized market processes, which can change the mix of supplying processes (from

---

Box 3.2 An example of linking to marginal production

Multiple electricity generation technologies may supply electricity to a given grid. In average modelling, one would account for the average grid mix, (i.e., that use a weighted average of the electricity generation technologies). For marginal production linkage, one would need to link to an electricity provider that will actually change its output as a response to the change in demand for electricity. By definition, this cannot be a constrained producer (e.g., hydro-electricity in a region where the hydro-electric potential is already fully used). If interested in short-term effects, the marginal producer will be the electricity producer able to increase the amount of electricity production with the existing capacity. If interested in the long-term, the marginal producer will be the electricity producer that will adapt the rate at which new capacity is installed.

3.4.4.2 Implementation of Linking Rules in for Unit Process Datasets

The modelling approach chosen should in principle be followed consistently throughout the modelling of the aggregated dataset, whether it is presented fully aggregated or as a modelled system of linked processes. The different modelling approaches generally

an average to a marginal mix, for example).

To facilitate linking, we strongly recommend that the names of intermediate flows in a database should be consistent across unit process datasets. The use of common intermediary flow names or reference flow classification schemes across databases would also facilitate interchangeability.

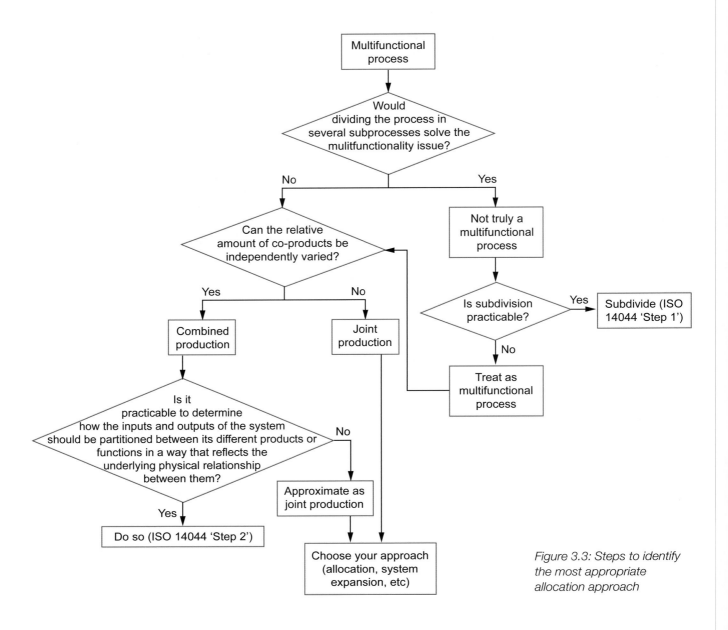

Figure 3.3: Steps to identify the most appropriate allocation approach

3.4.4.3 Allocation: Treatment of Multi-Functional Processes

Aggregated process datasets often have multiple functions (e.g., integrated chemical plants manufacturing a range of co-products, waste incinerators burning different types of waste, recycling facilities producing secondary materials while at the same time providing waste treatment services). For instance, an aggregation of the unit processes of a crude oil refinery shows the output of petroleum coke (from coking units) in addition to the primary reference flows such as gasoline or diesel fuel.

Therefore, the various inputs and outputs of the aggregated process dataset "oil refinery" need to make the aggregated process dataset mono-functional,

which can happen either through allocation or system expansion through the avoided burden approach. The use of system expansion to include additional functions into the system is not applicable in the context of developing datasets for LCI databases.

The allocation procedures described below are valid for co-production and recycling. As stated in International Organization for Standardization 14044 (ISO 2006, section 4.3.4.2), "whenever possible, allocation should be avoided."

The flow diagram (Figure 3.3) shows the steps to identify the most appropriate approach when dealing with multifunctional processes. If a multifunctional process can be subdivided, and this is practical, allocation can be avoided (e.g., identifying processes on a production site that contribute to specific production lines only).

If subdivision is possible, but not practical, the process is treated as if it were multifunctional (e.g., a subdivision of the processes in a chemicals production plant may theoretically be possible but not practical due to the constraints in time and human resources available for a more detailed analysis). In case the relative amounts of the co-products being produced can be varied independently, and it is practical to do so, physical relationships may be used as a basis for allocation (e.g., the dependency of fuel consumption and emissions of a lorry on the payload). If independent variation is either not possible or not practical, the multifunctional process represents joint production (e.g., electrolysis of sodium chloride).

When one is confronted with a case of (real or apparent) joint production for which none of the previous approaches are relevant (reaching the lowest box in the diagram), inputs and outputs should be attributed based on a procedure that is the best fit to meet aggregated dataset requirements.

Below is a list of commonly used procedures for addressing multifunctional processes, as stated, for example, in ISO 14044 (2006, section 4.3.4):

- Partitioning can be based on other relationships such as
    - physical properties such as mass, energy content, exergy content, or concentration;
    - economic value such as market prices of products and services, of primary materials, recycled materials, or scrap; or
    - number of subsequent uses..
- Avoided burden or system expansion can be based on
    - displacing average,
    - displacing marginal,
    - differentiating whether one is dealing with a determining or non-determining product flow, or
    - avoided burden followed by sharing of credit.

Whichever procedure is selected should be documented and explained, including, if available, information on the sensitivity analysis of the treatment of the multifunctional process. As far as feasible, allocation procedures should be applied consistently within and among the datasets available in an LCI database. For partitioning, the allocated inputs and outputs should equal unallocated inputs and outputs.

Existing databases handle allocation differently; some of these approaches are listed here, but it is not our intent to recommend one approach above another. The choice of allocation procedure should be in accordance with the stated goal and should be clearly documented. The ILCD (EC 2010) system differentiates micro-level (product, site), macro-level (policies,

strategies), and monitoring LCA applications. For the micro-level applications, it asks for system expansion via substitution of the superseded market mix with regard to recycling but also other cases of multifunctional processes. The development of sector- and product-specific allocation approaches is foreseen to complement the general guidance. The US LCI database guideline (NREL 2010) proposes to use substitution and best LCA practices in case of the consequential approach. The ecoinvent data v2.0 (Frischknecht et al. 2007) applies partitioning, in most cases based on economic value and exergy content (which correlates fairly well with economic value), and recycled content allocation with respect to recycling. The Advanced Industrial Science and Technology Database (AIST 2009) guideline asks for allocation, leaving the freedom to choose from either mass, energy, capacity, or cost. The Business Council for Sustainable Development and the World Resources Institute standard on product carbon footprint (WBSCD and WRI 2010) considers the allocation and the system expansion approaches as being equivalent. The GaBi 4.4 Database (PE International 2011) applies allocation on a case-specific basis and is based on the measure that reflects the intention of the processes most adequately (mass, energy, exergy, value, or individual partitioning) as well as substitution approaches where necessary.

3.4.5 Further Considerations in System Boundaries Definition

There are a number of choices of which the aggregator needs to be aware. Some of these choices may be driven by the database intended for the dataset being generated, others may be more dependent upon the system being modelled. These are discussed in the following sections.

3.4.5.1 What Cut-Off Rules to Apply

The ISO standard proposes using a percentage of total mass, total energy, and total environmental impacts as cut-off criterion (ISO 14044, 2006, clause 4.2.3.3.3). Some argue that the relative contribution can be quantified and that a relative threshold value can be defined against an estimated total environmental impact using similar processes and expert judgement (EC 2010). Others argue that the total mass, energy, or environmental impacts is unknown and a recommendation with a quantified percentage does not really help, from which they propose to use the environmental knowledge of experts to judge whether or not to include potentially negligible inputs or elementary flows (Frischknecht et al. 2003). An intermediate approach is followed by AIST (2009). They recommend excluding lightweight parts assuring coverage of 95% of the total weight of the products on one hand, and the exclusion of inputs for which a low environmental load can be proven.

3.4.5.2 Capital Equipment

Capital equipment can include cars, manufacturing machinery, factory halls, and the like. Infrastructure is assets such as power plants, transmission lines, pipelines, roads, and sewage systems. There are several common practices of including or excluding capital equipment and infrastructure in a product system. The AIST database takes capital equipment and infrastructure into account, in case the effect is considered to be large. The ecoinvent database explicitly and consistently includes capital equipment and infrastructure. The US database does flag capital equipment and infrastructure as not mandatory (NREL 2010). Other commonly used databases, e.g., GaBi 4.4, include infrastructure explicitly if a certain relevancy is traceable (such as like for wind power etc.). Ideally, infrastructure should be included where significant.

3.4.5.3 Environmental Incidents and Accidents or Maintenance

In principle, all accidents due to their fundamentally different nature are excluded from the regular LCI. However, smaller accidents of higher frequency (sometimes referred to as "incidents") are often invisibly included in the raw data and cannot easily be inventoried separately from the main LCI that relates to regular operation.[3]

While accidents are events that occur seldom but may cause large environmental damage, as was experienced with the explosion and oil spill at the Deepwater Horizon offshore platform in 2010, or the nuclear power core melt down at Chernobyl in 1986, incidents occur rather frequently. While there is consensus that LCA is not a tool suited for the quantification of low probability, high-impact events (better addressed through risk assessment), nevertheless it is advisable to account for incidents, which are considered as part of the "regular" if not normal operation.

We recommend a quantified distinction be established between accidents and incidents. If impacts from incidents are significant to the LCI results of an LCI dataset, we recommend including the incidents in the LCI dataset, if they are not already included in the annual totals.

Breakdown of end-of-pipe technologies such as flue gas treatment facilities or wastewater treatment plants cause higher emissions. We recommend that such breakdowns, either due to malfunction or intentionally (due to revision or maintenance), be included in the

annual emission flows determined, measured, or calculated for the respective production site and attributed to the annual production volume of the site.

3.4.5.4 Certificates

We recommend that carbon offset certificates and Renewable Energy Certificates (RECs) should not be included in aggregated process datasets (ISO draft 14067 [2011]) . Among other purposes, LCI databases are intended to be used to create models to support decisions such as whether to purchase RECs or carbon offsets. Mechanisms for compensating for the environmental impacts of products (e.g., prevention of the release of, reduction in, or removal of greenhouse gas emissions) are outside the boundary of the product system (ISO draft 14067 [2011], clause 3.9.4 on offsetting).

If one wants to communicate information on RECs and offset certificates, the associated flows shall be kept separate. If it is an elementary flow (e.g., a negative carbon dioxide flow), then it shall be reported as a distinct flow. If it is an intermediate flow (e.g., a purchase of renewable energy certificates), then it shall be non-terminated. Certified products (such as certified electricity) being purchased and used in processes within the product system can be accounted for, depending on the modelling approach.

3.4.5.5 Waste Management Processes

Waste management activities cover landfilling of different types of wastes (inert waste, municipal waste), underground storage (hazardous waste, nuclear waste), waste incineration, wastewater treatment, carbon capture and storage, etc. They are technical processes and thus should be part of the product system like any other process or activity. In terminated datasets, wastes should not be treated as elementary flows, except in cases where the respective waste treatment process is not part of the product system.

3.4.6 Calculate: Scale and Summation

Once the LCA model has been constructed, it is necessary to scale each unit process dataset to the reference flow and then sum the inputs and outputs of each scaled unit process dataset. This section deals specifically with vertical aggregation.

Depending on the scope of the aggregation, the resulting aggregated dataset will have different types of flows crossing the boundary. In all cases, one of the flows will be the reference flow. Beyond that, some aggregated processes will contain both intermediate flows and elementary flows (e.g., gate-to-gate aggregated dataset), mostly elementary flows and some selected

---

[3] The ILCD Handbook indicates that if the overall impacts from such small accidents are significant to the LCI results of an LCI dataset, then they need to be singled out and accompany the LCI as part of an optional, separate accident-related inventory.

intermediate flows (partially terminated aggregated process dataset) or only elementary flows (e.g., cradle-to-gate and cradle-to-grave aggregated process dataset).

There are different methods used to scale unit processes and to sum their inputs and outputs. The most intuitive method, which very closely follows the way product systems are usually depicted in flow diagrams, is the so-called "sequential approach." In this approach, unit processes are scaled in sequence, starting with the process supplying the reference flow, then scaling the unit processes supplying products to this unit process, then scaling the unit processes supplying them, and so forth. In addition to being intuitive, this approach has the advantage of facilitating interpretation, since the contribution of individual supply chains can be assessed very easily. Its main disadvantage is when it is used to calculate fully terminated or partially terminated systems from collections of single-operation or gate-to-gate processes. In these cases, the presence of feedback loops (coal production requires electricity, which in turn requires coal) implies that, unless the sequential approach is carried out infinitely, the resulting inventory will not be exact. The inventory may converge to an exact solution quickly, although this is not guaranteed. This issue tends to be less relevant in the case of datasets aggregated for confidentiality reasons on a gate-to-gate or partially aggregated basis.

A second method is the matrix approach (Heijungs and Suh 2002), whereby the inputs and outputs of unit processes are arranged in a matrix (representing the coefficients of a set of linear equations). In real-life product systems, matrix algebra can find exact inventories in all cases, even when there are many feedback loops. However, the matrix inversion approach complicates the exploration of individual branches and supply chains.

There are other approaches that exist (power series, hybrid approaches using both matrix inversion and sequential approach) that can be considered for LCA studies and LCA software. However, in the context of aggregating data for inclusion in a database, it can be said that the two main approaches described above are sufficient and well adapted. We recommend that

- the matrix approach be used when calculating partially or fully terminated aggregated process datasets using unit process datasets. The inability or difficulty to explore individual branches is not relevant in this context, and this approach will yield exact solutions.
- any approach be used for any other case, including calculating aggregated process datasets from other aggregated process datasets, noting in passing that the sequential approach may be the simplest approach (the matrix approach would imply some manipulation such as moving product flows to the elementary flow matrix to leave them out of the set of linear equations).

To allow aggregation of elementary flows, elementary flow nomenclature should be consistent. We also recommend not summing elementary flows that were disaggregated at the unit process level (e.g., do not aggregate polycyclic aromatic hydrocarbons [PAHs] into a sum amount if individual constituents were reported for one, some, or all of the unit process datasets).

Sometimes, unit process datasets carry information on the temporal and spatial distribution of emissions, ranging from generic tags (such as "long-term" or "urban") to very specific information (such as using specific time periods or a set of coordinates). This type of information can be very useful to refine the impact assessment phase.

If these elementary flows are simply summed according to their names (e.g., SO_2 to air), the resulting inventory will contain no information on the location or time aspects of the individual contributions (e.g., total SO_2 per unit reference flow will be available). It is therefore relevant to keep the temporal and spatial information by treating each combination of substance name, compartment (and sub-compartment), location, and timing of emission as individual elementary flows. This would mean that a single aggregated inventory process may have many instances of a specific elementary flow in the inventory, each associated with a different location (e.g., there would be as many SO_2-to-air flows as there are sites emitting SO_2 in the aggregated system).

This type of strategy could eventually lead to databases or datasets that are too large to manipulate easily, either because of machine computational limits (e.g., the datasets are so large that the computation of life cycles becomes too long or too demanding on normally used computers). If this becomes the case, then strategies will need to be explored, such as transforming LCI results of chosen horizontally averaged datasets to impact assessment results. While doing so, one may deviate from the strict ISO 14044–prescribed order carrying out an LCA (such as computing impact assessment for individual elements of the product system before the LCI proper would be calculated in order to judge if they can be eliminated from the LCI calculations), it may; however, greatly reduce the number of processes and the number of elementary flows handled.

3.5 Data Quality and Validation

Data quality of unit process datasets has been covered in Chapter 2 and should be taken into consideration when developing aggregated process datasets. This subsection elaborates the key points for ensuring data quality and validating the aggregated process datasets.

3.5.1 Data Quality

The unit process chosen for the reference flow of an aggregated dataset needs to be appropriately selected and modelled. All subsequent processes chosen should adequately represent what the preceding processes are actually consuming. When aggregating datasets, data providers need to ensure that all relevant processes have been included to fully represent the aggregated dataset reference flow, in accordance with the goal and scope of the study. All investigated datasets should be described in the report, and all necessary metadata and flow data should be available for each dataset.

In order to maintain a high level of data quality, data aggregation of unit processes should be undertaken by those with the relevant technical expertise in the system being modelled and with LCA expertise. In addition, an internal validation of the aggregated datasets and the methodology and aggregation process aims to ensure a high level of data quality.

Quantitative data quality information from the unit processes should be aggregated. In principle, one can quantify and aggregate qualitative data quality information or apply expert judgment. In addition, uncertainties in the quality of the dataset should be documented. Documentation is covered in Chapter 4.

The completeness associated with unit process datasets is covered in Chapter 2. The same rules can be taken into consideration for aggregated process datasets. Data providers need to ensure that all relevant processes have been included to fully represent the aggregated dataset reference flow, in accordance with the goal and scope of the study.

Aggregated dataset completeness can be evaluated in relation to the initially defined cut-off criteria in terms of process coverage, elementary flow coverage,

etc. All relevant datasets should be documented, and all necessary meta information and flow data should be available for each dataset. Final completeness should be documented as described in Chapter 4.

3.5.2 Validation

The generation of the aggregated datasets should be validated. This means that all unit processes and their interlinkages should be checked with regard to data plausibility and completeness, uncertainty, and methodological consistency. This validation process is carried out through a series of procedures to check if data are valid by assessing against the chosen data quality indicators.

The methods discussed in Chapter 4 on validation of datasets intended for databases can also be applied to an individual aggregated dataset of a gate-to-gate process. As with an LCI, the aggregated data provider should provide enough information so that the user can actually derive qualitative or, if possible, quantitative appropriateness information. As with unit process datasets, sensitivity analyses can help to validate the quality of an aggregated dataset.

3.6 Publications on Data Quality

There are many publications that can assist in the assessment of the data quality of aggregated datasets, and these include the following, in addition to the References in this chapter:

- Bauer C, editor. 2003. International Workshop on Quality of LCI Data; 2003 Oct 20–21; Forschungszentrum Karlsruhe.
- Huijbregts, AJ. 1998. A general framework for the analysis of uncertainty and variability in life cycle assessment. Int J LCA. (5):273-280.
- Weidema BP, Bauer C, Hischier R, Nemecek T, Vadenbo CO, Wernet G. 2011. Overview and methodology. Data quality guideline for the ecoinvent database version 3. Ecoinvent Report 1. St. Gallen (CH): The ecoinvent Centre.

3.7 References

[AIST] National Institute of Advanced Industrial Science and Technology. 2009. The database for research result presentations. [cited 2011 Feb 1]. Available from: http://www.aist.go.jp/aist_e/database/rrpdb/.

[BSI] British Standards Institution. 2011. PAS 2050 research report. London: BSI. ISBN 978 0 580 50995 7. [cited 2011 Feb 1]. Available from http://www.bsigroup.com/Standards-and-Publications/How-we-can-help-you/Professional-Standards-Service/PAS-2050/.

Dandres T, Carolinelt C, Tirado-Secod P, Samson R. 2011. Assessing non-marginal variations with consequential LCA: Application to European energy sector. Renewable and Sustainable Energy Reviews. 15(6):3121-3132.

[EC] European Commission – Joint Research Centre – Institute for Environment and Sustainability. 2010. International Reference Life Cycle Data System (ILCD) handbook - General guide for life cycle assessment - Detailed guidance. EUR 24708 EN. Luxembourg: Publications Office of the European Union. [cited 2011 Feb 1]. Available from: http://lct.jrc.ec.europa.eu/pdf-directory/ILCD-Handbook-General-guide-for-LCA-DETAIL-online-12March2010.pdf.

Ekvall T, Weidema BP. 2004. System boundaries and input data in consequential life cycle inventory analysis. Int J LCA. 9(3):161-171.

Frischknecht R. 1998. Life cycle inventory analysis for decision-making: Scope-dependent inventory system models and context-specific joint product allocation. 3-9520661-3-3. Zürich (CH): Eidgenössische Technische Hochschule. 255 p.

Frischknecht R, Jungbluth N, Althaus H-J, Doka G, Dones R, Heck T, Hellweg S, Hischier R, Nemecek T, Rebitzer G, Spielmann M. 2007. Overview and methodology. ecoinvent report No. 1, v2.0. Dübendorf (CH): Swiss Centre for Life Cycle Inventories.

Frischknecht R, Jungbluth N, editors. 2007. Overview and methodology, Ecoinvent Report No. 1. Swiss Centre for Life Cycle Inventories. Dübendorf (CH).

Frischknecht R, Stucki M. 2010. Scope-dependent modelling of electricity supply in life cycle assessments. Int J LCA. 15:806-816.

PE International. 2011. GaBi modelling principles. [cited 2011 Feb 1]. Available from: http://documentation.gabi-software.com/sample_data/external_docs/GaBi_Modelling_Principles.pdf.

Heijungs R, Suh S. 2002. Computational structure of life cycle assessment. Dordrecht (NL): Kluwer.

[ISO] International Organization for Standardization. 2006. ISO 14044. Environmental management — Life cycle assessment — Requirement and guidelines. [cited 2011 Feb 1]. Available from: http://www.iso.org/iso/iso_catalogue/catalogue_tc/catalogue_detail.htm?csnumber=38498.

[ISO] International Organization for Standardization. Under development 2011. ISO 14067. Carbon footprint of products., [cited 2011 Feb 1]. Information available from: http://www.iso.org/iso/iso_catalogue/catalogue_ics/catalogue_detail_ics.htm?ics1=13&ics2=020&ics3=40&csnumber=59521. Clause 3.9.4 on offsetting.

[NREL] National Renewable Energy Laboratory, Athena Sustainable Materials Institute, Franklin Associates, Ltd., Sylvatica. 2004. U.S. LCI Database Project – User's Guide Draft, February 2004, NREL/BK-35854. [cited 2011 Feb 1]. Available from: www.nrel.gov/lci/pdfs/users_guide.pdf.

[WBCSD and WRI] World Business Council for Sustainable Development and World Resources Institute. 2010. The GHG protocol product life cycle accounting and reporting standard. Geneva and Washington DC: WBCSD and WRI.

Weidema BP. 2003. Market information in life cycle assessment. 2.-0 LCA consultants for Danish Environmental Protection Agency. p 15. [cited 2011 Feb 1]. Available from: http://www2.mst.dk/common/Udgivramme/Frame.asp?http://www2.mst.dk/Udgiv/publications/2003/87-7972-991-6/html/kap00_eng.htm.

Data Documentation, Review, and Management

Atsushi Inaba

Angeline de Beaufort

Alberta Carpenter

Fredy Dinkel

Ivo Mersiowsky

Claudia Peña

Chiew Wei Puah

Greg Thoma

Marc-Andree Wolf (liaison)

CHAPTER

Key Messages

• A globally harmonized taxonomy (reference list of elementary flow names) is the primary condition for interoperability of datasets and databases. Data formats and software systems should differentiate data gaps from true numerical zero values.

• Each dataset needs to be clearly, but concisely documented so that users can understand what process it describes, what are the sources of the original data, how these data have been manipulated, what has been included and excluded, and what are the limitations or exclusions of use for the dataset. Furthermore, the uncertainties must be described.

• With regard to review of the dataset, the user should be able to understand what type of review has been performed on the dataset, what information in the dataset has been reviewed, and what were the conclusions of the dataset review (both the aspects or baselines against which the review was conducted and the metrics of the review). In the course of data validation and review, plausibility checks should be conducted in order to identify issues caused by data gaps and to quantify uncertainties.

• To facilitate understanding by the user community and to encourage preparation of datasets for inclusion, each database manager should prepare a protocol document describing the contents, format of datasets, method for feedback on datasets, and requisites for inclusion of datasets within the database.

• A life cycle inventory (LCI) database is a system intended to organize, store, and retrieve large amounts of digital LCI datasets easily. It consists of an organized collection of LCI datasets that completely or partially conform to a common set of criteria, including methodology, format, review, and nomenclature, and that allow for interconnection of individual datasets that can be specified for use with identified impact assessment methods in application of life cycle assessments (LCAs) and life cycle impact assessments (LCIAs).

When a user opens a new life cycle inventory (LCI) database or LCI dataset to complete work toward preparing an LCI, he or she will have certain questions pertaining to what the data represent and how reliable these data are in the context of his or her question. This chapter on data documentation, review, and management provides recommendations that can be used to communicate the information to the users in order to answer these questions. This information is also useful for those constructing datasets because it provides an understanding of the expectations for dataset documentation. Each topic is addressed below in more detail.

In the previous two chapters, guidance on constructing unit process and aggregated LCI datasets was provided. As a result of these activities, the user may have questions about the specific boundaries of a process model; the assumptions implicit in the process model; the data gaps in the model, whether chosen or because of lack of data availability; or the dataset review findings, as but a few examples.

4.1   LCI Database

An LCI database is a system intended to organize, store, and retrieve large amounts of digital LCI datasets easily. It consists of an organized collection of LCI datasets that completely or partially conform to a common set of criteria including methodology, format, review, and nomenclature. The database will allow for interconnection of individual datasets to create LCI models. The computed results can be used with identified life cycle impact assessment (LCIA) methods for life cycle assessment (LCA). Databases are managed using database management systems, which store database contents, allowing data creation and maintenance, search, and other access.

In contrast, a dataset library is a collection of datasets that may not conform to common criteria and do not allow for interconnections and common applications for LCA or LCIA purposes. An example of a dataset library is the United Nations Environment Programme/ Society of Environmental Toxicology and Chemistry (UNEP/SETAC) Database Registry.

A specific LCI database would cover situations where the datasets are looking at only limited interventions, such as carbon. These databases follow the same criteria for a general purpose LCI database but with a narrower scope. A database that houses type III Environmental Declarations (EDs) datasets for consumer use would be considered an ED repository. The datasets used to develop the EDs could potentially be part of a traditional LCI database.

An LCI dataset is a document or file with the life cycle information of a specified quantitative reference (reference flow, functional unit or other reference, e.g., product, site, process) including descriptive metadata and quantitative LCI or LCIA data (various sources).

4.2   Dataset Documentation

In a perfect dataset, all of the information or metadata needed to describe the quality and usability of a dataset for a given purpose would be included. Generally this level of detail is impractical because of considerations of cost or time.

4.2.1 General Documentation Considerations

Trade-offs will then need to be made in the process of documenting a dataset, balancing the need for transparency, opacity, and practicality. Transparency should be as high as possible to facilitate analysis, review, and interpretation. Opacity should be as low as necessary to protect sensitive business interests (confidentiality). Practicality is the balance between increased detail, which may help to improve the understanding of the process by the user and volume of information collected and processed, which will increase data collection and processing costs. For each dataset, these trade-offs will likely result in different levels of documentation. With these trade-offs in mind, the user should expect a certain level of documentation to be included with each dataset as described in the following subsections.

4.2.1.1 Name and Classification

We strongly recommend that each dataset be given a unique name and a unique ID that includes a version number as well as a product or process description. In addition, a classification, such as by NACE code (Nomenclature Générale des Activités Économiques dans les Communautés Européennes (EU classification system)), that may be useful to facilitate the creation of systematic and hierarchical database structures is recommended. The purpose of these recommendations is to provide an unambiguous means of identifying the process dataset within an LCI and communicating that to others.

4.2.1.2 Scope of the Dataset

We strongly recommend that the dataset include a system description (e.g., included processes, intended downstream use of the system outputs, specific single-plant or market average representation, suitability for consequential modelling). This enables the user to determine how the dataset fits within their current application context and to what processes, upstream or downstream, it logically connects as the LCI model is constructed.

4.2.1.3 Functional Unit or Reference Flows

Each dataset must have one of the following:

- functional unit in case of a (partial) product system with a defined use (which need not be quantified as a flow, but can be any quantified use, e.g., m^2),
- reference flow in the case of a single-output or allocated process, or
- several reference flows in case of an unallocated multi-output process.

No matter the case, the reference flows need to be clearly identified for the user.

4.2.1.4 Allocation

Where a process has multiple reference flows, allocation is the process of assigning process inputs and outputs to these reference flows. (Allocation is described in more detail in Chapters 2 and 3.) We strongly recommend that the documentation included with the dataset specify whether the process is unallocated or allocated. If allocated, the description is to include which allocation methods have been used: system expansion, that is, avoiding allocation, with details on replaced processes (and source of data); physical causality, such as mass, energy, or stoichiometric allocation; economic allocation, with cost information and source of data; or end of life or recycling, for example, 1:1 assignment to current and subsequent life cycle.

Further, we strongly recommend that the documentation included with the dataset specify whether there are any unallocated flows remaining. Finally, to facilitate review and allow sensitivity analysis, we recommend that when datasets are allocated the associated unallocated datasets also be provided.

4.2.1.5 Data Quality

There are a number of methods for assessing the quality of the data. This global guidance principles document offers the Data Quality Indicators (DQIs) (Table 4.1) as the recommended set. These DQIs represent the minimum set required for the user to assess fitness to purpose of the dataset. It is the responsibility of the dataset developer to prepare a self-assessment of the data against these indicators, which shall be confirmed in the course of the dataset review.

4.2.1.6 Hints on Interpretation

To facilitate the interpretation and use of the dataset by the user, we recommend that additional information about the dataset be included within the documentation if such data might be helpful in interpreting the result of the dataset in the context of an LCI. Such information might include discussions of the following: where datasets were updated, the differences between the current and the previous version of the dataset should be explained. For example, the documentation may comment on changes in technology. Where datasets represent complex processes, additional information should be provided, such as a detailed stoichiometric or energy balance of a chemical reaction.

4.2.2 Specific Requirements for Documentation of Unit Process Datasets

In addition to the general considerations discussed above, there are specific recommendations for documentation of both unit process datasets, provided in this subsection, and aggregated datasets, provided in the next subsection.

4.2.2.1 Data Sources

We strongly recommend that, for each flow within a dataset, the origin of the data be documented and references be provided. For primary data (for instance, collected by means of interviews, surveys, questionnaires, bookkeeping, tools, or measurements), the origin shall be denoted as measured, calculated, or estimated. For secondary data (for instance, assembled by means of interviews, statistics, or literature review), the references shall be appropriately cited.

4.2.2.2 References and Boundaries

The following items should be included as descriptive or textual content (in addition to the list of DQIs as per Table 4.1):

- geographic context, including spatial, reference region, or site.
- temporal context, including
  - reference year of data collection;
  - year of calculation;
  - daily, seasonal, or annual variations, as necessary;
  - other temporal information, such as the temporal profile of emissions (e.g., carbon provenance);
  - in case of combined references, the year best represented; and

- a temporal validity statement may be included (e.g., an expiry date »valid until …«).
- technology context, including
  - sectoral reference, technology coverage, represented technologies;
  - market mix and how it was established (e.g., regional);
  - annual production volumes (for processes and products); and
  - age of technology (as a list of pre-defined options, e.g., outdated).
- cut-off criteria, with justifications.
- other boundary descriptions, omissions, or exclusions, with justification.
- full documentation on whether the dataset is fully or partially terminated, and which flows apply for partially terminated datasets.

4.2.2.3 Calculation Models and Other Conventions

We strongly recommend the inclusion of assumptions, limitations, data gaps or missing information, and hidden or fixed inputs (e.g., load parameter of transport, detail on electricity mix used, transportation distances) used to support calculations, models, and other conventions. If the dataset has been reviewed, we strongly recommend the dataset contain the review documentation. The following administrative information should be included as part of the documentation: dataset commissioner, modeller, author, owner.

Table 4.1: Data quality indicators (DQIs) according to ISO 14040–44 (modified by adding no. 9)

N°	REQUIREMENT	ISO DESCRIPTION
1	Time-related coverage	Age of data and the minimum length of time over which data should be collected
2	Geographical coverage	Geographical area from which data for unit processes should be collected to satisfy the goal of the study
3	Technology coverage	Specific technology or technology mix
4	Precision	Measure of the variability of the data values for each data expressed (e.g., variance)
5	Completeness	Percentage of flows measured or estimated
6	Representativeness	Qualitative assessment of the degree to which the dataset reflects the true population of interest (i.e., geographical coverage, time period, and technology coverage)
7	Consistency	Qualitative assessment of whether the study methodology is applied uniformly to the various components of the analysis
8	Reproducibility	Qualitative assessment of the extent to which information about the methodology and data values would allow an independent practitioner to reproduce the results reported in the study
9	Sources of the data	ISO does not provide a description. Data sources defining the documentation of the data origin.
10	Uncertainty	Uncertainty of the information (e.g., data, models, and assumptions)

4.2.3 Specific Requirements for Documentation of Aggregated Process Datasets

In addition to the suggestions and recommendations provided above, in the case of aggregated datasets there are further recommendations and suggestions. These are meant to provide the user with a high degree of understanding of the aggregated dataset, through which fitness to purpose can be determined.

4.2.3.1 Materiality (Transparency)

We recommend that unit processes within an aggregated process dataset which materially contribute to one or more relevant impact categories be fully transparent (exposed or made available for examination outside the aggregated dataset). A further recommendation is that impact categories and methods that were used have also to be documented. We strongly recommend that information should be provided on the key contributors to the resulting dataset, and further that a sensitivity analysis of the key contributors should also be provided.

4.2.3.2 Minimum Documentation Requirements

The level of detail provided in the inventory of each of the unit process datasets used to prepare the aggregated process inventory should be maintained. For example, if the unit process lists each polycyclic aromatic hydrocarbon (PAH) as individual flows rather than the combined flow of PAHs, these should be maintained as separate flows and not combined to total PAHs, to maximize usability of the dataset.

We strongly recommend that the following additional information be provided for aggregated process datasets:

- a description of how the engineering-based models (gate-to-gate) used to prepare the aggregate dataset have been developed, where necessary;
- methods for aggregation of unit process inventory-level DQIs into aggregated process inventory-level DQIs (as per Table 4.1);
- the kind of unit process inventories used (e.g., average or marginal dataset), their source, and documentation;
- whether these unit process inventories are available, which specific datasets have been used, and how they have been linked (e.g., consequential approach);
- the aggregation method, for example, vertical or horizontal averaging of datasets, matrix inversion, or sequential approach;

- an assessment of the uncertainty as discussed in Chapter 2;
- documentation of the calculation process;
- a discussion of how the results of the aggregation are sensitive to the method of allocation applied to the underlying unit process datasets;
- where the unit process datasets are not given, an assessment of the relevant influences;
- where unit process datasets have been modified, full documentation recording the actual changes made. Examples include regionalising a specific dataset and updating of a dataset (e.g., [partially] updating industry data).

4.2.4 Key Issues of Dataset Documentation: Caveat on LCI Data Gaps and Uncertainties

LCI datasets may contain gaps (missing data) or uncertainties (variance or spread of data). Data gaps, such as the limits in the number of elementary flows covered, may effectively preclude the application of impact assessment methods, because the required LCI data are not found. Data uncertainties may impinge on the quality of impact assessment results as variability is further compounded by uncertainties in impact factors.

While database operators will generally strive to ensure internal consistency of the database by avoiding gaps and indicating uncertainties, this problem is especially relevant when combining datasets from different databases (synthesized datasets); for instance, data gaps may occur in different places.

The following strategies address this problem:

- We recommend the use of a globally harmonized reference list of elementary flow names as the primary condition for interoperability of datasets and databases;
- We recommend that data formats and software systems differentiate data gaps (e.g., »n/a« or »null«) from true numerical zero values;
- We recommend, in the course of data validation and review, plausibility checks be conducted in order to identify issues caused by data gaps and to quantify uncertainties.

4.3 Data Review

The subject of the review is a single dataset, either unit process or aggregated process. The fundamental purpose of dataset review is twofold: first, to ensure that the data quality and characteristics are consistent with the database general requirements, and second, to provide sufficient information to dataset consumers to support their evaluation of the applicability of the dataset for their specific goal and scope requirements. To help achieve these goals the following sections provide suggestions ad recommendations on specific aspects of the review process and personnel.

4.3.1. Reviewer Qualifications

Independence, expertise, and experience of the reviewers are vital. The four main qualification aspects for reviewers are 1) LCA methodology expertise, 2) knowledge of applicable review rules, 3) review or verification experience, and 4) technical, engineering, scientific, or economic expertise on the process or product that is represented by the dataset that is to be reviewed.

4.3.2. Minimum Review Requirement

The review concepts from ISO 14044 are useful general guidance; however, single datasets are not used for comparative assertion, and may generally not undergo a third party or external, three-person panel review. Independent internal or external review of datasets is considered common practice. Those datasets that are part of the product systems of a full LCA study and that have been explicitly reviewed as part of the LCA study review on the level of unit process inventory need not be reviewed again.[1]

For datasets that are used internally and not intended for public use or disclosure, the review requirements are managed by the organisation. We strongly recommend that datasets that will be made publicly available (freely or for a fee) undergo as a minimum an independent review. Further, we recommend that this review be conducted by external reviewers.

4.3.3 Coordination of Review

The commissioner of a review can be either the dataset provider[2] or the database manager.

For the dataset provider, if a specific database is selected, we recommend that the criteria specified by the database manager regarding dataset characteristics be adopted by the dataset provider.

For the database manager, datasets that have been previously reviewed and included in another database (which may have different criteria) can be subjected to an additional review prior to acceptance, or alternatively, the review documentation of the dataset can be evaluated to determine acceptability to the database manager.

4.3.4 Cost Considerations

We recommend a streamlined review procedure and report to minimize duplication of review efforts and costs associated with conducting reviews of datasets.

4.3.5 Purpose of Review

The target audience for dataset review documentation is an LCA practitioner. The database manager is also a consumer of the review report; however, the use of the report by database managers carries a different set of requirements than that of the practitioner. LCA practitioners require sufficient documentation of the dataset review to establish the accuracy of the activity and elementary flows as reported. The additional documentation from the dataset provider regarding the data

quality characteristics is also necessary for the practitioner to determine if the dataset is acceptable for their intended use. Database managers' requirements for review documentation are primarily associated with the need to ensure both the quality of the data and completeness of the metadata for the dataset.

The critical review gives added value to datasets, providing datasets with a higher level of confidence (credibility and reliability) for the users downstream by

- providing assurance of consistency with the goal and scope of the LCI;
- providing validation and verification of the datasets;
- ensuring ISO-established data quality parameters are correct (technological, geographical, and temporal representativeness; completeness; uncertainty; methodological appropriateness; and consistency as per validation and review criteria); and

---

[1] In case the full LCA is a comparative assertion intended to be published, the datasets that are part of the product systems need to undergo an additional panel review according to ISO 14044.
[2] The dataset can be provided to a database by the owner, developer, or author of the dataset.

- ensuring the correctness and consistency of applied nomenclature (nomenclature, compartments, measurement units, etc.) and terminology.

4.3.6   Procedures of Review

A number of recommendations and suggestions on the structure and process of dataset review are given in the following sections. These differ only from the review for an LCA in the limited scope.

4.3.6.1 Type of Review

To do an adequate review, the reviewers need a technical understanding of the process described by the dataset (including specific geographic and temporal knowledge), experience in LCA, and knowledge of the LCA review process and requirements. If one expert can fulfil all of these criteria, the review can be conducted by one reviewer. If not, at least two experts (technical and methodological) are needed.

4.3.6.2 Standard of Review

All reviews must be conducted relative to a set of quality standards. For datasets targeted for inclusion within a specific database, the database manager will impose standards against which the quality of the data and documentation must be assessed. In other cases, a more general set of standards can be used.

4.3.6.3 Review Criteria

We strongly recommend that the review determine whether the dataset fulfils the criteria of ISO 14040, as well as the additional criteria listed below, and any additional requirements imposed by a database manager. Further, we recommend the reviewer evaluate whether all the needed background information is given in the metadata so that the user can decide if the process is adequate for his needs. To complete a sensitivity analysis, it can be crucial that descriptive information about the unit process is given in order for the user to understand which parameters to vary and the extent over which they may vary.

In the best case the dataset fulfils all these criteria, and the criteria are documented in the review document. In this case the database provider has just to verify the contents of the review. If not all requirements are met a further iteration and perhaps a further review process could be required.

If the dataset is to be included in one or more databases, the reviewer must confirm if the dataset fulfils the criteria of the database. The following more-specific criteria will usually be set by the database manager in order to ensure consistency of process datasets within the database:

- Dataset classification follows database requirements (subcategorisation or database structure).
- Nomenclature is correct and consistent with applied nomenclature (naming rules, compartments, measurement units, etc.) and terminology.
- Modelling method is consistent with the requirements of the database, for example, infrastructure is included or not within a process dataset.
- Scope and boundary is consistent with the requirements of the database, for example, geographic or life cycle stage boundaries.
- Information regarding the DQIs (list of DQIs as per Table 4.1) is appropriate.
- The appropriateness, correctness, extent of documentation, and the metadata information in the dataset are consistent with the requirements of the database.

If a dataset validation check has not been documented in a previous review, the following procedures can be applied:

- Plausibility test, for which these procedures are recommended:

  - Calculate relevant impacts and compare it with the LCIA of processes covering similar technologies or services, for example, same production process in another region or similar product produced with comparable technology.
  - Determine plausibility of the magnitude of the mass and energy flows.
  - Assess whether the emissions and resources cover the relevant impacts according to current knowledge.

- Sensitivity analyses of specific data items (emissions, inputs from technosphere, or resources) or assumptions like allocations.

4.3.6.4 Other References for Review

Other references that may be used during the review process as comparative data or sources against which to validate data may include databases from associations, other databases of the same sectors, and other world level databases.

4.3.7   Review Documentation

The review documentation is prepared by the reviewers, summarising the scope and outcome of the review. It becomes part of the dataset, which means the process of dataset preparation is recursive. The review is conducted on the dataset, and the review is documented in the (thus modified) dataset.

The purpose of the review documentation is to enable the database operator to assess whether the dataset is compliant with the standard or criteria underlying the database and to enable the data user to ascertain that the dataset complies with certain criteria and hence to use the dataset with confidence.

We strongly recommend that the review documentation comprise the items described in the following subsections.

4.3.7.1 Identity of Reviewer

The name and affiliation (institution) of reviewers and their qualifications, along with the role or assignment of each reviewer (technical or methodological) should be included in the documentation.

4.3.7.2 Type and Scope of Review

The type of review undertaken by the dataset developer, either internal or external, should be provided and should indicate precisely which elements of the following were included in the scope of the review:

- goal and scope definition of dataset,
- raw data,
- LCI methods,
- LCIA methods that are applicable,
- unit process inventory,
- aggregated process inventory, and
- dataset documentation.

To this aim, we recommend the use of a checklist (Table 4.2). Each of the above entries can be assessed by using one or more of the following default elements as applicable:

- compliance with ISO 14040–44,
- cross-check with other dataset or source,
- energy or mass balance, and
- expert judgement.

Especially in emerging economies, costs need to be taken into consideration when deciding the level of review.

Table 4.2 Example of a scheme for a review report, which can be used to summarize the review. (In the case of quality indicators, each value or level will need to be defined in the review guidance.)

Type of review	Internal review, External review
Elements of review	Goal and scope definition
	Raw data
	Unit processes, single operation (unit process inventory)
	Aggregated process inventory
	LCI results or partly terminated system
	LCIA methods that are applicable
	Dataset documentation
	Check of the data quality indicators (DQIs)
Conclusions	Confirmation that all performed checks have been passed
Reviewer name and institution	Name, affiliation, and roles or assignments of the reviewers
Review details	Procedural details of the review process
Review summary	Overall review statement

4.3.7.3 Results of Review

We strongly recommend that the review documentation also summarize the results of the review, indicating where or how requirements of the applicable standards or criteria of the database were met. In case of PDF or printed reports, we strongly recommend that the review documentation be a distinct chapter or annex. In the case of electronic datasets, it is recommended that at least an abstract of the review documentation be integrated into the data format as a series of dedicated data fields, with the full review report available to users through other means. We strongly recommend that the review documentation confirm whether the dataset is actually consistent with its metadata and whether all performed checks have been passed; if the check has not been passed, the review document shall indicate what is missing or has to be changed.

We suggest that, where necessary or appropriate, procedural details about the review process be provided in greater detail. We recommend that the reviewer state exceptions where requirements of the standards or criteria were not met. Further, it is recommended the reviewer provide comments and recommendations, for example, how to resolve any exceptions or limitations on the applicability of the dataset.

We strongly recommend that the reviewer provide an overall review statement as a condensed report.

4.3.8 Key Issues of Review

In the dataset review process, there are two key issues: the need for validation and the need for independent review. First, we strongly recommend that, before an LCI dataset is included in a LCI database, it undergoes a defined validation process in order to confirm that it is consistent with the LCI database protocol. Second, we strongly recommend that, before an LCI dataset is included in a publicly available LCI database, it undergoes an independent review, which should be external.

4.4 Database Management

Database management requires consideration of criteria for the inclusion of data and datasets in a particular database, the communication and updating of changing data, and the period reevaluation and maintenance of included data.

4.4.1 General Database Management Considerations

In general, there are three important considerations in database management: ensuring a high level of internal consistency among datasets in a database, clearly defining the roles and responsibilities of the key players, and planning for the long-term viability of a database.

4.4.1.1 Database Criteria

A database can be characterised by its content (datasets), structure, and function. The database operator must clarify these and other characteristics of the database discussed in the following subsections in order to ensure the highest feasible level of internal consistency of datasets.

The structure of the database includes the terminology such as the systematic naming of unit process inventories, for example, United Nations Standard Products and Services Code (UNSPSC) or North American Industry Classification System (NAICS), and the systematic naming for activity and elementary flows.

We recommend that the database management team (DBMT) make clear the criteria for inclusion of datasets in the database in a protocol document. Further the DBMT should make the protocol document available for all data providers and data users. Some suggested elements of the protocol include

- formats in which a dataset is available to the users.
- format in which the datasets should be provided to the database (post-review with full documentation).
- documentation required with a dataset (see also Section 4.2), including
  - required metadata, for example, boundaries, processes, representativeness of technology, allocation, aggregation, geography, completeness, time;
  - comprehensive list of types of processes generally found in the database, regions typically covered, date of last full review; and
  - quality assurance process for datasets and database, specifically validation and review procedures for dataset inclusion (Figure 4.1[3]).

4.4.1.2 Roles and Responsibilities

The development and management of a database and the datasets within the database require discrete activities and defined roles:

- The database manager or the database management team may or may not own some or all of the datasets, but will hold and distribute them for public use, and has ultimate responsibility for database consistency. The database manager

---

[3] For Figure 4.1, the following definitions, which are specific to this chapter, apply: Validation: Either a manual or an automated software routine process for evaluating LCI datasets in the framework of the database against established validation criteria. Review: A manual, systematic, independent, and documented process for evaluating LCI datasets in the framework of the database against established validation and review criteria.

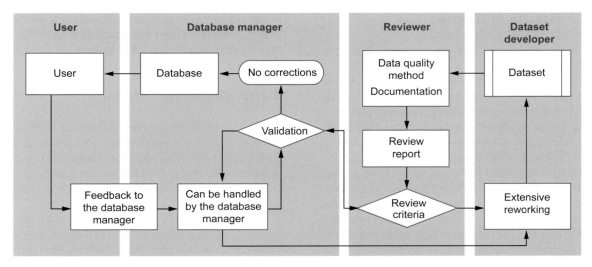

Figure 4.1: Sample flowchart of database management, specifically validation and inclusion process

may stipulate requirements for the qualification of the reviewer, define the requirements for the review, and operate an accreditation scheme. The database manager is also responsible for organising the review of updated datasets.

- The dataset owner (commissioner) is the person or organization paying for the data collection and ultimately is responsible for the accuracy of the dataset.
- The dataset developer is the group or individual who collects or compiles raw data and normalizes the raw data relative to a quantified reference into a unit process inventory, who is responsible for data quality, and who may or may not also be the author or owner of the dataset.
- The dataset author enters the data into the dataset format and fields and may also be the dataset developer or dataset owner.
- The dataset reviewer is a service provider who may or may not be independent of the database, and who reviews datasets according to Section 4.2.4 and database protocol guidance for dataset owners or database manager.

4.4.1.3 Long-term Planning

Long-term planning is very important for maintaining the viability of a database. For this viability to be achieved, it is important to have a vision of how manage the database, taking into account resources, the need for updates and communication, flexibility of structure, how to deal with changes in methodologies, and information technologies.

4.4.2 General Management Responsibilities: Communicating Changes

Drivers causing the need for updates of the data contained in a database include changes in technology, regulations, and LCA practice. The management of changing data will require the DBMT to have a plan and a process for communicating and deploying changes to the user and data developer communities. Examples of different updates include the

- recalculation of aggregated process datasets due to updated unit process datasets,
- updated unit process datasets and aggregated process datasets reflecting new or changed technology,
- updated unit process datasets and aggregated process datasets reflecting improved raw data, and
- updated unit process datasets and aggregated process datasets reflecting additional elementary flows.

In communicating with the user community, the DBMT will need to state the type of update that has been completed. This may be as simple as stating no update is required because upon review the dataset is still current, or it may require full or partial updates of the datasets.

Datasets may also be incrementally added to the database. We recommend that the database manager provide a mechanism for users to access these additions, possibly through a web portal. We strongly recommend that the database manager maintain control of the contents of the database, including detailed descriptions of changes.

We recommend that any new updates or revisions to datasets within the database be communicated to data users in a timely manner. For example, if an error were found and addressed in a specific dataset for coal mining by the data provider, we recommend that not only this correction but also the consequences for other related datasets be communicated to the data user.

With each change, the database manager needs to communicate the level of review that has been conducted for each changed dataset and provide the review results (as defined in the review requirements Section 4.3 and the supporting documentation of the review for the users). We recommend that there will be a mechanism for the data users to provide feedback on the datasets or database to include questions, comments, or notes on possible errors or inconsistencies in the datasets.

4.4.3 General Maintenance Responsibilities

The DBMT is responsible for maintaining a schedule of reviews for the datasets, which may or may not lead to updates. This schedule of reviews can be evaluated at appropriate intervals, and may be dependent on the maturity of the technologies being reviewed .The DBMT has the responsibility for managing the periodic re-evaluation of potentially outdated datasets. When updates to datasets are required, the DBMT is responsible for

working with the dataset owners on dataset reviews and updates. When the DBMT and dataset owner are the same, they can look at questions, comments, or problems identified with the dataset and make corrections to the dataset internally, and subject the revised dataset to the appropriate review. When a third party has ownership of the dataset, the DBMT must coordinate the examination of questions, resolution of comments, or problems identified with the dataset with the owner and provide a mechanism for tracking revisions within the database. There may be cases where the ownership is mixed between the DBMT and a third party. In that case, the third party and DBMT first need to define roles and responsibilities for review and update, and then proceed.

4.4.4   Key Issue of LCI Database Management: LCI Database Protocol

We strongly recommend that the DBMT issue a written protocol that defines the requirements for LCI datasets to be included in the database.

4.5   Further Information

Further information concerning the documentation and review can be found in the guidelines of the different providers (see Annex 3).

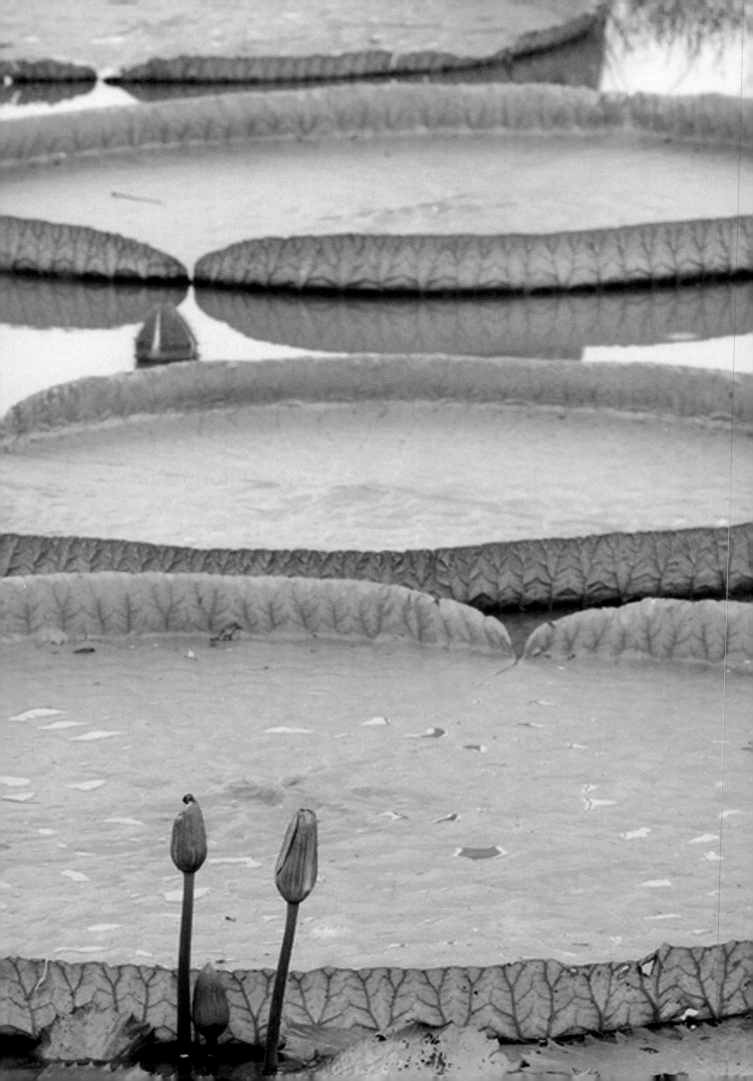

Adaptive Approaches

Jim Fava
Laura Draucker
Greg Foliente
Henry King
Joon-Jae Lee
Toolseeram Ramjeawon
Sangwon Suh
Reginald Tan
Bo Weidema (liaison)

CHAPTER

5

Key Messages

• Life cycle assessments (LCAs) should use the most appropriate datasets and modelling approaches to meet the specific goal and scope required to satisfactorily answer the questions posed.

• Current LCI databases often are sufficient to provide the required information to meet many consumer, industry, and government objectives. However, additional details on the current data as well as supplemental data sources will likely be needed to provide satisfactory answers to emerging questions in the fields of LCA and sustainability.

• The continuing evolution in consumer preferences, market and industry imperatives, and public policy forces continuous development and improvement of datasets and methodologies for LCA to meet these needs. This continuous development includes adapting and extending data collection and modelling methods.

There is increasing consumer interest and market demand for improved information on a product's environmental performance, and for industry to meet these needs through cleaner production methods and greener supply chains. In some sectors, this could also mean greater whole-life product stewardship (e.g., end-of-life management of electronic products). In addition, an increasing number of governments and organizations are now incorporating principles of life cycle management in strategic and operational decision-making. Four typical outcomes (e.g., enhanced public policy, sustainable production, sustainable consumption, and eco-efficient organizations and businesses) reflect what different stakeholders may seek (Figure 5.1). These are representative and are by no means the only outcomes that stakeholders are seeking. After the first questions in search of these outcomes are answered, more or expanded questions follow, which in turn demand more comprehensive and complete data and information. Stakeholder needs, and thus the need for better or more data, will continually evolve.

Life cycle assessments (LCAs) should use the most appropriate datasets and modelling approaches (as discussed in Chapters 2 through 4) to meet the specific goal and scope required to satisfactorily answers the questions posed[1]. Current life cycle inventory (LCI) databases are often sufficient to provide the required information to meet many consumer, industry, and government objectives. However, additional details on the current data as well as supplemental data sources will likely be needed to provide satisfactory answers to emerging questions in the fields of LCA and sustainability. The continuing evolution in consumer preferences, market and industry imperatives, and public policy forces continuous devel-opment and improvement of datasets and methodologies for LCA to meet these needs. This development includes adapting or extending data collection and modelling methods.

The purpose of this chapter is to identify the additional requirements for LCI datasets and databases to meet the evolving stakeholder needs, and to fulfil the specific goal and scope of an assessment. The overall guiding principle in extended and adaptive approaches (i.e., this chapter) is summed up well by David Friend (Palladium Group):
"I'd rather be generally correct than precisely wrong".

The specific LCI database properties needed to meet current and emerging needs are

- completeness of information in the databases (e.g., whole systems view) and
- flexibility in data organization within a LCI database (e.g., capturing critical information in datasets, enabling alternative modelling approaches, facilitating the linkage with other data sources).

The primary focus of this chapter is on LCI data and database requirements, not on the questions that may be asked where LCA may provide information.

To address emerging and wider stakeholder questions, it may be worth noting that LCA could be just one of the available tools and should not be seen as the only tool that should be used. In response, LCI databases need to support the evolving development

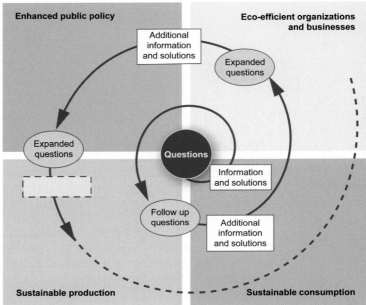

Figure 5.1: Expanding data requirements to meet evolving representative stakeholder needs (none of these needs are deemed more important than the other, nor are these meant to be inclusive)

of LCA as a tool in a kit to be used for answering certain questions. It should be recognized that the value of additional information has to be balanced against the costs of generating, collecting, and maintaining it. Using the most appropriate tools in a toolbox to get a job done should always be considered rather than endeavouring to develop an all-in-one super tool at any cost.

This chapter is organized as follows: The data and database properties needed to undertake consequential modelling are introduced and described first. Then the additional data and database properties needed for geographic and temporal assessments are

---

[1] The International Organization for Standardization (ISO) also indicates that the data quality requirements "shall be specified to enable the goal and scope of the LCA to be met" (ISO 14044:2006).

identified. To provide a more complete assessment, the use of national statistical data on supply-use and environmental emissions is presented, both alone and in conjunction with existing LCI databases. Finally, the emerging data demands for undertaking social and economic assessments are briefly identified.

5.1 Additional Database Properties For Consequential Modelling: Key Considerations

Consequential modelling within an LCI or LCA study aims to describe how environmentally relevant flows for a product system will change in response to possible decisions on production volumes or alternative technologies in response to a change in demand. For example, a consequential modelling approach would be appropriate if one seeks to understand the potential changes to life cycle environmental impacts associated with implementing an in-house production technology innovation on the product supply chain (Finnveden et al. 2009).

The consequential modelling approach requires information on the scale and time horizon of the changes considered, market delimitation, trends in volumes of the affected market, and relative competitiveness of alternative suppliers or technologies.

To support the use of a consequential modelling approach within an LCI or LCA study, we recommend that the following data characteristics be included in the LCI datasets: technology level, trends in production volumes, and access to disaggregated data.

5.1.1 Technology Level

Changes in production volume may lead to a shift in preferred production technology. For example, old or obsolete technologies could foreseeably be replaced by more recent ones. To enable the modelling of such changes, we recommend that the process-level data include a quantitative or qualitative description of the relative competitiveness, level of sophistication, or assessment of the state of development of the production technology used.

5.1.2 Trends in Production Volumes

Changes in production volume within one product system may lead to time-related changes in the same or a different product system. For example, short-term fluctuations in demand for a product could affect the capacity utilization of old production technology until

such time that new production technology is installed. If demand is forecast to increase continuously, longer-term results may need to be modelled by an accumulation of short-term variations. To model the time-effect of such consequential changes, it is recommended that the production data include, to the extent possible, historical, temporal, and time-sensitive aspects of the data, for example, expressed in the form of a time-series.

5.1.3 Access to Disaggregated Data

In general, the consequential modelling approach is best supported by access to disaggregated datasets. When aggregated data are provided, we recommend that the levels and rules of aggregation be clearly documented so that the data can be disaggregated if needed.

5.2 Additional Database Properties for Geographical and Temporal Information

There is an increasing desire or demand to include geographic and temporal information in the LCIs to

- improve the quality of impact assessments;
- meet the requirements of some applications of life cycle thinking, such as carbon and water footprinting;
- improve the quality and specificity of decision-making; and
- support scenario-based assessments.

The need for representativeness is defined by the International Organization for Standardization (ISO), and the lack of adequate descriptors may prevent or limit the use of the data (ISO 14044:2006). Conversely, the desire for greater specificity within databases and datasets has implications for both data owners and database managers. It may add complexity to the database structure and process modelling, and require additional data collection efforts to create datasets with greater geographic and temporal specificity. Therefore the need for such information has to be balanced against the costs of generating and maintaining it.

5.2.1 Geographic information

Geographic descriptors of a unit process, an aggregate process or an emission are crucial for reliable applications of life cycle impact assessment (LCIA) for the impact categories that are affected by geographic characteristics. Geographic information includes

- information on the location,
- geographical conditions, and
- non-geographic, site-specific properties.

Information on the location can be in the form of coordinates (longitude and latitude information or polar coordinates), administrative districts (a city, a prefecture, a county, a state, or a nation), or regions or continents (Europe, sub-Saharan Africa, or Arctic region).

A description of geographical conditions in addition to the location information is useful and sometimes even necessary for certain applications. Information on the current and the past land use and cover type, for instance, is necessary to assess greenhouse gas (GHG) emissions associated with land conversion. Some of the geographical conditions can be retrieved from data sources outside the typical LCI databases such as topographic or land cover data from geographic information system (GIS) databases. Geographic conditions can also be useful for transport analysis and for determining the most appropriate data for location-specific aspects like electricity-grid fuel mixes or use and end-of-life impacts.

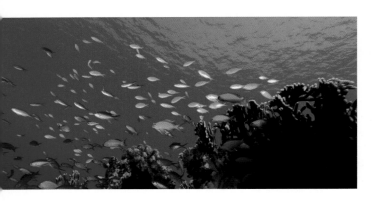

For certain applications, provision of additional site-specific information that is not pertinent to geographic properties is helpful. For instance, stack height, population density, or urban versus rural distinction may influence certain LCIAs.

We suggest that when providing geographic information for non-point source emissions (including area emissions and line emissions) data owners and providers consider additional descriptions such as the identity (name) of the receiving water body and rural versus urban distinction. However, LCI data providers must weigh the trade-offs between cost associated with collection and maintenance of such data relative to their usefulness in subsequent applications. We recommend that when aggregating unit process LCI data, geographic descriptors of unit processes should be preserved, forming separate elementary flows (as discussed in Chapter 4). Data manageability issues may require other solutions to be developed.

The following are key considerations for geographic information:

- We recommend that the choice of the location descriptor consider the granularity of the location information and its relevance for subsequent applications.
- We recommend that when assessing location-sensitive impact categories such as eutrophication, acidification, toxicity, water withdrawal and consumption, land use, and biodiversity, database providers make the necessary geographic descriptors available to the users in order to facilitate adequate assessment of these impacts. For instance, in the case of water consumption or nutrient emissions where the impacts are location dependent, the inclusion of a detailed location descriptor would facilitate subsequent LCIA applications.
- We recommend that, when the unit process or the aggregate process data involves significant land use and land cover change, information on the current and the past land use and land cover types be included to adequately assess GHG emission associated with land conversion (see also Section 5.2.2)
- We recommend that data providers consider balancing the costs and efforts to collect and maintain geographic information against its value in potential applications.
- Some processes such as transportation may not be easily defined by a single geographic reference point (a single longitude and latitude descriptor). In such a case, we suggest that providing alternative descriptions such as the geographic region (e.g., country) or location name (e.g., receiving water body) or other descriptor (e.g., urban or rural distinction) be considered.
- We recommend that when conducting process aggregation, data providers consider how to retain the specificity of the geographic information.

5.2.2 Temporal Information

Temporal, or time-relevant, information is crucial as a descriptor of a unit process, an aggregate process, or an emission within a dataset for the reliable application of LCIAs for some impact categories and in some studies (i.e., determined by the goal and scope). Temporal information is also relevant for understanding the technology level of the unit process. Temporal information includes

- information on the time-relevancy of a dataset as defined by ISO 14044:2006 (the common metric is calendar year) and

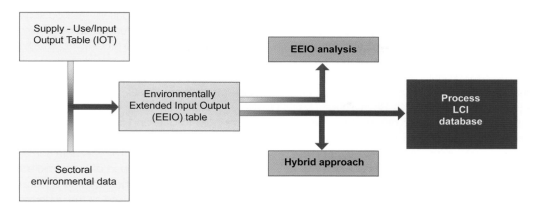

Figure 5.2: Illustration of the inputs and uses of supply use tables and sector environmental data

- information on when inputs or emissions within a unit process or aggregated process occur in time, for example, where the impact assessment varies over a defined time period, such as the relationship between water withdrawal or demand and the seasonal availability of water, and land-use GHG emissions changes over time.

As a key consideration regarding temporal information, we recommend that time-relevant descriptors and datasets be required when

- the unit process or the aggregate process data show strong inter-annual variations (e.g., agriculture) to ensure sufficient time-related representativeness (see Section 5.2.1).
- time-sensitive impact categories are assessed, such as water withdrawal and consumption, land-use GHG emissions, or photochemical oxidant creation potential (POCP). In such cases, we recommend that the database make the necessary temporal descriptors available for assessing these impacts.
- data owners and providers assess whether the aggregation of temporal information prevents broader applications due to the loss of temporal specificity.

5.3 Additional Data from National Statistics

LCAs need to use the most appropriate datasets and modelling approaches to meet the specific goal and scope, and that this assessment may require data beyond that which currently exists in typical LCI databases. One approach for filling data gaps in LCI databases is Input-Output Analysis (IOA)[2]. Input–output

analysis is a top–down economic modelling technique that aims to understand the interactions among economic sectors, producers, and consumers within a national economy. One of the advantages of IOA is that government statistical offices in most countries and municipalities compile input–output tables (IOTs) in a standard format specified by the United Nations (UN et al. 2003). These data are known as "national statistics".

Ideally in certain instances, an IOT can be adapted for use by the LCA practitioner when information on average resource use and environmental emissions for each sector is added to the table. These adapted IOTs are also known as environmentally extended input output (EEIO) (Finnveden et al. 2009). Due to its economy-wide approach, EEIO allows for the allocation of impacts along the production and supply chain to the consuming sector or groups of final products. This allocation has the advantage of covering all sectors of the economy and avoiding cut-off issues commonly associated with process–based LCA. Input–output analysis is a way to fill data gaps. It can also be a stand-alone application to provide environmental information to support policy-level decisions and for screening-level assessments as organized in a series of steps to create and use the information (Figure 5.2). However, there are certain issues for consideration linked to this approach as discussed below.

5.3.1 National Statistical Data on Supply-Use: Input-Output Tables

The compilation of IOTs as part of national accounts by national statistical agencies is now a routine practice governed by a UN standard. The IOTs state, in average monetary terms and for each economic sector, how much a sector buys from each of the other sectors, for each unit produced in the sector. It gives an overview of the transactions in a national economy. The number of sectors and their definition vary from country to country. At the national level, several countries produce input–

---

[2] Using proxy data from other process-based data sets is another approach for filling data gaps that does not involve national statistics.

output (IO) or EEIO tables with around 50 to 100 sectors. The United States and Japan produce IO tables with a resolution of about 500 sectors. The calculations are based on data for industrial sectors, and will thus provide results for the "average product" from the sector. The computational structure of IOT is functionally the same as that of LCA (Heijungs and Suh 2002). Because data are used as approximations for specific products or product groups from the sector, the precision of these approximations depends on whether the studied product or product group is typical of other products in this sector.

The major issues for consideration are these:

- Monetary unit: The monetary unit in an IOT is used to represent the flow of product and services in a supply chain, and with a homogenous price, the results of an LCA are insensitive to the unit. The results are distorted when the LCA includes inputs or outputs with price heterogeneity. However, IOT is compiled in the producer's price, which is more homogeneous across the consuming sectors.
- Allocation: IOA has long been using both economic value-based allocation and system expansion (or substitution method). With additional data, IO and hybrid approaches (combinations of EEIO and process-based LCA, see Section 5.3.4 for more discussion) can accommodate other allocation approaches such as energy content-based allocation.
- Aggregation: This is an inherent problem under the current IO practice. Some sectors are more aggregated than others, resulting in low sector resolution. If the data quality degradation due to low resolution outweighs any benefits of using IO data, other alternative approaches should be considered.
- Import assumptions: IOTs are compiled with the assumption that imported commodities are produced using the same technology and structure as domestic industries. Thus results of input-output analyses of countries that rely heavily on imports are subject to higher uncertainty. In this case, multi-regional IOTs or linking imports to appropriate data would be desirable.
- Data age: Available IOTs are generally several years old, and thus rapidly developing sectors and new technologies may introduce errors because of base-year differences between the product system under study and IO data. For such sectors and technologies, examining data age of the corresponding unit process or aggregated datasets should be considered.

From the above list, the major aspect of IOA that has inherent differences as compared to the pro-

cess approach is aggregation. Methodologically, all other issues listed above are functionally equivalent to issues that can occur using the process approach (i.e., data age and assumptions).

Key considerations for use of national statistical tabulate data are these:

- Up-to-date and comprehensive IO databases are essential for applying IO and hybrid techniques for LCA. The IOA data come from national statistics as part of economic accounts developed within the statistical agencies and thus are only as accurate as the underlying data and processing routines. The primary data reported from industries are aggregated by the national statistical agencies, partly to maintain confidentiality of the individual industry data, but also simply to limit the size of the resulting tables. The aggregation makes the data less useful and more uncertain for use in IOA and LCA.
- One main problem is that data are not gathered in consistent classification systems. At statistical agencies, much effort is currently spent on transposing sector and product data from one classification to another, rather than on gathering data themselves. Input–Output Tables in many countries have a low sector resolution and getting detailed input-output data require a more detailed classification, which ideally should to be standardized.
- Better documentation and reporting by statistical agencies would assist in the interpretation of uncertainty and use of the data, preferably in each cell in the supply-use tables.
- If the IOT significantly lacks the quality required in accordance with the goal and scope of the study, alternative data sources should be considered.
- Increasing the frequency of IOT publication and reducing the time lag before the publication can facilitate timely provision of data for LCA.
- Input–output tables are derived by statistical agencies from supply-use tables and direct requirement tables. The use of supply-use tables is preferable to the use of derived IOTs.

5.3.2 Environmental Data Sources for Completeness

To achieve environmental data completeness, applicable sectoral environmental data are needed to complement the national statistical data on supply and use. In most cases, the availability of these data relies on

- governmental or international agencies with regulations or agreements in place to collect the information,

- compliance or enforcement of the regulation or agreement, and
- the ability (or willingness) of the government or agency to make the information publicly available.

A compilation of sectoral environmental data source examples is given in Suh (2005).

A key consideration for assessing and using sectoral environmental data is the limitation that it is not readily available in many countries. Furthermore, even if the information is available, often it is not in a ready-to-use format and may not be complete. For example, small and medium-sized enterprises (SMEs) and non-point sources may only register in part.

There are ways in which the completeness of national and sectoral environmental data can be improved. If national, regional, or sectoral energy-use data exist, it can be converted into environmental flows using published emission factors. For example, the International Energy Agency (IEA) calculates CO_2 combustion emissions using energy data and default methods and emission factors from the Revised 1996 IPCC Guidelines for National Greenhouse Gas Inventories (IEA 2010). For other air emissions, the US Environmental Protection Agency (USEPA) AP-42 publishes emission factors for several source categories (i.e.. a specific industry sector or group of similar emitting sources) (USEPA 2011). This information can be adapted for use in other countries by considering differences in fuel characteristics and technologies. Sector or resource specific data (e.g., used agricultural models, land-use statistics) can also be used to fill gaps in national environmental data.

There are also techniques one can use to validate the completeness of environmental data. For CO2 and other GHG data, the United Nations Framework Convention on Climate Change (UNFCCC) database can be used to verify that when summed together, the sectoral environmental data are consistent with the national GHG inventory (UNFCCC 2011). Material flow analysis can be used to track resource flow through the sectors and draw attention to any imbalances between inputs to a sector and releases to the environment.

In many countries the data have been collected, but no environmental information system exists to sort, organize, and upload the data for public use. The mining of these data would improve the global completeness of sectoral environmental data.

5.3.3 Linking Input-Output Tables with Environmental Data

Linking IOTs with environmental data is a necessary first step to integrating within current databases (Section 5.3.4) and becoming a useful tool for achieving database completeness as discussed in Section 5.3. The outcome of this linkage is referred to as "EEIO."

The UN, European Commission (EC), International Monetary Fund (IMF), Organisation for Economic Co-operation and Development (OECD), and the World Bank

have produced, as a part of the Handbook on National Accounting, the publication *Integrated Environmental Economic Accounting*, commonly referred to as "Socio-Economic and Environmental Assessment" (SEEA) (UN et al. 2003). The handbook provides a common framework for the inventory and classification of economic and environmental information, and can be helpful to countries or organisations that want to create EEIO tables. Additionally, Lave et al. (1995) show how national IOTs can be used in connection to with LCA studies, while Suh et al. (2004) give a survey of existing EEIO tables.

The limitations of sectoral aggregation (as discussed in Section 5.3.1) can be exaggerated in EEIO tables, particularly when the environmental impacts of products within a sector vary widely. For example, an aggregated livestock sector includes ruminate and non-ruminate animals that have different GHG impacts. In an EEIO table, these impacts are averaged in the sector, causing emission data for ruminates and non-ruminates to be under- and over-estimations, respectively. Additionally, if one sub-sector within a sector engages in emission reduction activities while others do not, aggregated EEIO tables will average those reductions among all sub-sectors. In these cases, disaggregated EEIO table or process-based data are more representative.

5.3.4 How to Use with Current LCI Databases: Hybrid Approach

For many practitioners input-output (IO)-LCA is not an attractive alternative to process-LCA for detailed product LCA because the sector resolution is too coarse. What has emerged is a hybrid technique combining the advantages of both process-LCA and IOA (Suh et al. 2004). The use of IOA through hybrid techniques helps to provide a complete picture in relation to the system boundaries. The IOA is used for all upstream processes to estimate LCA data and reduces the truncation errors that arise in process-LCA. There are three types of hybrid approaches:

1) tiered-hybrid approach (Moriguchi et al. 1993),
2) IO-based hybrid approach (Joshi 1999), and
3) integrated hybrid approach (Suh 2004).

Suh and Huppes (2005) provide a review of these hybrid approaches and their advantages and disadvantages. In a hybrid assessment, aggregated data from the IOA are substituted iteratively by specific, detailed process data for the most important system-specific activities, thus continuously making the inventory more reliable and accurate. Whenever process data or resources are unavailable or the required level of uncertainty is achieved, the process part can be truncated and the remaining requirements covered by input-output analysis. Thus the boundary delineation of a hybrid assessment task can be tailored to suit requirements of specificity, accuracy, cost, labour, and time. Hybrid LCA and the process approach share the same computational structure, given appropriate datasets. However, care needs to be taken when constructing a hybrid data set to avoid miscalculation (e.g., double counting, leaked emissions).

Note that different hybrid approaches have different strengths and weaknesses, and the choice of method should be made considering various factors, including data requirements, required time and resources, the relevance of imports for a national economy, and the level of aggregation in a national IOT. Also note that besides data for the waste treatment sector, IOA typically does not include data downstream of production and therefore the hybrid nature does not apply for the use and end-of-life stages where only process-level data are available.

5.4 Emerging Demands from Social and Economic Assessments

For the purpose of a more general sustainability assessment, the environmental assessment typically considered in LCA and its extensions described in the preceding sections ultimately would be balanced with social and economic assessments. Specialized tools and data sources (i.e., not based or dependent on the LCI database) for these additional analyses are often used, but at other times, an LCA-based or LCI-based methodology may be preferred, especially in the production of specific goods (UNEP 2009). In the latter case, their implications to LCI database development are briefly explored in this section.

5.4.1 Social Information

ISO 26000 (2010) provides the broad scope for considering the contributions and impacts of social factors in sustainable development. The United Nations Environment Programme/Society of Environmental Toxicology and Chemistry (UNEP/SETAC) Life Cycle Initiative has attempted to incorporate many of these factors in an LCA framework in the *Guidelines for Social Life Cycle Assessment of Products* (UNEP 2009). The social and socio-economic LCA (or S-LCA) Guide "presents key elements to consider and provides guidance for the goal and scope, inventory, impact assessment and interpretation phases of a social life cycle assessment" and "highlights areas where further research is needed."

The S-LCA guide not only provides comparisons with traditional environmental LCA, but also identifies S-LCA's specific limitations, including dealing with qualitative, informal, uncertain, and/or incomplete data. These limitations may have relevance to other types of LCA (not necessarily S-LCA) that need to deal with the same issues.

In particular, in relation to the inventory data for S-LCA, while the traditional LCI database framework and structure may be the same, the inventory and aggregated data are different (and so are the intermediate and end impact categories for impact assessment). The types and nature of S-LCA inventory data that need to be collected (and how) and organised in the database are outlined in the Guide. In practice, this may mean separate database compartments or fields for S-LCA data. This data collection is in its infancy. A first comprehensive database with social working environment information has recently been made available as part of the GaBi databases (PE 2010).

5.4.2 Cost Information

In practice, life cycle costing (LCC) is a common method independent of LCA, which is employed for economic or value-based decision-making. A SETAC working group (Hunkeler et al. 2008) described environmental LCC, and a guideline for LCC has been published by SETAC (Swarr et al. 2011). LCC uses price information for intermediate inputs and outputs to establish monetary balances for each unit process and for the product system. The system boundaries for LCC correspond to those of the product system in LCA.

LCA already incorporates a portion of the economic externalities by modelling the physical causalities within the product system. In some instances, LCA is extended to include estimates of the external costs such as costs paid by parties not operating or in control of the reported activities, and not part of the price of the products.

5.5 Summary

The list below summarises the key messages relating to adaptive approaches:

- Stakeholder needs and demands are evolving, and additional information is allowing both old and new questions to be answered.
- Key considerations are given on additional database properties for consequential modelling, geographic and temporal information, additional data using national statistics, and emerging demands from social and economic assessments.
- LCA is only one available tool to address these broader needs, and LCA database managers should consider what information can be included in the databases and made available to LCA tools, and what should remain external and the domain of other tools.
- The value of additional information has to be balanced against the costs of generating, collecting, and maintaining it.

5.6 References

Finnveden G, Hauschild M, Ekvall T, Guinee J, Heijungs R, Hellweg S, Koehler A, Pennington D, Suh S. 2009. Recent developments in life cycle assessment. J Environ Manag. 91:1-21.

Heijungs R, Suh S. 2002. The computational structure of life cycle assessment. Dordrecht:. Kluwer.

Hunkeler D, Lichtenvort K, Rebitzer G. 2008. Environmental life cycle costing. Pensacola (FL) USA: Soc of Environmental Toxicology and Chemistry (SETAC). ISBN 978-1-880611-83-8.

[IEA] International Energy Agency. 2010. CO_2 emissions from fuel combustion. [cited 2011 Feb 10. Available from: http://www.iea.org/publications/free_new_Desc.asp?PUBS_ID=1825

[ISO] International Organization of Standardization. 2006. ISO 14044:2006: Environmental management - Life cycle assessment - Requirements and guidelines. [cited 2011 Feb 1]. Available from: http://www.iso.org/iso/catalogue_detail?csnumber=38498.

[ISO] International Organization for Standardization. 2010. ISO 26000: Guidance on social responsibility. Geneva: ISO.

Joshi S. 1999. Product environmental life cycle assessment using input-output techniques. J Ind Ecol. 3:95-120.

Lave L, Cobas-Flores E, Hendricksion C, McMichael F. 1995. Using input-output analysis to estimate economy-wide discharges. Environ Sci Tech. 29:420-426.

Moriguchi Y, Kondo Y, Shimizu H. 1993. Analyzing the life cycle impact of cars: The case of CO_2. Ind Env. 16(1-2):4-45.

PE INTERNATIONAL AG. 2010. GaBi 4 Software and database for Life Cycle Engineering, (computer program). Version 4.4. Leinfelden-Echterdingen, Germany.

Suh S. 2004. Functions, commodities and environmental impacts in an ecological economic model. Ecol Econ. 59:7-12.

Suh S. 2005. Developing a sectoral environmental database for input-output analysis: the comprehensive environmental data archive of the US. Economic Systems Research. 17(4):449-469.

Suh S, Huppes G. 2005. Methods for life cycle inventory of a product. J. Cleaner Prod. 13:687-697.

Suh S, Lenzen M, Treloar GJ, Hodo H, Horvath A, Huppes G, Jolliet O, Klann U, Krewi W, Mouchi Y, Msgaard J, Norris G. 2004. System boundary selection in life cycle inventories using hybrid approaches. Environ Sci Tech. 38:657-664.

Swarr TE, Hunkeler D, Klöpffer W, Pesonen H-L, Ciroth A, Brent AC, Pagan R. 2011. Environmental life cycle costing: A code of practice. Pensacola (FL), USA: Soc of Environmental Toxicology and Chemistry (SETAC).

[UN] United Nations, European Commission, International Monetary Fund, Organisation for Economic Co-operation and Development, World Bank. Handbook of national accounting: Integrated environmental and economic accounting. 2003. Final draft circulated for information prior to official editing. [cited 2011 Feb 1]. Available from http://unstats.un.org/UNSD/envaccounting/seea2003.pdf.

[UNEP] United Nations Environment Programme. 2009. Guidelines for social life cycle assessment of products. UNEP/SETAC Life Cycle Initiative report. Paris: UNEP.

[UNFCCC] United Nations Framework Convention on Climate Change. 2011. GHG from UNFCCC (website and links). [cited 2011 Feb 1]. Available from: http://unfccc.int/ghg_data/ghg_data_unfccc/items/4146.php.

[USEPA] United States Environmental Protection Agency. 2011. Emissions factors & AP-42: Compilation of air pollution emission factors (website and depository). [cited 2011 Feb 1]. Available from: http://www.epa.gov/ttnchie1/ap42/.

Cooperation and Capacity Building

Sonia Valdivia
Guido Sonnemann
Bruce Vigon
Atsushi Inaba
Mary Ann Curran
Mark Goedkoop
Bo Weidema
Surjya Narayana Pati
Cássia Maria Lie Ugaya (liaison)

CHAPTER

6

Key Messages

• Governments are requested to launch national life cycle assessment (LCA) training and awareness activities in their respective countries.

• Global coordination among life cycle inventory (LCI) dataset developers and LCA database managers has been identified as a priority, together with capacity building and data mining, to move toward a world with interlinked databases and overall accessibility to credible data.

• Huge amounts of relevant raw data, and even developed LCI datasets, currently are not easily accessible for LCA studies. LCA database managers and LCA practitioners for particular studies should do data mining by working with actors who routinely collect data.

• All stakeholders, including governments, industry associations, and commercial parties that manage and supply databases, should strongly increase their cooperation and coordination.

Chapters 6 and 7 differ from the previous chapters because they do not provide actual guidance principles, but instead offer some thoughts and ideas for the future. The group considered it important not only to deliver guidance on life cycle inventory (LCI) data and datasets, but also to present these relevant future perspectives in the Global Guidance Principles.

6.1 Vision

The vision for the global life cycle assessment (LCA) database guidance process, as mentioned in the prologue, is to

- provide global guidance on the establishment and maintenance of LCA databases, as the basis for future improved interlinkages of databases worldwide;
- facilitate additional data generation (including for certain applications such as carbon and water footprint creation) and to enhance overall data accessibility;
- increase the credibility of existing LCA data, through the provision of such guidance, especially as it relates to usability for various purposes; and

- support a sound scientific basis for product stewardship in business and industry, and life cycle-based policies in governments, and ultimately, to help advance the sustainability of products.

From the vision, a clear need can be derived for cooperation and capacity building. These Global Guidance Principles can be considered as a first step towards a world with interlinked databases and overall accessibility to credible data. Furthermore, we recognize there is a need to address confidentiality and quality issues.

The principles discussed in this guidance document can be upheld and the vision can be reached by enhancing capabilities for LCA dataset development and database management worldwide, promoting a broader dissemination of data, and providing for stronger coordination of efforts, which results in better recovery of existing data and more efficient allocation of resources.

Life cycle approaches have got relevance not only in the business world where sustainability is emerging as a megatrend, but has also gained stronger political dimension by being included in sustainable consumption and production policies around the world.

6.2 Capacity Building

The term "capacity building" is used with respect to a wide range of strategies and processes. When executed, these strategies and processes will contribute to a better understanding of the benefits of quality life cycle data, how to use these data, and how to start up, run, maintain, document, and review life cycle databases. The development of technical expertise is considered essential, especially in developing and emerging economies.

Capacity building is meant to address researchers, policy makers, and industry in order to create a critical mass of experts in all parts of society. These increased capabilities ultimately result in a broader use of LCA, and thus influence market development and the benefit–cost ratio of life cycle data management.

Governments are called on by the workshop participants to launch national LCA training and awareness activities in their respective countries. National bureaus dealing with data management and generation, such as statistics offices and infrastructure services (e.g., hospitals and waste and water treatment plants), are specially called to be part of the capacity development efforts. In developing countries and emerging economies, because resources are lacking, international and intergovernmental organizations are called upon by the workshop participants to support the national efforts hand-in-hand with essential local partners such as national life cycle networks, centres of excellence, national cleaner production centres, chambers of commerce, and industrial associations. Following United Nations (UN) principles, sectoral and gender balance should be pursued, and they should be taken into account when designing the training activities.

Examples of capacity building at the international level include the following activities:

- Projects in developing countries and emerging economies are supported through the United Nations Environment Programme/Society of Environmental Toxicology and Chemistry (UNEP/SETAC) Life Cycle Initiative Award that provides, among other benefits, free licenses for LCA databases and coaching services in support of capabilities development. PRé Consultants, PE International AG, ifu Hamburg GmbH, and the ecoinvent Centre have supported this activity since 2006.
- Workshops on enhancing the capabilities for LCA in developing countries of the Asia/Pacific region are conducted regularly and are organized by Advanced Industrial Science and Technology (AIST) and Japan Environmental Management Association for Industry (JEMAI).
- Meetings are organized among national LCA database projects for exchanging experiences and for mutual learning on database development and maintenance.
- A Latin America project is funded by the UNEP/SETAC Life Cycle Initiative, which aims to enhance capabilities in five countries (Chile, Argentina, Brazil, Mexico, and Peru) regarding development of life cycle inventories of national energy systems (Red Iberoamericana de Ciclo de Vida, no date).

6.3 Coordination and Partnerships

Global coordination among LCI dataset developers and LCA database managers has been identified together with capacity building and data mining as priorities in a move towards a world with interlinked databases and overall accessibility to credible data. There is a need for global coordination among LCI dataset developers and LCA database managers to ensure that these guidance principles are upheld. This could be accomplished through a roundtable or a series of periodic meetings of key actors during international events. The coordination exercise could lead to a widely accepted global dataset library (such as envisaged with the UNEP/SETAC registry). Furthermore, processes at various levels could be set up to facilitate direct interlin-

kages between databases. Important elements of such a process would be

- recognition of differences between existing LCA databases;
- analysis of the sources of these differences, which may lead to an understanding that the differences are mainly due to different system boundaries and allocation rules, plus different geographic and related technical conditions, different "histories," organisational preferences, etc.; and
- adoption of the same system boundaries and allocation rules to facilitate interlinkages.

Finally, a strengthened coordination could also lead to an improved alignment of data formats that result in better-functioning data format converters or even a common data format worldwide.

The creation of partnerships is a vital complement of support and funding. Partnership is based on an agreement between two or more LCI database stakeholders to work together in the pursuit of common goals as provided in this guidance document. Teamwork for consensus and consultation, sharing of power, risks and responsibilities, respect of the expectations and limits, as well as of the missions and self-interests of each partner, and commitment are key principles to hold and successfully accomplish the goals of the partnerships. Some examples of non-profit partnerships include the UNEP/SETAC Life Cycle Initiative (2010) and the Sustainability Consortium (2011).

6.4 Data Mining

There are huge amounts of relevant raw data, and even developed LCI datasets, available that are currently not easily accessible for LCA studies. LCA database managers, and also LCA practitioners for particular studies, should do data mining by working with actors who routinely collect data about the inputs and outputs of unit processes and related life cycle information. Several important pathways for access to data and datasets should be considered.

Governments maintain vast numbers of databases, some of which contain portions of the data needed to create a unit process dataset. Such data are distributed across many external databases, often managed by different agencies. It is worthwhile to note that these databases do not contain LCIs or even LCI data. However, they can serve as sources of generally useful information (raw data) for later use in constructing an LCI dataset. This is unlike the input–output (IO) data described in Chapter 5, which is intended to augment or extend the data in an LCI database. Governments and international agencies, such as the Food and Agriculture Organisation (FAO) and the World Health Organization (WHO), are rapidly making more of their databases available for use via the Web, including projects to make these data available in Resource Description Framework (RDF) (Semantic Web) form. Also, open source tools are publicly available for converting standard data formats such as text, spreadsheets, and relational databases into RDF. Moreover, numerous research projects with public funding have generated a huge amount of relevant raw data and also a fairly important number of unit process and aggregated datasets and will continue to do so in the future. Public funding agencies are encouraged to ensure that the data and datasets resulting from research projects are publicly available for future use in LCA databases.

6.5 Funding and Support

Funding and support is essential in order to maintain the momentum that has been generated by the recent international developments in life cycle databases and life cycle–based information. These support mechanisms are especially important for the continuous development, maintenance, and updating of databases in order to ensure their sustainability and persistence.

To increase the priority of these principles within the political agenda of emerging economies and developing countries, support of intergovernmental organizations such as UNEP is advisable. This support could include any of a number of activities, such as

- framing of enabling mechanisms for the development and maintenance of databases;
- design and implementation of programs and activities to increase the demand for life cycle data and databases, including sustainable public procurement, design for environment, and eco-labelling programs; and
- promotion of activities that encourage the use of environmental footprints, including carbon and water footprinting for decisions and reporting within organizations and in external communication.

In the past, common funding sources have included government and private industry and trade associations. In addition to direct funding from these sources, support can be realized in the form of in-kind contributions (such as providing data directly to a database).

Governmental policies and market mechanisms have promoted database development. Their long-term viability depends on business models that ensure obtaining at least that minimum level of resources which

is required to maintain the life cycle database systems from revenue sources such as charges to the users of data, to data providers, to companies clustered in associations, or through additional governmental funding. The challenge for the future is to bring more data into the public domain, while ensuring the minimum funding required for maintenance, updates, etc.

The assumption is that the increasing number of independently managed databases will help to minimize the funding needs for the creation and support of information storage. A further assumption is the costs associated with the efforts to collect, provide, and check data will spread across an increasing number of users, with the resulting incremental cost to any one user expected to be very small.

6.6 Language and Nomenclature Aspects

Language is an issue of concern worldwide. Although English is often used in LCA databases, there are many databases developed in other languages (e.g., in Japanese). To reach out to small and medium-sized companies and to involve individuals throughout the world, attention should be paid to the use of other broadly used languages. The language issue refers not only to the text used in documentation, but also to the nomenclature or naming of LCI parameters, processes, and products.

A few, but certainly not all, options have been identified for addressing these aspects:

- Use automated translation systems as they are currently used in websites. This will probably work reasonably well for documentation, but does not seem to work well when translating LCI parameters and product or process names.

- Use international standardised systems for products and services. Two options are the United Nations Standard Products and Services Code (UNSPSC) or CAS numbers; however, these options should be augmented by additional systems because there will still be a group of LCI parameters, such as resources and land uses, that cannot be referred to by using the UNSPSC codes or CAS numbers. The use of international standardisation systems would be a very important feature to enhance data conversion between systems.

6.7 References

Red Iberoamericana de Ciclo de Vida (Life Cycle Iberoamerican Network). No date. Inventarios de Ciclo de Vida en América Latina [Internet]. [cited 2011 Feb 3]. Available from http://rediberoamericanade-ciclodevida.wordpress.com/inventarios-de-ciclo-de-vida-en-latino-america/.

The Sustainability Consortium. 2011. The Sustainability Consortium [Internet]. [cited 2011 February 3]. Available from: http://www.sustainabilityconsortium.org/.

UNEP/SETAC Life Cycle Initiative. 2010. The Life Cycle Initiative [Internet]. [cited 2011 Feb 3]. Available from: http://lcinitiative.unep.fr/.

Outlook: Future Scenarios for Knowledge Management

Mary Ann Curran
Mark Goedkoop
Scott Butner
Katsuyuki Nakano
Greg Norris
Surjya Narayana Pati
Cássia Maria Lie Ugaya
Sonia Valdivia
Martin Baitz (liaison)

CHAPTER

7

Key Messages

• Three important, and largely independent, trends can potentially influence the way the future of life cycle assessment (LCA) data and databases develop:

1) Governments, industry associations, and other database providers will take strong action to improve mutual cooperation.

2) Many new stakeholders will join the LCA community as they need more life cycle inventory (LCI) data, which creates a new dynamic.

3) A very important revolution in the way Internet communities now generate and manage data is occuring.

• Current trends in information technology will shape users' expectations regarding data, software functionality, and interoperability. These trends will also alter the scope of what can be done with LCI data in very basic ways. While the LCA community should not be distracted too strongly by these technological trends, to ignore them may be at our peril.

• Three scenarios are envisioned for plausible futures about how LCI data might be collected, managed, accessed, and used. The scenarios serve as the basis for discussion about what each might imply for LCI data along the dimensions of utility, accessibility, and composability:

1) Scenario L. Based on a linear projection of current trends into the near future, LCI databases continue to be created and operated largely as activities independent from one another, but are increasingly easy for users to locate and access. The recommendations made in previous chapters have helped to improve data quality and consistency, both within and among databases.

2) Scenario C. The way in which data are managed — primarily through curated, independently managed databases — continues, but the aggressive adoption of Web 2.0 technologies enables significant changes in the way that data may be accessed by users. LCI databases in this scenario often provide an open, web-accessible application programming interface (API) which enables users and third party developers to mash up' data from multiple sources, or to create federated search tools which can locate LCI data stored in multiple databases from a single query. LCI database developers are eager to implement these APIs because they greatly expand the utility of their data by making them easier to find and use.

3) Scenario I. Holders of raw data adopt, at a major scale, new technologies that introduce new pathways for the creation of LCI data, and these data find their way to users through both existing channels of national and independently managed databases, as well as new parallel pathways. For example, governments and other holders of large external (non-LCI) databases adopt technology that makes it much easier for researchers (including the managers of existing LCI databases) to use external data to create new unit process datasets and update or expand existing unit process datasets. Also, companies widely make use of tools that increase the bottom-up collection of unit process data and the transmission of these data to data reviewers and aggregators.

• New knowledge management technologies, combined with significant societal trends in the way that knowledge is being created and managed, are likely to change our ideas about what constitutes LCA data, and these changes very likely will pose significant challenges to LCA database providers. The providers will be expected to create LCA knowledge management frameworks in which data are more distributed, more mobile, more democratic, and less standardized, yet providers will also be expected to make sure that data continue to be interoperable between applications and platforms.

This chapter identifies ways to manage and implement the Global Guidance Principles in the future. While it is not the aim to predict the future, three future scenarios are presented here without knowing which scenario, or combination of scenarios, will develop into practice. In addition, three important drivers have been identified that can potentially influence the way the future of life cycle assessment (LCA) data and databases develop:

1) Governments, industry associations, and other database managers will take strong action to improve mutual cooperation.
2) Many new stakeholders will join the LCA community, as they need more LCI data, which creates a new dynamic.
3) A very important revolution in the way internet communities now generate and manage data is occuring.

This chapter makes recommendations for all stakeholders who want to contribute to generating high-volume, high-quality, reviewed LCI data. Stakeholders can also use this information to develop action plans to support desired developments.

7.1 New Ways of Identifying and Accessing LCI-relevant Information

Currently, societies live and work in a time of rapid changes in information technology. More importantly, perhaps, this is a time when changes in information technology are impacting the lives of people around the world. From the advent of social computing, to the proliferation of "smart" phones and other mobile computing devices, to pervasive Internet connectivity found even in less-developed parts of the world, these trends are altering the way people work, play, and relate to one another.

What relevance, if any, do these trends have for LCA? How might these trends be harnessed to build upon the foundation laid by LCI data providers and users to date, and the recommendations provided in the preceding chapters? Those are the questions that this chapter is intended to address.

While the LCA community should not be distracted too strongly by these technological trends, to ignore them may be short-sighted. The fact is that current trends in information technology will shape users' expectations regarding data availability, software functionality, and interoperability. These trends also will alter the scope of what can be done with LCI data in very basic ways.

Faced with a wide range of future scenarios and emerging technologies, one group in the workshop was given the task of screening potentially interesting trends towards the future of LCI databases and knowledge management from the basis of a simple value proposition:

"We wish to promote uses of life cycle assessment (and LCI data) which improve products and processes. We believe that there are current trends in information technology and knowledge management that can support this goal by fundamentally changing the cost–benefit ratio of using LCIs, either by reducing the cost of collecting, managing, and using LCI data, or by increasing the value of those data. Our explorations focus on technologies, which can deliver on this promise in the 3- to 5-year time frame, and on plausible transition paths to allow these ideas to be incorporated within the context of existing data systems".

Where examples are cited — from both existing and hypothetical future tools — of future functionality that could be delivered by LCI databases, these examples are intended as notional, not specific recommendations (unless so noted). They are included solely to help illustrate the kinds of requirements or constraints that might be faced by LCI databases of the future.

One of the core messages within this chapter is that new knowledge management technologies offer the potential for increased data "mobility": data can more easily find its way into LCA databases from other sources, and out of LCA data resources for application to other uses.

At points in this chapter, suggestions are made on the potential for LCA dataset developers and database managers to facilitate exterior applications. In addition to the needs of LCA database managers, the needs of users within the LCA field are also addressed. Moreover, the audience for this chapter includes policy makers, business associations, and stakeholder representatives who want to investigate how to uphold these guidance principles under different scenarios and who want to take actions to support their desired scenario.

7.2 Three Scenarios

Three different future scenarios are developed with the aim to of exploring how current trends in information technology can affect the future of LCI databases and their management. The approach is to use a scenario-based planning approach, in which plausible future scenarios about how LCI data might be collected, managed, accessed, and utilised are developed. These scenarios then serve as the basis for discussion about what each scenario might imply for the future of LCI data along each of these dimensions.

The three scenarios, which are discussed in detail in subsequent sections, are as follows:

- Scenario L. The first scenario is based on a linear projection of current trends into the near future. LCI databases continue to be created and operated largely as activities independent from one another, but are increasingly easy for users to locate and access. The recommendations made in previous chapters have helped to improve data quality and consistency, both within and between databases.
- Scenario C. This scenario assumes that the way in which data is managed – primarily through curated, independently managed databases – continues to be the case, but the aggressive adoption of Web 2.0 technologies enables significant changes in the way that data may be accessed by users. LCI databases in this scenario often provide an open, web-accessible application programming interface (API) which enables users and third-party developers to "blend" data from multiple sources, or to create federated search tools which can locate LCI data stored in multiple databases from a single query. LCI database developers are eager to implement these APIs because they greatly expand the utility of their data by making them easier to find, and easier to use.
- Scenario I. In this scenario, holders of "raw data" adopt, at a major scale, new technologies which introduce new pathways for the creation of LCI data, and these data find their way to users both through the existing channels of national and independently managed databases, as well as new parallel pathways. For example, governments and other holders of large "external" (non-LCI) databases adopt technology, which makes it much easier for researchers (including the managers of existing LCI databases) to use external data to create new unit process datasets and update or expand existing unit process datasets. As another example, companies widely make use of tools that increase the bottom-up collection of unit process data, and the transmission of these data to data reviewers and aggregators.

The scenarios developed are informed by two sets of core assumptions: One pertains to what are believed to be key attributes of LCI data which are important to achieving the vision laid out in this chapter, and the other pertains to key information technology trends that will have a strong influence on the evolution of LCI databases over the planning period.

The first set of assumptions, key attributes of LCI data, are aspirational. The assumption for each of the scenarios is that the objective is to improve the state of LCI data along the following three dimensions:

1) Accessibility may be thought of as related to the question "how easy is it to find and access the data needed to prepare an LCI?" Improved accessibility of data suggests that it exists, that is, that data are available for a wide range of products, processes, and services; that they can be found easily, regardless of where they exist; and that they are affordable (or at least, that the cost of the accessing the data is small relative to the value that the data provides).

2) Utility addresses the question "how useful are the data that are found?" Improved utility of data means that they will be of good quality (and sufficiently transparent that the user can make informed judgements about data quality and modelling methodology); that data will be presented in formats that allow them to be incorporated into other tools; and that the data are is provided with sufficient metadata such that an informed user can clearly understand any limitations or constraints on their use.

3) Composability is a dimension that is perhaps most unique to LCI data, because it addresses the question of "how easily can these data be combined with data from other sources to model a larger system?" This is, of course, a defining aspect of the LCI task: composing system descriptions from a collection or aggregation of smaller units.

The second set of assumptions that guided scenario development regarded information technology trends that are viewed to most likely shape the way in which people use information in the future, including LCI data. Just as the advent of the World Wide Web forever changed the nature of software by making the web browser a primary platform for application deployment, these and other trends are believed to have pervasive impacts on how people access, use, and think about data:

- service-oriented architecture (data as a service),
- semantic Web technologies (moving from data to knowledge),
- social computing (the data user adds value to the data), and
- mobile computing (data everywhere).

7.3 Scenario L

In Scenario L (Figure 7.1), data are stored and databases are managed independently. Dataset providers are responsible for developing LCI datasets, and reviewers guarantee the conformance of the LCIs according to its individual quality assurance guidelines as set forth in the goals and scope of each LCA. New technologies are not aggressively adopted in this scenario. The database managers are responsible for ensuring that their guidelines follow the principles in this guidance document.

Therefore, the challenge in Scenario L is to overcome such limitations and develop a model of governance with a better collaboration and easier information exchange through development of

- common methodological, documentation, and review aspects under these Global Guidance Principles;
- a solution for overcoming differences in data formats; and
- a mutual understanding of differences in objectives and interests of the database managers.

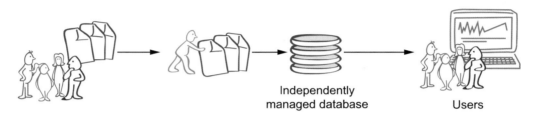

Figure 7.1: Scenario L

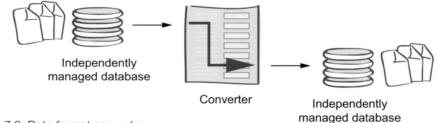

Figure 7.2: Data format converter

7.3.1 Description of the Scenario

The current LCI infrastructure builds on a number of independent databases from more or less independent database developers.[1] Some of these developers are governmental, others private, including commercial and non-profit organisations. In this scenario, users can count on reliability according to each individual database's principles and guidelines, and the accessibility is up to database managers.

The existence of these databases has contributed to the more widespread use of LCA because of the ease of access to process data. On the other hand, these independently managed databases (IMDs) lack standardised methodologies and formats.

7.3.2 Interchangeability Tools of Data Sources

Currently there are several data formats for LCA data, but only a few formats that are used as exchange formats, including ecospold and the International Reference Life Cycle Data System (ILCD; EC 2011) format. To improve the exchange and global use of LCA data, conversion tools (Figure 7.2) available such as the OpenLCA converter developed under United Nations Environment Programme/Society of Environmental Toxicology and Chemistry (UNEP/SETAC) leadership. Currently this tool is able to convert fairly well between ecospold 1.0 (Hedemann and König 2007) and the IL-

---

[1] Database developers are individuals or teams who organise and set up a database but who may not continue to manage that database.

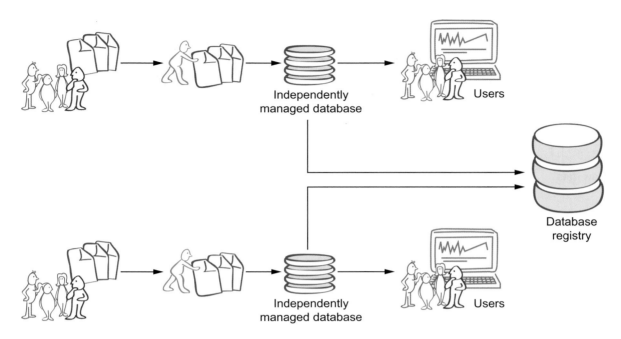

Figure 7.3: A life cycle database registry

CD-predecessor format, as well as the ISO@Spine format and some commercial software programs. A new version is being developed to allow conversion from and to ILCD and ecospold 2.0 (ecospold 2011) formats. Conversion is not a final solution because complete conversion is currently not possible due to differences in the data models. For instance, if one format has a field that describes the date of creation, and the other format has a field containing the expiration date for the user, the converter cannot "judge" how to convert one field to the other.

A logical step forward is to encourage the "owners" of the formats to further harmonise their format.

7.3.3 Example: Life Cycle Database Registry

A database registry (Figure 7.3) can be visualised as a hub of databases that allows users and providers of process datasets to offer what they have and to find what they need. Its aim is to connect life cycle data users with life cycle dataset providers, to allow users to find data, and to allow dataset providers to contact users worldwide[2]. A database registry is centrally managed by an organisation. As an extension, the registry itself could also have a section where any organisation or individual can upload data. The idea behind this latter effort is to develop a basic first "open source" database. A small guidance team would oversee the development of this database and check if the basic data requirements are met. But this action of basic

data checking and evaluation then moves the activity toward being a database and not simply a registry.

One example is the UNEP/SETAC Database Registry (http://lca-data.org). The website has two sections: one provides a search or query option, and the second provides a repository of resources, including data and web pages of individual dataset providers. Each dataset provider is free to select whether to join the registry or not, and is further free to select the level of detail that is made available to the registry. Dataset providers have the option to update their own web pages. Users are able to comment and rate datasets, although this process does not and should not take the place of critical peer review. The ability to allow users to comment in such an open process has both advantages and disadvantages. On one hand, updates can be done quickly, efficiently, and inexpensively (provided the comments are known to the dataset providers). On the other hand, putting this activity in the hands of a large group is harder to regulate and ensure that quality is maintained.

The UNEP/SETAC Database Registry is supported by moderators who have the role to follow up on updates and uploaded content to verify if it is in line with the overall goal of the registry. It has the option of open source modality, and includes the software converter between three LCI data formats. Additional potential functionalities are based on the adoption of emerging technologies such as the crowd-sourcing option and the interlinking of databases and registries.

---

[2] The word 'registry' is most often used to describe a searchable listing (such as a library) but it also includes the ability to accept uploaded data sets.

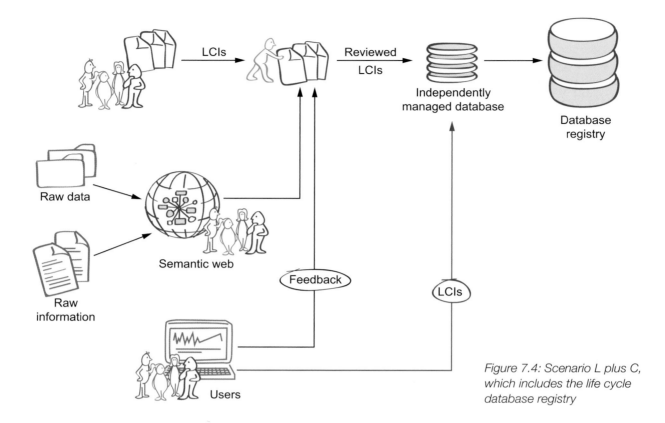

Figure 7.4: Scenario L plus C, which includes the life cycle database registry

Another example refers to the Japanese database registry that is managed by the LCA Society of Japan (JLCA). It consists of inventory datasets collected by industry associations, the secretariat of the Japan Environmental Management Association for Industry (JE-MAI), and researchers. Each dataset must be reviewed by the LCA promotion committee of JLCA, based on the data collection manual (JLCA 2000), before the data are registered. The dataset's provider is accountable for the data published, and the user of the dataset is accountable for the results based on the data that are used.

7.3.4 Policy Options to Strengthen Implementation of Global Guidance Principles under Scenario L

In Scenario L, the current IMDs carry a large responsibility to actually facilitate the development of the scenario. This means that all stakeholders, like governments, industry associations, and commercial parties that manage and supply databases, should start to strongly increase their cooperation and coordination. No one can specify exactly what the results of this cooperation must be, but it can cover a whole range of options, from better alignment of methods, to coordinated review procedures, to providing for interlinkages between datasets, etc. As the principles in this guidance document are made available to the general public and the same

methodological rules are applied, it becomes easier for stakeholders to cooperate with one another. A further point to address is the improvements needed in the process of resolving the problems around incompatibilities between data formats.

Successful implementation of this scenario requires strong support to build, develop, strengthen, and improve capacities and capabilities, especially in developing nations (see Chapter 6). When the stakeholders act effectively on improving the collaboration, they create the opportunity to develop a very good alternative to Scenarios C and I, as the need for developing these scenarios will diminish when high-quality data can be provided in abundance through the joined forces of the database managers. For example, the Provincial government of Québec has decided to create its LCI database in collaboration with and integrated into the ecoinvent database. Similarly, working towards a compatible structure but otherwise independent, the Malaysia government works for its national LCA database with ILCD format and elementary flows, the same as, for example, the Brazilian national project. Such efforts to harmonise databases and support a common data structure will improve the LCI database landscape even if the technologies in scenarios C and I are not, or are only slowly, introduced.

7.4 Scenario C

Scenario C preserves much of the L scenario: data are stored and managed primarily through curated, IMDs, whether developed by governmental interests or commercial ones, and conformance to these principles is primarily the responsibility of these database managers (see Figure 7.4 and compare and contrast to Figure 7.1).

7.4.1 Description of the Scenario

Scenario C departs from Scenario L in the ways in which data may be accessed by users. These changes stem largely from the accelerated infusion of key Web 2.0 concepts by database providers, including (but not limited to) the

- adoption of service-oriented architectures to expose the data — partially or fully — to third-party applications. This exposure would typically be done via a Web-based API, which is a common means of exposing program functionality to third-party developers, while maintaining control over the code and data. However, this can be accomplished through other means as well, including via file-based techniques where each accessible data record is presented as a unique uniform resource identifier (URI). An excellent example of where open APIs have been used to extend functionality while preserving the integrity of developers' code and data is the CAPE-OPEN (Co-LAN 2011) API for the chemical process simulation industry.
- user's role in the data value proposition. Arguably, the most significant aspect of Web 2.0 technology is not a technology at all, but a shift in paradigm about the role of users with respect to data. In Web 2.0 applications, users become an integral part of the data value proposition, whether as direct dataset creators (e.g., Flickr, Wikipedia) or as dataset evaluators and commentators (e.g., user feedback and social recommendation tools incorporated into many e-commerce sites such as Amazon.com). Under Scenario C, users are not envisioned to be primary creators of LCI data, but are anticipated to add value to datasets via user feedback, annotation, or comments. And because of the use of service-oriented architectures that allow access to managed datasets via third-party platforms, these user-generated data do not have to be stored or endorsed by the dataset owners.

Under Scenario C, LCI database managers are eager to implement these APIs because the use greatly

expands the utility of their data by making the data easier to find and easier to use. Central database registries still exist to help users find databases, and many users will continue to use the native interfaces to these databases to locate that data they need. In addition, however, third-party developers (or the dataset owners themselves) can also create new ways of searching, aggregating, packaging, and disseminating LCI data. These may include

- an intergovernmental group, government, or trade association that creates a "federated" search tool to locate unit process data from any of several national databases that contain the process, and to rank them according to objective criteria such as geographic constraints, how recently the data were developed, or the level of scrutiny to which they have been subjected.
- a subject matter expert who creates verified "packages" of LCI data which have been culled from a variety of databases, and which have been independently reviewed by the expert and assembled in a single location (which could be as simple as a Web page containing links to the individual data records) for use in a particular LCA or in a cluster of related LCAs that reuse the same data many times.
- a nongovernmental organisation (NGO) that develops a social ranking system for LCI data, allowing its users to rank data at the unit process level, as well as to comment on it. Because the ranking refers only to a link to the data that exist in the national database, it is not endorsed by the data owner, but allows other stakeholders to view the data through the lens of the NGO.

Because these new ways of accessing the information in IMDs do not change where the data are stored (only the ways in which users may access the data), database managers will want to adopt certain technologies that facilitate this approach. For instance, the so-called RESTful Web service is an approach that gives each data record (for instance, a unit process) its own unique URI, which can now be used as a persistent "bookmark" to those data.

Under this scenario, dataset developers still bear the responsibility for creating LCI data, as they do in Scenario L. They also retain the primary responsibility for assuring that their data are in conformance with these principles. Many users will continue to access the data via the native interfaces that the database managers provide. But increasingly, users will find, and potentially access, data from these databases through other applications including those developed by third parties. Because data in the databases can be referenced at the individual record level (via a unique URI), the market is opened up to a whole new layer of service providers, who work to evaluate data independently from the database manager, on behalf of themselves or their clients. This trend actually helps to improve the overall quality of data in the IMDs by providing more opportunities for competent technical review, as described in Chapter 4, and feedback about the data.

While not a radical departure from the status quo, this scenario does require the infusion of existing technology into existing LCI database applications. This infusion implies a certain degree of coordination that will be required, especially in defining a minimal set of API functionalities that databases should expose. The above descriptions of technology advances are under development and will soon be implemented by the primary data providers[3].

7.4.2 Policy Options to Strengthen Implementation of Global Guidance Principles under Scenario C

The current IMDs carry a large responsibility to actually facilitate the development of Scenario C. This responsibility means that all stakeholders, such as governments, industry associations, and commercial parties, who manage and supply databases should start to strongly increase their cooperation and coordination. Exactly what the results of this cooperation must be cannot be specified, but it can cover a whole range of options, from better alignment of method, coordinated review procedures, and providing for interlinkages between datasets. These principles provide a very good opportunity on which to base cooperation.

A further point to address is the strong support that is needed for capacity building, and the improvements needed in the process of resolving incompatibilities between data formats (see Chapter 6). The role of a database registry system also becomes even more important than in Scenario L because data will be located in many different database systems.

The dynamic described under Scenario C also requires more flexibility, because many more stakeholders may be expected to enter this area. Because the number of stakeholders is expected to increase, the current stakeholders should develop a policy for including newcomers, and ways to make it attractive for such newcomers to enter collaboration under these principles; otherwise, new communities may emerge and then diverge along their own path of data and database development. In the same line of thought, those of the current stakeholders who are currently not investigating new information technology (IT) developments should start to understand the threats and opportunities, and develop policies to influence the direction with respect to LCI datasets and databases. When the stakeholders act effectively on improving the collaboration, they have the opportunity to develop a very good alternative to Scenario I, because the need for developing this scenario will diminish when high-quality data can be provided in abundance through the joined forces of the new and current database managers.

7.5 Scenario I

The demand for additional LCA data has increased in recent years. Current practices for the development of LCI data require time and money to engage the services of multiple individuals or groups (e.g., a national database program, industry association, research institute, or consulting firm), who in turn will design and conduct the survey, review as described in Chapter 4, aggregate the data received, and integrate the results into its database.

7.5.1 Description of the Scenario

Whereas Scenario C sees the adoption of technologies which expand user interaction with LCI data, Scenario I sees holders of raw data adopting new technologies which introduce new pathways for the creation of LCI data (see Figure 7.5). Of course Scenario L is the basis of Scenarios C and I, which could happen in combination. There is nothing about Scenario C that lessens the potential for Scenario I to occur and vice versa; they might even reinforce each other.

Two important new data creation pathways to consider as examples within Scenario I are

1) the application of technology by governments and other holders of large external (non-LCI) databases, which makes it much easier for researchers (including the managers of existing LCI databases) to use external data to create new unit process datasets and update or expand existing unit process datasets, and

---

[3] The ecoinvent network and the International Reference Life Cycle Data System (ILCD) are actively working on the implementation of the enabling technologies mentioned in Scenario C.

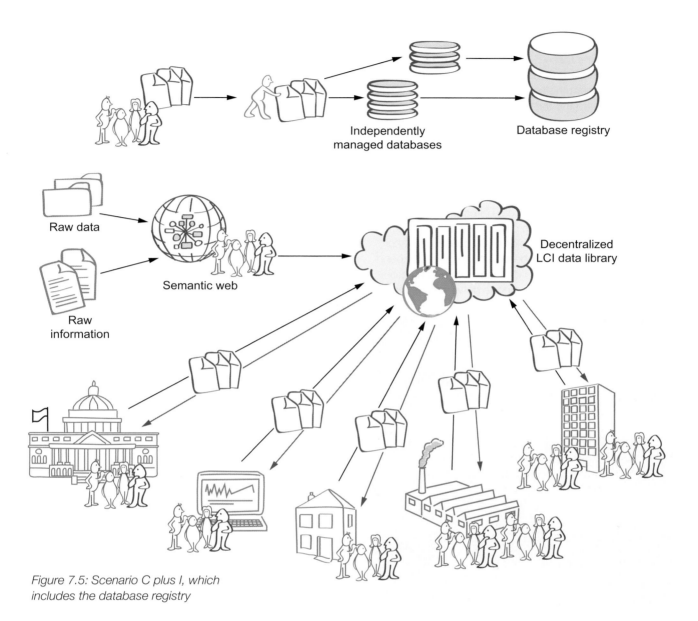

Figure 7.5: Scenario C plus I, which includes the database registry

2) the adoption of technology by companies to increase the bottom-up collection of unit process data, and the transmission of these data to data reviewers and aggregators.

Each of these two examples is described in more detail below.

Example 7.1: Enhanced conversion of external data into LCI databases

Unit process datasets contain comprehensive information on elementary and technosphere flows, per unit of process output, for a given unit process type.

Currently (and in the future within Scenario L), the way in which these data are collected for process-level databases is via surveys by one or more operators of databases such as governments, industrial associations, research institutions, non-profit organisations, or commercial entities, that develop LCI datasets.

But LCI dataset developers are not the only entities routinely collecting data about the inputs and outputs of unit processes. Governments maintain vast numbers of databases, some of which contain portions of the data needed to create a unit process dataset. Such data are distributed across many external data-bases, often managed by different agencies.

Currently, it is difficult (i.e., quite time-consuming) to

- find the best available data from which to construct a unit process dataset;
- combine these data into a unit process dataset, all referenced to the process output; and
- document the sources used and the steps taken to create the dataset.

It doesn't have to be this way. One promising solution for nearly automating the conversion of relevant external data into unit process data is the application of Semantic Web technology. This technology tool kit includes the use of formal ontologies, and linked data frameworks. These technologies already have had an impact in related modelling disciplines: for instance, the OntoCAPE ontologies developed by the University of Aachen in Germany have been used to greatly expand the ways in which process data can be used by providing a common language bridge between chemical

process instrumentation, chemical process simulation tools, and enterprise-level tools. Indeed, OntoCAPE provides a potential pathway for helping to generate raw data inputs to process LCIs directly from process control instrumentation.

Governments such as those in the United Kingdom and United States of America, and international agencies including the World Health Organization, are rapidly making more of their databases available for use via the Web, including projects to make these data available in RDF (Semantic Web) form. Also, open source tools are publicly available for converting standard data formats such as text, spreadsheets, and relational databases into RDF.

Example 7.2: Increased Bottom-Up Collection of Unit Process Data

New applications of available technology could enable a large number of the production activities in the world economy to become able, and incentivised, to collect the basic unit process data for their own operations. In this "LCI crowd-sourcing" scenario, the tasks that remain to be completed include

- review of these data (to ensure quality and accuracy according to Chapter 4), and
- aggregation of these data across producers of the same or similar products to form horizontally aggregated, or "generic," datasets, thereby protecting business sensitive information.

In this context, there can be a competitive marketplace for review and aggregation services. Once review and aggregation are completed, managers of existing databases could decide to integrate the newly available generic data into their databases; indeed, the database managers themselves could undertake either or both of the review and aggregation tasks. At the same time, newly available generic and reviewed data can also be made available as a free-standing generic dataset for a unit process (i.e., not yet integrated into a existing database).

Open source projects, such as Earthster (www. earthster.org), enable and incentivise bottom-up collection of unit process data worldwide. As mentioned above, companies must be capable and incentivised to collect on-site data in order for the system to work. This in turn requires that the benefits to companies for doing so exceed the costs of doing so, which can be brought about by lowering costs and increasing benefits.

Ways to lower the cost of bottom-up data collection include

- making free the download and use of LCA software or an editor in which you can collect and document software.
- designing the system to be very simple to use.
- making the software code open source, meaning that programmers can do such things as
  - make the user interface available in all languages;
  - create user interfaces adapted to specific user groups, sectors, etc.; and
  - continually innovate the user interface to enhance usability.

Ways to increase the benefits of bottom-up data collection include

- helping companies quickly understand the life cycle impacts of their products, understand relative contributions of each input to impacts, visually identify hot spots in the supply chain, etc.
- enabling the exchange of cradle-to-gate LCA results across companies (and software platforms) within supply chains, including
  - sharing of cradle-to-gate results with actual and potential customers, while keeping unit process data confidential; and
  - allowing a user the ability to manage access to the data, to update the data, and even to "de-publish" data.
- making use of user input to present the user with opportunities for sustainable innovation. For example, the software could automatically query regionally relevant databases that contain data on hundreds of different sustainable manufacturing resources, including technical assistance and financing for investments.
- providing the ability to report progress over time, and to assess the impacts of progress in the supply chain of a company's own product's cradle-to-gate impacts.

The key to this scenario example is that advances in software and in data-sharing services enable the benefits of unit process data collection and on-site use to exceed the costs of doing so. Free software for on-site use of such data, and free services for sharing results within supply chains, may make the benefit–cost ratio greater than 1. Once this is true, the activity can become widespread, especially given the network dynamic of data demand within supply chains. And once the activity becomes widespread, existing and new actors within the LCA community can offer services for review according to Chapter 4 and aggregation of the unit process data according to Chapter 3, so that it becomes relevant and valuable for use in LCAs.

7.5.2 Policy Options to Strengthen Implementation of Global Guidance Principles under Scenario I

In this scenario, the current IMD providers still have an important role to play. How important it is depends on the effectiveness of the response to the developments described in this scenario. However, if this scenario develops, it is still advisable to try to provide guidance. The way guidance is provided in this very difficult-to-control scenario has to be innovative. Important lessons can be learned from some of the examples mentioned in this and the previous scenario description, such as the following:

- Provide capacity building that incorporates a strong focus on these principles, in order to ensure that the principles are well understood by many contributors (the crowd) (see Chapter 6).
- Develop communities built on social computing principles to create a community of raw data providers.
- Facilitate a very advanced registry system in order to locate the distributed data.
- Update these principles in case it is necessary to cope with this new dynamic scenario, such as developing guidelines or certification schemes for the community of reviewers envisaged under Scenario I.

When the stakeholders act effectively on improving the collaboration, they have the opportunity to develop leadership in this complex scenario.

7.6 References

CO-LaN. 2011. The CAPE-OPEN laboratories network. [cited 2011 Feb 1]. Available from: http://www.colan.org.

[EC] European Commission – Joint Research Centre – Institute for Environment and Sustainability. 2010. International Reference Life Cycle Data System (ILCD) handbook - General guide for life cycle assessment - Detailed guidance. EUR 24708 EN. Luxembourg: Publications Office of the European Union. [cited 2011 Feb 1]. Available from: http://lct.jrc.ec.europa.eu/pdf-directory/ILCD-Handbook-General-guide-for-LCA-DETAIL-online-12March2010.pdf.

Ecospold. 2011. Ecospold data documentation format 2. [cited 2011 Feb 1]. Available from http://www.ecoinvent.org/ecoinvent-v3/ecospold-v2/.

Hedemann J, König U. 2007. Technical documentation of the ecoinvent database. Final report ecoinvent data v2.0, No. 4. Dübendorf (CH): Swiss Centre for Life Cycle Inventories. (formerly 2003 v1.01).

[JLCA] Life Cycle Assessment Society of Japan. 2011. 2000: Data collection methodology, 1st Japanese National LCA project (in Japanese). [cited 2011 Feb 1]. Available from: http://lca-forum.org/database/offer/.

Integration
and Synthesis

Guido Sonnemann
Bruce Vigon
Martin Baitz
Rolf Frischknecht
Stephan Krinke
Nydia Suppen
Bo Weidema
Marc-Andree Wolf

CHAPTER

8

This Global Guidance Principles document resulted from the intensive efforts of an international group of experts to identify key issues for the development, review, documentation, management, and dissemination of datasets contained in life cycle inventory (LCI) databases. A careful evaluation of the existing guidance from dozens of regional- and national- level references was brought to a focused analysis process. Findings and recommendations on six individual areas of current and possible future practice are presented in the previous chapters. However, these topics are not stand-alone in how they influence the primary objective of the document. This chapter provides an integration and synthesis as well as key messages of the topics covered. One element of this integration encompasses all of the aspects of current practice. A systematic treatment of data from the earliest stages of data sourcing and collection through inclusion of reviewed datasets into databases, maintaining a clear view of the requirements of those databases is highly important to provide the best support to database users and strongly recommended by the guidance principles.

8.1 Data Collection

Data sourcing and data collection are the starting points of any unit process and aggregated process dataset, and of any life cycle assessment (LCA) database as well. The importance of data sourcing and data collection is often underestimated, and the International

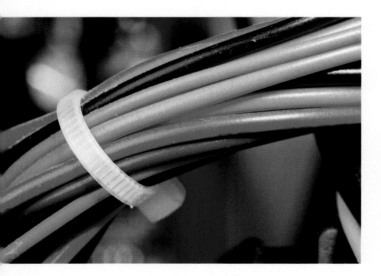

Organization for Standardization (ISO) standards on product LCA do not address it sufficiently. This guidance principles document explains the principles of raw data collection for LCA. "Raw data" is understood as data that has not yet put into relation to an LCI process

dataset. Starting at this early point helps ensure that the resulting LCI datasets will have the desired quality and extent of documentation.

Data collection is defined as the process of gathering data for a specific purpose or purposes. Data collection has the aim to "deliver" data needed for one or several specific unit process datasets: both the input and output flows and metadata that describe the processes. A broad range of data collection methods exist, ranging from direct on-location primary measurements to various secondary and estimation techniques. Some that may be most important are explained in Chapters 2 and 3, and references for further reading are provided. Some aspects of good practice for data collection procedures are given as well. The identification of good practice, wherever it is possible to do so, helps with the consistency and interchangeability of datasets that this guidance document strives to provide. However, in some areas, there may not be a single good practice or the experts may not have been able to reach consensus.

Data collection is closely linked to unit process development. Life Cycle Inventory unit process development procedures specify data (and supplemental information for data documentation) that is required, and the ensuing data collection effort tries to provide this information. In parallel with collection of the raw data, there needs to be proper documentation, to be able to later derive the required documentation at the next steps of unit process and aggregated datasets development.

Data collection is also closely linked to validation and quality assurance. The validation process starts from data as they are used in the process model. Results of the validation process may lead to the conclusion that further data are needed, or that the data used are insufficient. Validation at the dataset level serves to ensure that the model represents the actual process. Specifics steps to validate datasets are described.

8.2 Development of Unit Process and Aggregated Process Datasets

Using the ISO standards as a starting point, this guidance document makes a key distinction between "unit process dataset" and "aggregated process dataset." The Shonan Guidance Principles provide recommendations at a global level regarding the process of converting raw data into a unit process dataset, including the phases goal and scope definition (as applicable to the intended purpose of dataset development), dataset generation, validation, verification, and documentation.

In principle, the creation of a unit process dataset should be guided by the intended application specified in the goal and scope phase of the data development activity. We recommend keeping the content of the unit process dataset flexible so that it can be used in different application contexts. In particular, we recommend that multi-functional datasets be provided in their unallocated form, which allows the end user to apply either allocation or system expansion as is appropriate for their decision context.

There are good reasons to provide datasets on a unit process level. First, unit process data provides maximum transparency, allowing the users of the database to understand which unit processes are used in the life of a given reference flow, and how these unit processes are linked. Secondly, unit process data makes the database flexible and adaptable in the sense that specific unit processes in a specific LCI life cycle inventory can better reflect the situation to be assessed. Thirdly, unit process data can improve the interpretation of life cycle studies because the high resolution of unit process--based assessments allows a user to identify the key unit processes to perform sensitivity analysis by varying methodological and other assumptions as well as parameters, inputs, and outputs.

The credibility of LCA databases very much depends on the quality of raw data used and the unit process datasets developed from those data. The creation of unit process datasets, as well as the modelling of aggregated process datasets, requires technical, scientific, engineering, and economic knowledge, as well as familiarity with LCA methodology. We recommend an independent verification be conducted on unit process datasets provided as stand-alone datasets in an LCI database, and of those unit process datasets used to generate aggregated process datasets along with the product system model used.

There are several reasons to aggregate datasets. First of all, when answering questions typically addressed by LCA, it is often more convenient to work with aggregated process datasets (cradle-to-gate, cradle-to-grave) in a number of LCA software systems and in simplified tools because their use can reduce calculation time and memory requirements. Furthermore, from a user perspective, it can be beneficial to work with aggregated or even LCI system-level datasets if the user does not have the technical or engineering know-how to model a complex process chain, such as a steel plant or a refinery. Finally, the aggregation of datasets may be required for confidentiality reasons. Confidentiality may be ensured by different levels of aggregation (e.g., by establishing an industry average, by aggregating some selected unit process datasets along the supply chain, or by aggregating unit process datasets with selected inputs being followed from the cradle). For these cases an aggregated, reviewed dataset with comprehensive documentation can be an appropriate choice.

For the first time, this guidance document shows in a graphical and self-evident way the various methods by which unit process datasets can be aggregated.

Datasets (from databases) can be used in different modelling approaches: attributional, consequential, and decisional. Consistency is key to allow these choices to be made by users. Different approaches exist to model product systems. These approaches can be the basis for generating aggregated cradle-to-gate or cradle-to-grave process datasets. The modelling approaches are different, and one approach cannot be recommended as the general best approach. We recommend that users make the decision about modelling approach by looking at the explicit decision context of their LCA study. We recommend too that aggregate process datasets be modeled as consistently as necessary and that inconsistencies be documented when relevant. We recommend that the dataset provider be very clear about the modelling approach used when creating aggregated process datasets.

Next to consistency and drawing on good documentation, the accuracy of the datasets that will be combined into a life cycle model deserves special attention. The technological, geographic, and temporal representativeness determine whether the modelled life cycle is sufficiently descriptive of the system it is meant to represent. Datasets of sufficient representativeness are recommended. We strongly recommend to proper documentation and consideration of the potential loss in accuracy due to using datasets whose individual scopes differ from each other and the scope of the life cycle model being constructed. These recommendations signal to data developers and database managers that increased consistency is desirable and even essential since users increasingly want global product and service systems to be accurately captured in life cycle inventories.

The documentation of aggregated process datasets is highly important. We strongly recommend that sufficient information be provided and that the process be as transparent as possible. The provision of the unit process datasets used in the product system of an aggregated process dataset is preferable. When there is sufficient motivation not to provide the unit process level data and the associated documentation, we strongly recommend that other information in the aggregated process dataset be included. This may include key drivers of the overall environmental impacts, data sources used, assumptions, key process operational figures, and any other information that may help the user understand the utility of the dataset for their particular modelling purpose.

Thus, these Global Guidance Principles recognize that there may be valid technical, business, or practical reasons for having aggregated datasets in an LCI database. At the same time, a recommendation is made to provide unallocated unit process data as much as possible. Even when aggregated datasets are deemed necessary or preferable, additional documentation (as well as verification and review) is recommended to ensure credibility.

8.3 Documentation and Review

Data documentation and review are key elements in these guidance principles. The primary target audience for these guidance principles was identified as database managers. They have the role and responsibility to decide not only what the datasets themselves must include but also what additional information is required and what would be considered recommended or necessary in terms of validation and review prior to being stored in the database. To accomplish these functions, it is strongly recommended that the database management team issues a written protocol to define these requirements.

While providing accurate and complete measurements or estimates of flows into and out of a process or product system is obviously critical to the usability of an LCI dataset, we felt this was not sufficient. The workshop participants strongly support the view that only complete documentation makes a dataset. Complete documentation may be achieved by supplying all unit process datasets with associated verification documentation and conducting an external review. For aggregated datasets, the recommendation is to supply complete documentation to the reviewer of all underlying unit process datasets, and additional specific documentation to facilitate analysis, review, and interpretation is recommended. To respect confidentiality, and cost issues, documentation and review should be as concise as possible but as detailed as needed. Some flexibility in the provision of the documentation is allowed, depending on the form in which the dataset is delivered.

Due to the need for datasets to be both accurate depictions of reality and compliant with the requirements of the database they reside in, validation and review are considered to be critical. This guidance describes a number of ways in which validation, as an internal "quality-check" process or mechanism, and review, as a more formal and often external procedure, should take place. In particular, this guidance recommends that before a dataset is included in an LCI database, it undergoes a defined validation process to ensure it meets the database protocol (as well as the process reality check noted above). Additional processes are recommended to review the dataset to provide the user with the necessary quality assurance.

This guidance document recommends where and how the review procedure fits best in the data flow. It also recommends that the validation be done by an independent person and the review be done externally. Specifics on how and who should conduct a review in various circumstances are spelled out, with the goal being to provide users of datasets from different databases the knowledge that a coherent level of quality assurance has been given to the data. Criteria for the review are also listed, as are qualifications for reviewers, and the circumstances which would lead to an individual versus a panel-type review. All of these elements of guidance should foster greater exchangeability and consistency of LCI datasets from different LCI databases worldwide.

Lastly, the recommended content of review documentation is described. In this way, not only can users rely on a set of documentation from the dataset provider but also can receive an independent and sometimes external verification of what a dataset is about and its quality. We recommend that the review documentation or at least an abstract is made available with the dataset documentation.

8.4 Database Management

The terms "LCI dataset" and "LCI database" are commonly used, sometimes with completely different meanings. This guidance document provides definitions and the related implications to avoid misunderstandings.

An LCI database is an organized collection of ISO 14040- and 14044-compliant LCI datasets that sufficiently conform to a set of criteria including consistent methodology, validation or review, interchange format, documentation, and nomenclature, and allow for interconnection of individual datasets. Life cycle inventory databases store LCI datasets allowing creation, addition, maintenance, and search. Life cycle inventory databases are managed by a responsible management team, who has the responsibilities for the database creation, content, maintenance, and updating. In contrast, an LCI dataset library contains datasets that do not sufficiently meet the above criteria, and care must be taken when using them jointly in a life cycle model.

If the aspects above apply, but the scope of a database is limited regarding covered impact categories (e.g., only covers carbon footprint information) or has a specific focus for certain applications or schemes, this guidance document refers to a specific database, such as a carbon footprint database or a water footprint database.

Another issue is provision of LCI data for processes, technologies, and materials where no LCI data exist or they are not in an accessible form. Especially for new (non-commercial) technologies, there are often only few or no LCI data available. While it is no less important to have accurate and complete LCI datasets for these processes, methods and tools for creating datasets for developmental (not yet commercial-scale) processes were not discussed much during our workshop in Shonan Village and thus remain a topic for the future.

Other experts are invited to offer dataset developers, database managers, and the LCA practitioner community solutions to this challenge.

Databases can be seen as continuously evolving and never as finalized systems, even though the contained datasets have been reviewed. Maintenance, updating, and expandability are relevant elements of database management together with other stated responsibilities on the part of the database management team, for example, coordination and communication with users and other database managers.

8.5 Adaptive Approaches

Some Shonan workshop participants identified a need for additional data and data management to allow LCA databases to provide more comprehensive answers or to answer more comprehensive questions, such as spatially differentiated models, developments over time, and issues related to social and economic impacts. Another aspect addressed was the filling of data gaps with data estimations from non-process–based approaches.

The workshop participants analysed the different data sources, such as geographic data, data from national environmentally extended economic Input-Output Tables (IOTs) and environmental accounts, data on social indicators, and data on costs. In general, we found that all of these data sources could be used in a way complementary to existing raw data in the development of unit process datasets. If the actual data from the alternative data sources differ in scope, method, or resolution, any resulting limitations in the suitability to model the product system (for example, if a dataset has environmentally extended input output (EEIO) data and process data at different levels of aggregation) are strongly recommended to be documented as would be the case for any set of mixed data.

The additional data may add complexity to the LCA model structure and process modelling, and may require additional data collection. Therefore, the value of the additional information has to be balanced against the costs of generating, collecting, and maintaining it.

8.6 Role of Technology in the Future

Current trends in information technology are expected to shape users' expectations regarding data, software functionality, and interoperability in ways that will alter the scope of what can be done with LCA data. It is important to anticipate these trends, along with market drivers, in order to be better prepared to properly manage the development of life cycle information, and the trend towards providing quality data as a reliable basis for decision support. In both developed and developing countries, the increased potential for data mobility will allow data from various sources to more easily find its way into LCA databases, and then out of the LCA databases into a wide range of new applications. Such applications can potentially bring significant progress toward sustainable consumption and production.

Information technology will bring new ways to access the information in LCA databases, which may not change where the data are generated or stored, but the way in which users access the data. While not a radical departure from the status quo, the infusion of new technologies into existing database applications is occurring now and will continue into the near future.

8.7 Vision and Roadmaps

This guidance document affirmed many of the current practices relating to data and databases. In fact, as was recognized before the LCA databases workshop and mentioned in Chapter 1, a significant percentage of guidance in this area is not contentious. In a number of areas, the global guidance principles are recommendations that are neither confirmation of current ways of handling data and datasets or affirmation of how databases are set up and managed.

This guidance document can be considered as a first step towards a world with interlinked databases and overall accessibility to credible data, in line with the established vision of global LCA database guidance, that is, to

- provide global guidance on the establishment and maintenance of LCA databases, as the basis for future improved interlinkages of databases worldwide;
- facilitate additional data generation (including for certain applications such as carbon and water

footprint creation) and to enhance overall data accessibility;

- increase the credibility of existing LCA data, through the provision of such guidance, especially as it relates to usability for various purposes; and
- support a sound scientific basis for product stewardship in business and industry and life cycle-based policies in governments, and ultimately, to help advance the sustainability of products.

Life cycle approaches have got relevance not only in the business world where sustainability is emerging as a megatrend, but has also gained stronger political dimension by being included in sustainable consumption and production policies around the world.

Global coordination among LCI dataset developers and LCA database managers, together with capacity building and data mining, have been identified as priorities in the move towards a world with interlinked databases and overall accessibility to credible data. There is a need for global coordination among LCI dataset developers and LCA database managers to ensure that the principles discussed in this guidance document are upheld. This coordination could be done through a roundtable or a series of periodic meetings of key actors during international events. The coordination exercise could lead to a widely accepted global dataset library. Furthermore, processes at various levels could be set up to facilitate direct interlinkages between databases. Important elements of such a process would be

- recognition of differences between existing LCA databases;
- analysis of the sources of these differences, which may lead to an understanding that the differences are mainly due to different system boundaries and allocation rules, plus different geographic and related technical conditions, different "histories," organizational preferences, etc.; and
- adoption of the same system boundaries and allocation rules to facilitate interlinkages, and promote construction of adaptable datasets that can meet requirements of multiple databases.

A strengthened coordination could also lead to an improved alignment of data formats which result in better-functioning data format converters or even a common data format worldwide.

Capacity building concerning global guidance on LCA databases has been identified as another priority to ensure overall accessibility to more credible data (and its use). Capacity building is particularly relevant in emerging economies and developing countries where LCA databases have yet to be established. Therefore, it is a goal to convert this guidance document into train-ing material that can be used together with existing UNEP/SETAC material in targeted training events. With regard to capacity building, the strengthening of existing and the development of new regional and national life cycle networks is important. They facilitate the coordination and mutual empowerment of pioneer life cycle experts.

Moreover, it is imperative that universities develop courses on life cycle assessment and management so that companies, public authorities, and research institutions can hire young professionals with this expertise, and a number of them can become consultants, creating markets for life cycle information. Finally, as indicated by Sonnemann and de Leeuw (2006), it is especially important to strengthen the capacity of the weakest economic actors in the global supply chains to tackle environmental requirements. It can be expected that, in the future, subject matter experts at companies in developing countries will have to provide raw data for LCI datasets in their supply chains. Therefore, these experts and companies will have to be empowered by capacity-building efforts through intermediary agencies like National Cleaner Production Centers and the Chamber of Commerce, in addition to training provided by the companies located in the more developed economies who are purchasing these goods and services. Overall the international community is asked to support these capacity building efforts and also to provide further technical assistance. Because a main driver for capacity building is the demand for life cycle information, industry and government in the more economically developed countries should be informed about the specific benefits of life cycle approaches, so they can promote the development via the pull of their supply chains and policies, respectively.

There are huge amounts of relevant raw data and even developed LCI datasets available that currently are not easily accessible for LCA studies. LCA database managers, and also LCA practitioners for particular studies, should mine data by working with actors who routinely collect data about the inputs and outputs of unit processes (not necessarily for LCI) and related information to characterize the life cycle. Several important pathways for access to data and datasets should be considered.

Governments maintain vast numbers of databases, some of which contain portions of the data needed to create a unit process dataset. Such data are distributed across many external databases, often managed by different agencies. Governments and international agencies are rapidly making more of their databases available for use. Moreover, numerous research projects with public funding have generated a huge amount of relevant raw data and also a fairly significant number of unit process and aggregated datasets and will continue to do so in the future. Public funding agencies are encouraged to ensure that the data and datasets resulting from research projects are publicly available for future use in LCA databases.

Adoption of technology by companies can increase the bottom–up collection of unit process data, and the transmission of these data to data collectors and reviewers. New applications of currently available technology could enable a large number of global producers to be enabled and incentivised to collect basic unit process data for their own operations. Competitive markets can promote review and aggregation services. Once compiled and reviewed, the newly available generic dataset can be integrated into existing centrally managed LCA databases at the managers' discretion; furthermore, database managers could themselves undertake the review task. At the same time, newly available generic and reviewed datasets can also be made available as free-standing generic datasets for unit processes in a dataset library. It can be expected that datasets generated through the adaptive approaches, as introduced in this document, will gain importance. Open questions with regard to ensuring

credible data derived from these approaches might still need to be discussed at appropriate international forums.

These various possible roadmaps have been put together to highlight how life cycle experts could contribute to moving forward towards the vision of a world with coordination between LCA databases and broad accessibility to credible LCI datasets. Ultimately, the principles in this global guidance document help to develop a common understanding and provide a guide along a path towards global use of life cycle information to inform design, production, and consumption of greener products in the future.

8.8 References

Sonnemann G, de Leeuw B. 2006. Life cycle management in developing countries: State of the art and outlook. Int J LCA. 11(1):123–126.

Participants of the Workshop on Global Guidance Principles for Life Cycle Assessment Databases

Martin Baitz (PE International AG), Angeline de Beaufort (Independent Consultant), Clare Broadbent (World Steel Association), Scott Butner (Knowledge Systems Group, Pacific Northwest National Laboratory, USA), Armando Caldeira-Pires (UNI Brasilia, Brazil), Alberta Carpenter (NREL, USA), Andreas Ciroth (GreenDeltaTC), David Cockburn (Tetra Pak), Mary Ann Curran (US EPA-ORD), Fredy Dinkel (Carbotech AG), Laura Draucker (WRI), Jim Fava (Five Winds International), Greg Foliente (CSIRO, Australia), Rolf Frischknecht (ESU Services), Pierre Gerber (FAO), Mark Goedkoop (Pré Consultants), Reinout Heijungs (CML Leiden University, The Netherlands), Atsushi Inaba (Kogakuin University, Japan), Henry King (Unilever), Stephan Krinke (Volkswagen), Joon-Jae Lee (KEITI, Korea), Pascal Lesage (CIRAIG, Quebec, Canada), Ken Martchek (Alcoa Inc.), Charles Mbowha (University of Johannesburg, South Africa), Ivo Mersiowsky (DEKRA Industrial on behalf of PlasticsEurope), Thumrongrut Mungcharoen (Kasetsart University and National Metal and Materials Technology Center, Thailand), Katsuyuki Nakano (Japan Environmental Management Association for Industry), Greg Norris (Harvard University, USA/ Sylvatica), Surjya Narayana Pati (National Council for Cement and Building Materials, India), Claudia Peña (Chilean Research Center of Mining and Metallurgy), Chiew Wei Puah (Malaysian Palm Oil Board), Toolseeram Ramjeawon (University of Mauritius), Olivier Réthoré (ADEME, France), Abdelhadi Sahnoune (ExxonMobil Chemical Co.), Guido Sonnemann (UNEP), Martha Stevenson (World Wildlife Fund), Sangwon Suh (University of California, Santa Barbara, USA), Nydia Suppen (Center for Life Cycle Assessment and Sustainable Design – Mexico, CADIS), Kiyotaka Tahara (National Institute of Advanced Industrial Science and Technology, Japan), Reginald Tan (National University of Singapore), Greg Thoma (The Sustainability Consortium), Ladji Tikana (European Copper Institute), Cássia Maria Lie Ugaya (Federal Technological University of Paraná, Brazil), Sonia Valdivia (UNEP), Bruce Vigon (SETAC), Hongtao Wang (Sichuan University, China), Bo Weidema (Ecoinvent), Marc-Andree Wolf (EC JRC). In addition, staff of the Society of Non- Traditional Technology (SNTT) provided logistical and organisational support for the workshop.

ANNEX 1

Glossary

TERMS	DEFINITION
Adaptable (flexible)	Ability to adapt, change, or replace specific unit processes in a life cycle inventory or product system to better reflect the product life cycle that the model is meant to represent.
Aggregated dataset (accumulated system dataset)	An activity dataset showing the aggregated environmental exchanges and impacts of the product system related to one specific product from the activity. (Weidema et. al. 2011)
Aggregation	The action of summing or bringing together information (e.g., data, indicator results) from smaller units into a larger unit. (e.g., from inventory indicator to subcategory). (Benoit and Mazijn 2009)
Allocation (partitioning)	Partitioning the input or output flows of a process or a product system between the product system under study and one or more other product systems. (ISO 2006)
Attributional approach	System modelling approach in which inputs and outputs are attributed to the functional unit of a product system by linking and/or partitioning the unit processes of the system according to a normative rule.
Average LCI dataset	LCI dataset obtained via averaging (producer-) specific LCI datasets. Typically referring to horizontally averaged data of complete product systems (e.g., global average steel billet data), unit processes (e.g., EU air transport fleet mix), or partly terminated systems (e.g., Australian average wastewater treatment plant). Also used for so-called "vertically averaged data," i.e., LCI result datasets. (European Commission - Joint Research Centre - Institute for Environment and Sustainability 2009)
Average technology (also called 'production mix')	The average technology (mix) is represented by a technology (mix) used to cover the demand for a certain functional unit within a specific area and a certain time period (e.g., a calendar year). (ESU-services Ltd. 2009)
Background system	The background system consists of processes on which no or, at best, indirect influence may be exercised by the decision-maker for which an LCA is carried out. Such processes are called "background processes." (Frischknecht 1998)

TERMS	DEFINITION
By-product	Ability to adapt, change or replace specific unit processes in a life cycle A marketable good or service that is not the primary good or service being produced. (European Commission - Joint Research Centre - Institute for Environment and Sustainability 2009) Note: "primary good or service" = reference product (see definition provided in this glossary)
Capacity building	A wide range of strategies and processes that contribute to a better understanding about the benefits of counting on good-quality life cycle data, how to use it, and how to start up, run, maintain, document, and review life cycle databases.
Completeness check	Process of verifying whether information from the phases of a life cycle assessment is sufficient for reaching conclusions in accordance with the goal and scope definition. (ISO 2006)
Composability (of data)	Dimension of LCI data concerning its ability to combine data from one source with data from other sources to model or compose a larger system.
Consequential approach	System modelling approach in which activities in a product system are linked so that activities are included in the product system to the extent that they are expected to change as a consequence of a change in demand for the functional unit.
Consistency check	Process of verifying that the assumptions, methods, and data are consistently applied throughout the study and are in accordance with the goal and scope definition performed before conclusions are reached. (ISO 2006)
Constrained supplier	Supplier that is unable to increase production as a result of an increase in demand for its product. These constraints can be due to a number of factors such as regulation (e.g., quotas), shortage in raw materials or other production factors, and market failures. The use of the output of a constrained producer results in the output being unavailable to another potential user. (Based on the definition of "constrained technology"; Weidema et al. 1999)
Consumption mix	The weighted average of the suppliers providing a specific product to a geographical area, equal to the production mix plus imports minus exports of products produced in the territory.
Co-product	Any of two or more products coming from the same unit process or product system. (ISO 2006)

TERMS	DEFINITION
Cradle-to-gate	An assessment that includes part of the product's life cycle, including material acquisition through the production of the studied product and excluding the use or end-of-life stages. (WRI and WBCSD 2010)
Cradle-to-grave	A cradle to grave assessment considers impacts at each stage of a product's life cycle, from the time natural resources are extracted from the ground and processed through each subsequent stage of manufacturing, transportation, product use, recycling, and ultimately, disposal. (Athena Institute & National Renewable Energy Laboratory draft 2010)
Critical review	Process intended to ensure consistency between a life cycle assessment and the principles and requirements of the International Standards on Life Cycle Assessment. (ISO 2006)
Crowd sourcing	The act of outsourcing tasks, traditionally performed by an employee or contractor, to an undefined, large group of people or community (a "crowd"), through an open call.
Cut-off criteria	Specification of the amount of material or energy flow or the level of environmental significance associated with unit processes or product system to be excluded from a study. (ISO 2006)
Data collection	The process of gathering data. (UNECE 2000)
Data commissioner	Persons or organizations which commission the data collection and documentation. (ISO 2002)
Data documentation format	Structure of documentation of data (NOTE: this includes data fields, sets of data fields, and their relationship). (ISO 2002)
Data field	Container for specified data with a specified data type. (ISO 2002)
Data gaps	Data (elementary flows) that are missing in a dataset and that impair the data quality (completeness criteria) of the dataset required for the LCI database and/or the application of impact assessment for a certain impact category.
Data management	Administrative process by which the required data is acquired, validated, stored, protected, and processed, and by which its accessibility, reliability, and timeliness is ensured to satisfy the needs of the data users. (Business Dictionary no date)

TERMS	DEFINITION
Data mining	Generally, data mining [...] is the process of analyzing data from different perspectives and summarizing it into useful information [...]. Technically, data mining is the process of finding correlations or patterns among dozens of fields in large relational databases. (Palace 1996)
Data quality	Characteristics of data that relate to their ability to satisfy stated requirements. (ISO 2006)
Data source	Origin of data. (ISO 2002)
Database developer	Database developers are the ones who build or develop databases and may not be only owners or the providers.
Dataset (LCI or LCIA dataset)	A document or file with life cycle information of a specified product or other reference (e.g., site, process), covering descriptive metadata and quantitative life cycle inventory and/or life cycle impact assessment data, respectively. (European Commission - Joint Research Centre - Institute for Environment and Sustainability 2009)
Dataset author	The person who enters the data into the dataset format and fields (this person may also be the dataset developer or dataset owner).
Dataset review	A manual, systematic, independent, and documented process for evaluating LCI datasets in the framework of the database against established validation and review criteria.
Decisional approach	System modelling approach in which activities in a product system are linked to anticipated future suppliers with which one may establish financial and contractual relations even if the said suppliers are constrained.
Elementary flow	Material or energy entering the system being studied that has been drawn from the environment without previous human transformation, or material or energy leaving the system being studied that is released into the environment without subsequent human transformation. (ISO 2006)
Energy flow	Input to or output from a unit process or product system, quantified in energy units. (ISO 2006)
Environmental aspect	Element of an organization's activities, products or services that can interact with the environment. (ISO 2004a)
Environmentally extended input-output data (environmentally extended input-output / environmentally extended input-output tables)	The data presented by national statistical agencies as supply-use tables (also known as "make-use tables") and direct requirements tables. The environmental extension is an inventory of the elementary flows for each unit process in these tables.

TERMS	DEFINITION
Evaluation	Element within the life cycle interpretation phase intended to establish confidence in the results of the Life Cycle Assessment. (ISO 2006)
Foreground system	The foreground system consists of processes which are under the control of the decision-maker for which an LCA is carried out. They are called foreground processes. (Frischknecht 1998)
Generic data	Data that is not site or enterprise specific. (Benoit and Mazijn 2009)
Goal and scope	The first phase of an LCA; establishing the aim of the intended study, the functional unit, the reference flow, the product system(s) under study and the breadth and depth of the study in relation to this aim. (Guinée 2002)
Horizontal averaging	A type of aggregation in which multiple unit processes (or aggregated datasets) supplying a common reference flow are combined in order to produce an averaged dataset.
Input-output table	A means of presenting a detailed analysis of the process of production and the use of goods and services (products) and the income generated in that production; they can be either in the form of (a) supply and use tables or (b) symmetric input-output tables. (UNSD 1993)
Intermediate product	Output from a unit process that is input to other unit processes that require further transformation within the system. (ISO 2006)
Interpretability	The extent to which information or data can be easily translated into useful application, in the case of LCA to support decision-making.
Intrinsically linked database (or "aggregatable") life cycle inventory database	Databases that are structured in such a way that it is possible for software to automatically create aggregated process datasets. These databases contain datasets for which one process input is linked, directly or through a set of rules contained in an algorithm, to another process output, and treats all multifunctional processes (through allocation or system expansion) such that fully terminated aggregated process datasets have only one reference flow.
Inventory dataset	A set of input and output data of a process. All of them are related to the same reference of this process. Usually, an inventory dataset also contains metadata describing, for example, geography, time reference, and ownership of the dataset. The process can be a unit process or an aggregated process.

TERMS	DEFINITION
Life cycle	Consecutive and interlinked stages of a product system, from raw material acquisition or generation from natural resources to final disposal. (ISO 2006)
Life cycle assessment	Compilation and evaluation of the inputs, outputs and the potential environmental impacts of a product system throughout its life cycle. (ISO 2006)
Life cycle database registry	A global database in which quality life cycle databases can be registered.
Life cycle dataset library	A global database of registered and searchable life cycle datasets.
Life cycle impact assessment	Phase of Life Cycle Assessment aimed at understanding and evaluating the magnitude and significance of the potential environmental impacts for a product system throughout the life cycle of the product. (ISO 2006)
Life cycle interpretation	Phase of Life Cycle Assessment in which the findings of either the inventory analysis or the impact assessment, or both, are evaluated in relation to the defined goal and scope in order to reach conclusions and recommendations. (ISO 2006)
Life cycle inventory analysis	Phase of Life Cycle Assessment involving the compilation and quantification of inputs and outputs for a product throughout its life cycle. (ISO 2006)
Life cycle inventory database	A system intended to organize, store, and retrieve large amounts of digital LCI datasets easily. It consists of an organized collection of LCI datasets that completely or partially conforms to a common set of criteria, including methodology, format, review, and nomenclature, and that allows for interconnection of individual datasets that can be specified for use with identified impact assessment methods in application of life cycle assessments and life cycle impact assessments.
Long-term changes	Changes are classified long-term if the factors of production are variable and one may choose between different technologies available. The performance of the technologies available is given. Long-term corresponds to the extension or downsizing of production capacities within a couple of years to a few decades to follow the predicted development of demand. (ESU-services Ltd. 2009)
Marginal technology (production)	A marginal technology is represented by a technology or technology mix which is put in or out of operation next due to a short- or long-term change in demand. (ESU-services Ltd. 2009)

TERMS	DEFINITION
Market mix	The weighted average of the suppliers providing a specific product to a specific market. This can be equal to a consumption mix when the market boundaries and the geographic boundaries are equal. When the market is global, the market mix is equal to the global production mix.
Metadata (descriptor)	Data that defines and describes other data and processes. (ISO 2004b)
Mobile computing	A trend towards accessing data from mobile devices via wireless connections to the Internet or other network systems. This includes the use of smart phones, tablet computing devices, and laptops but ultimately can also include devices not normally considered "computers" but which have a need to access data. While we did not directly address mobile computing in our scenarios, it is likely that this trend will have some degree of impact on how LCI data are consumed and/or used. For instance, it is possible, using current mobile technology, to conduct a study of personal travel habits by harnessing geoinformation provided by smart phones, and these data could be used to help improve the assumptions used in a transportation system LCA.
National statistical data	Data collected on a regular basis (by survey from respondents, or from administrative sources) by survey statisticians in the national statistical system to be edited, imputed, aggregated and/or used in the compilation and production of official statistics. (SDMX 2008)
Nomenclature	Set of rules to name and classify data in a consistent and unique way. (ISO 2002)
Primary data	Data determined by direct measurement, estimation or calculation from the original source. (Weidema et al. 2003) NOTE: primary or original source is the source of initial physical or chemical appearance and not the initial literal appearance.
Process	Set of interrelated or interacting activities that transforms inputs into outputs. (ISO 2005)
Product	Any goods or service. (ISO 2006)
Product flow	Products entering from or leaving to another product system. (ISO 2006)
Product system	Collection of unit processes with elementary and product flows, performing one or more defined functions, and which models the life cycle of a product. (ISO 2006)

TERMS	DEFINITION
Production mix	The production-volume-weighted average of the suppliers of a specific product within a geographical area. (Weidema et al. 2011)
Raw data	Data used in unit process inventory modelling to deliver inventory data at the end, which are extracted from various data sources, such as bookkeeping of a plant, national statistics, or journal literature.
Raw material	Primary or secondary material that is used to produce a product. (ISO 2006)
Recycling	The use of a by-product output of one product system as input to another product system.
Reference flow	Measure of the outputs from processes in a given product system required to fulfil the function expressed by the functional unit. (ISO 2006)
Reference product	Product of an activity for which a change in demand will affect the production volume of the activity (also known as the determining products in consequential modelling). (Weidema et al. 2011)
Releases	Emissions to air and discharges to water and soil. (ISO 2006)
Representativeness	Qualitative assessment of degree to which the data reflect the true population of interest (NOTE: considerations could include, e.g., geographical, time period and technology coverages). (ISO 2002)
Review criteria	Criteria to ensure the correctness of the dataset. This might be published in the database protocol document.
Reviewer (independent external reviewer / independent internal reviewer)	A competent and independent person or persons with responsibility for performing and reporting on the results of a dataset review. (**independent external reviewer:** A reviewer recognized by the database manager, who was not involved in the definition or development of the reviewed case and is therefore independent. The reviewer has no affiliation with dataset provider or the study commissioner. This includes both the reviewer as a person and their employer as an organization.) (**independent internal reviewer:** A reviewer recognized by the database manager, who is not involved in the study to be reviewed, or quantitatively relevant parts (e.g., background data) but can be part of the organization that performed or commissioned the LCI work.) (Latter two definitions taken from European Commission - Joint Research Centre - Institute for Environment and Sustainability 2009)

TERMS	DEFINITION
Scaling	Adjusting process input and output flows in relation to the functional unit.
Semantic web technologies	A collection of technologies (including, e.g., formal ontologies, and the Resource Description Framework mark-up language) which are being used to allow data to be represented in ways which make their meaning (their underlying semantics) explicit and machine readable. A specific example is the inclusion of geotagging information on photographs; by presenting the location that the photograph was made in a semantic web–enabled format, that information is available to other applications such as mapping tools.
Sensitivity analysis	Systematic procedures for estimating the effects of the choices made regarding methods and data on the outcome of a study. (ISO 2006)
Sensitivity check	Process of verifying that the information obtained from a sensitivity analysis is relevant for reaching the conclusions and giving recommendations. (ISO 2006)
Service-oriented architecture	An approach to software design that presents software functionality via a web-based interface, called a "web service." This allows the underlying functions of the software (e.g., a query utility) to be accessed by other programs using common Internet protocols. Service-oriented architectures can, if desired, facilitate the development of third-party applications that extend a data provider's tools without compromising the integrity of the data or software.
Short-term changes	Changes are classified short-term if the factors of production and the technology available are fixed. Short-term corresponds to a one time only change in demand and helps to better use existing production capacities. (ESU-services Ltd. 2009)
Social computing	A pervasive trend towards the construction of web-based applications that link together users in extended social networks and harness the data that are generated by their use of the application. For instance, social recommendation tools found on many e-commerce sites ("customers who bought this book also enjoyed…") are a form of social computing, as is the "tagging" (addition of textual metadata to photos) by users of popular social sites such as Flickr or Facebook.

TERMS	DEFINITION
Substitution	Solving multi-functionality of processes by expanding the system boundaries and substituting the non-reference products with an alternative way of providing them, i.e., the processes or products that the non-reference product supersedes. Effectively the non-reference products are moved from being outputs of the multi-functional process to be negative inputs of this process, so that the life cycle inventory of the superseded processes or products is subtracted from the system, i.e., it is "credited." Substitution is a special (subtractive) case of applying the system expansion principle. (Definition prepared by merging the definitions from ISO 14040ff and the European Commission - Joint Research Centre - Institute for Environment and Sustainability 2010)
System boundary	Set of criteria specifying which unit processes are part of a product system. (ISO 2006)
System expansion	Expanding the product system to include the additional functions related to the co-products. (ISO 2006)
Terminated (partly or fully) aggregated process datasets	A fully terminated aggregated dataset is a dataset that comprises within its boundaries an entire product system, such that the only flows crossing the system boundaries are the reference flows and elementary flows. All other intermediate exchanges are generated and consumed within the system boundaries and hence are not represented in the terminated aggregated dataset. These datasets are equivalent to (cradle-to-gate or cradle-to-grave) LCIs.

A partly terminated aggregated process dataset, on the other hand, purposely does not link some of the intermediate flows to a dataset (in other words, the processes that produce these intermediate flows are outside the aggregation boundaries). As such, these partly terminated aggregated process datasets do not represent a life cycle inventory. In order to calculate a life cycle inventory, these intermediate flows must be linked to fully terminated aggregated process datasets or systems of linked unit processes that allow the calculation of life cycle inventories. |
| Uncertainty | Quantitative definition: Measurement that characterizes the dispersion of values that could reasonably be attributed to a parameter. (adapted from ISO 1995)
Qualitative definition: A general and imprecise term which refers to the lack of certainty in data and methodology choices, such as the application of non-representative factors or methods, incomplete data on sources and sinks, lack of transparency, etc. (WRI and WBCSD 2010) |
| Uncertainty analysis | Systematic procedure to quantify the uncertainty introduced in the results of a life cycle inventory analysis due to the cumulative effects of model imprecision, input uncertainty and data variability. (ISO 2006) |
| Unit process | Smallest element considered in the life cycle inventory analysis for which input and output data are quantified. (ISO 2006) |

TERMS	DEFINITION
Unit process input	Product, material or energy flow that enters a unit process. (ISO 2006)
Unit process model	A group of mathematical relations that transforms raw data into a unit process dataset.
Unit process modeling	Procedures of defining mathematical relations and collecting raw data to obtain a unit process dataset.
Unit process output	Product, material or energy flow that leaves a unit process. (ISO 2006)
User	Person or organisation responsible to construct an LCA model from one or more unit process datasets and/or aggregated process datasets taken from databases and/or personal or organizational investigations. The user is responsible for presentation and interpretation of the LCA results and the linked recommendations within a decision process. The user is not necessarily the decision maker.
Utility (of data)	A summary term describing the value of a given data release as an analytical resource. This comprises the data's analytical completeness and its analytical validity. (Statistical Disclosure Control 2011)
Validation	Ensuring that data satisfy defined criteria.
Verification	Confirmation, through the provision of objective evidence that specified requirements have been fulfilled. (ISO 2005)
Vertical aggregation	A type of aggregation involving the combination of unit processes that succeed each other in a product life cycle, connected with intermediary flows.
Waste	Substances or objects which the holder intends or is required to dispose of. (ISO 2006)
Web 2.0	A collection of information technologies (primarily web-based) and a set of operating principles that build upon these technologies to change the way in which users interact with web-based applications. The term was coined in the early 2000s by Tim O'Reilly, and has come to mean web-based applications that involve their users in an active role, often by allowing them to easily add information in the form of comments, ratings, or other evaluations of data found online.

Glossary – Reference List

Athena Institute and National Renewable Energy Laboratory. 2010. U.S. LCI database overview and data submission requirements version (draft) 2.

Benoit C, Mazijn B, editors. 2009. Guidelines for social life cycle assessment of products. Geneva (CH): UNEP/SETAC Life Cycle Initiative.

Business Dictionary. No date. Data management. [Internet] [cited 2011 Jan]. Available from http://www.businessdictionary.com/definition/data-management.html.

European Commission – Joint Research Centre – Institute for Environment and Sustainability. 2010. International Reference Life Cycle Data System (ILCD) handbook - General guide for life cycle assessment - Detailed guidance. EUR 24708 EN. Luxembourg: Publications Office of the European Union. [cited 2011 Feb 1]. Available from: http://lct.jrc.ec.europa.eu/pdf-directory/ILCD-Handbook-General-guide-for-LCA-DETAIL-online-12March2010.pdf.

European Commission - Joint Research Centre - Institute for Environment and Sustainability. 2009. International Reference Life Cycle Data System (ILCD) Handbook – Terminology. Initial draft.

Frischknecht R, Stucki B 2010. Electricity use and production in Veolia environment activities - Scope dependent modeling of electricity in life cycle assessment, ESU-services Ltd. final report, v1.

Frischknecht R. 1998. Life cycle inventory analysis for decision-making: Scope-dependent inventory system models and context-specific joint product allocation [PhD thesis, ETH Zürich]. Uster (CH): Rolf Frischknecht. ISBN 3-9520661-3-3.

Guinée J.B. editor. 2002. Handbook for life cycle assessment. Operational guide to the ISO standards, Series: Eco-Efficiency in industry and science, 7. Dordrecht (NL): Kluwer. 708 p.

[ISO] International Organization for Standardization. 1995. Guide to the expression of uncertainty in measurement (GUM). Standard Reference Number: ISO/IEC Guide 98:1995.

[ISO] International Organization for Standardization. 2002. Environmental Management — Life Cycle Assessment — Data Documentation Format. Standard Reference Number: ISO/TS 14048:2002(E).

[ISO] International Organization for Standardization. 2004a. Environmental management systems -- Requirements with guidance for use. Standard Reference Number: ISO 14001:2004.

[ISO] International Organization for Standardization. 2004b. Information technology -- Metadata registries (MDR) -- Part 1: Framework. Standard Reference Number: ISO/IEC 11179-1:2004.

[ISO] International Organization for Standardization. 2005. Quality management systems -- Fundamentals and vocabulary. Standard Reference Number: ISO 9000:2005.

[ISO] International Organization for Standardization. 2006. Environmental management — Life Cycle Assessment — Requirements and Guidelines. Standard Reference Number: ISO 14044:2006(E).

Palace B. 1996. Data mining. Technology nNote prepared for Management 274A: Anderson Graduate School of Management at UCLA. [Internet] [cited June 2011]. Available from http://www.anderson.ucla.edu/faculty/jason.frand/teacher/technologies/palace/datamining.htm.

[SDMX] Statistical Data and Metadata Exchange. 2008 draft. Annex 4: Metadata common vocabulary, [Internet] [cited 2011 Feb 1]. Available from: sdmx.org/.../sdmx_annex4_metadata_common_vocabulary_draft_february_2008.doc

Statistical Disclosure Control. 2011. Glossary on statistical disclosure control. [Internet] [cited January 2011]. Available from http://neon.vb.cbs.nl/casc/glossary.htm.

[UNECE] United Nations Economic Commission for Europe. 2000. Glossary of terms on statistical data editing. Conference of European Statisticians Methodological Material. Geneva (CH): UN. [cited January 2011]. Available from http://ec.europa.eu/eurostat/ramon/coded_files/UN_Glossary_terms_stat.pdf.

[UNSD] United Nations Statistics Division. 1993. Glossary of the system of national accounts 1993. [Internet] [cited 2011 Jan]. Available from http://unstats.un.org/unsd/nationalaccount/glossresults.asp?gID=633.

Weidema BP, Bauer C, Hischier R, Mutel C, Nemecek T, Vadenbo CO, Wernet G. 2011. Overview and methodology. Data quality guideline for the ecoinvent database version 3. Eecoinvent Report 1. St. Gallen (CH): The ecoinvent Centre. [cited 2011 Feb]. Available from http://www.ecoinvent.org/fileadmin/documents/en/ecoinvent_v3_elements/01_DataQualityGuideline_FinalDraft_rev1.pdf.

Weidema BP, Cappellaro F, Carlson R, Notten P, Pålsson A-C, Patyk A, Regalini E, Sacchetto F, Scalbi S. 2003. Procedural guideline for collection, treatment, and quality documentation of LCA data. Document LC-TG-23-001 of the CASCADE project.

Weidema BP, Frees N, Nielsen AM. 1999. Marginal production technologies for life cycle inventories. Int J LCA 4(1):48-56.

[WBCSD and WRI] World Business Council for Sustainable Development and World Resources Institute. 2010. The GHG protocol product life cycle accounting and reporting standard. Geneva and Washington DC: WBCSD and WRI.

Peer Review Report of the Global Guidance Principles for LCA Databases

Introduction

This annex provides the peer review findings prepared by the chair and co-chair of the Technical Review Committee (TRC) of the UNEP/SETAC Life Cycle Initiative: Reinout Heijungs (CML Leiden University, the Netherlands) and Michael Hauschild (Technical University of Denmark). The present report produced evaluates and summarizes both the process and the peer review comments received.

The peer review did not concentrate on the document as such, because the Pellston process (to be described below) emphasizes the role of the workshop participants and the mutual understanding and consensus that has been achieved between these participants during the workshop. Substantial changes of the document are therefore impossible after the workshop has closed. Whenever peer reviewers bring up important limitations, these cannot be solved textually, but are listed here, as a part of the peer review report.

The peer review basically consists of two parts. Part 1 is based on the observations by the TRC chair during the workshop, as well as on teleconferences and emails before and after the workshop. It concentrates on the process aspect. Part 2 is a more classical peer review of a draft document for which a TRC was established. The TRC co-chairs have sent the different draft chapters to TRC members and has produced a synthesis of their findings. The TRC consisted of following experts who did not participate in the workshop and who gratefully provided feedback on specific chapters within a very tight deadline:

Pablo Arena (University of Mendoza, Argentina), Terrie Boguski (Harmony Environmental LLC, U.S.A.), Joyce Cooper-Smith (University of Washington, U.S.A.), Amy Costello (Armstrong World Industries), Shabbir H. Gheewala (King Mongkut's University of Technology, Thailand), Jean-Michel Hébert (PwC), Walter Klöpffer (Editor in Chief of the International Journal of Life Cycle Assessment), Yasushi Kondo (Waseda University, Japan),

Todd Krieger (DuPont), Kun-Mo Lee (Ajou University, Korea), Deanna Lizas (ICF International), Martina Prox (IFU-Hamburg, Germany), Isabel Quispe (Pontifical Catholic University of Peru), Gert van Hoof (P&G)

Part 1
Peer Review of the Pellston process

We refer to the Pellston process as three phases:

- the preparatory phase, roughly from 2009 to 29 January 2011;
- the workshop itself, from 30 January to 4 February 2011;
- the editorial phase, from 5 February 2011 to June 2011.

In the first phase, the purpose and set-up of the workshop was defined and discussed, and the list of invited contributors was made. The chair of the TRC has been involved in some of the meetings and has received copies of some of the emails, but does not possess a complete archive of everything that was discussed. Nevertheless, the TRC chair has been able to get an idea of this phase. The discussion on purpose, set-up and participant list has been well organized. Many meetings of the Coordinating Committee of the UNEP/SETAC Life Cycle Initiative and the International Life Cycle Board (ILCB) have devoted time to find a good balance between the interests of business, industry, academia and other stakeholders. Likewise, the list of participants reflected a balance in terms of affiliation, continent, and gender. A critical note is the observation that the more political interest that UNEP is trying to follow may be in conflict with the desire to achieve a high quality result in scientific terms. To be specific, some persons or groups with a long experience in LCA databases were not represented, whereas they might have contributed to a document of a higher quality, but probably on the expense of less endorsement. The participants were extensively informed on the Pellston process[1] and the purpose of the workshop, and they also received a set of rules, e.g., on how to deal with minorities. They also received a draft table of contents parallel to a division into 6 workgroups, with a precise description of the Terms of Reference of these workgroups.

In preparing and during the workshop, the role of a Steering Committee should be mentioned. It served to define the topics to be addressed, to provide the basic structure of the document, and to guide the authors in shifting some of the topics between chapters. Moreover, a leadership team was formed in which workgroup chairpersons and liaisons could inform on obstacles and inconsistencies in the original planning.

The workshop itself took place in Shonan, Kanagawa, Japan, in a conference venue with a large plenary room and a number of rooms for the workgroups. An agenda had been sent out in advance, including plenary introductions, workgroup writing activities, and plenary discussion discussing preliminary findings and issues of cross-cutting interest. Every workgroup was assigned a chairperson, and a number of liaison persons were involved in two workgroups in order to finetune the division of work and to safeguard consistency between the workgroups. The TRC chair itself was not a member of a workgroup, and was not active in writing, so that he could freely move from one group to another, observe the discussions, and speak with participants on the process. The TRC chair was impressed by the constructive atmosphere created by the participants, and by the professional chairing of the workgroups. In most cases, the chairpersons dealt appropriately and effectively. In a limited number of cases, the TRC chair observed smaller of (rarely) bigger clashes, but these in the end turned right after some time. The organisation managed to keep a good balance between adhering to the original agenda and table of contents on the one hand, and introducing changes whenever required. Altogether, the positive and constructive atmosphere was maintained unto the end of the workshop.

Immediately after the workshop, the organisation and chairpersons met to discuss about the process of finalization of the document. A timeline was agreed, and a procedure was created. Subsequent emails of draft chapters and teleconferences were held until the beginning of May 2011. The atmosphere is best described as critical but constructive. As far as can be seen by the TRC chair, no pressure has been exerted on authors to change their opinion.

---

[1] The Pellston process refers to SETAC's use of a concentrated workshop to produce a monograph; see http://www.setac.org/node/104. The first workshop of this type was held in Pellston, Michigan, in 1977.

Part 2
Peer Review of the draft document

On 10 May, the UNEP secretariat started to set out the different draft chapters to TRC members. There were typically two peer reviewers per chapter, and most reviewed only one chapter. The peer reviewers were given one week to provide their comments to the text and judge the quality of the text against five questions:

- Is the Chapter thorough and complete?
- Is the text in general consistent and understandable?
- Does the document/chapter advance the technical practices associated with LCA databases, and/or does it provide an indication of where/ how the practices should advance?
- Are the definitions present in the glossary, (relevant for your chapter), appropriate, precise, understandable and consistent?
- Are all important references listed?

Together with the answer to the questions above, the chapter peer reviewers provided their comments to the text to the TRC co-chair who went through the report and the comments provided and processed them to arrive at the recommendations from the TRC.

Conclusions

Overall the peer review comments given by the TRC members are positive and many of them are of an editorial nature aimed at enhancing the readability and usefulness of the document to the reader. Many comments are also aimed at enhancing the information provided by the text by adding information to that already provided by the text. These comments have been handed to the editorial committee with the aim improving the draft into the finalized version you are now reading.

A few comments were judged to be of a more fundamental character and these are summarized below together with some more general observations for each of the report chapters.

Chapter 0 (prologue) and Chapter 1

The chapters were not reviewed, but from a reader friendliness point of view, the prologue could be shortened somewhat assuming that a reader of a technical guidance on LCI databases already is motivated to work on life cycle approaches.

Chapter 2

A guidance document on creation of LCI databases should require a specific nomenclature system for the elements of the unit process database to avoid the continuous development of databases that are not compatible. It should also support the harmonization of database structure and in general address the aspects of current practice that leads to incompatibility of LCI databases.

In addition the guidance needs to be strengthened on

- the preparation of uncertainty data
- unit process data parameterization, perhaps within the context of section 2.3.2
- modeling of closed loop processes

Chapter 3

The discussion of attributional vs. consequential LCA modeling needs more description and quantitative examples of how different modeling approaches and the associated different allocation techniques lead to substantially different results. Proposals are given in the peer review comments.

On the very important choice of allocation principle, a more clear guidance should be provided: The choice of allocation procedure in an LCA study should be in accordance with the stated goal. For the developer of a unit process database it is therefore important to make sure that it is clearly documented what is done in terms of allocation for multi-output processes, and it should be made clear that providing unallocated data increases the flexibility of the database for different uses. It should also be recommended that in case of doubt on how to handle multi-output processes, a sensitivity analysis should be performed of the different alternatives.

For cut-off rules, there is no guidance given, only a review of what is done in a number of LCI databases. This is a central assumption for a unit process data developer and guidance must be provided to make the guidance document of assistance.

Chapter 4

The chapter is rather general in its discussion of the review of LCI dataset. There are many lists but little guidance to the user on points that are not obvious anyway, and the added value of this part of the chapter is not clear to the TRC chair. The chapter could be abbreviated with this in mind, and anyhow needs a thorough editorial editing. Apart from this there are no really substantial peer review comments.

Chapter 5

The introduction to the chapter is very long and has a lot in common in both scope and goal with the introduction to the whole report. It is recommended that it is reduced to what is really necessary to prepare the reader for the contents of this chapter and to see why it is relevant. In particular why the (very useful) parts on requirements for consequential modelling and on geographical and temporal information is provided in this chapter and not in Chapter 2 where these topics are also dealt with.

Chapter 6

The text on cooperation and capacity building is found important by the peer reviewers although more concrete guidance is requested in particular on how capability development can be strengthened.

Chapter 7

The chapter is an inspiring discussion of possible future developments of the conditions for LCI databases and the policy options to strengthen the implementation of the recommendations given in the guidance report under each of these potential developments.

Chapter 8

The chapter was not peer reviewed, but as a more structural observation it would seem appropriate to move it to the front of the report where it would work well as a sort of executive summary of the whole report.

Conclusions

As a whole, the TRC acknowledges that the Pellston process has been able to provide an impressive document on an important topic. People from different backgrounds and affiliations have collaborated in a fruitful way to deliver these global guidance principles for LCA databases. While understanding that no definitive guidance can be produced, the TRC is still convinced that the present book will help to bring together data suppliers and data users, enhancing the world-wide applicability of LCA and increasing the transparence and credibility.

Note from the editors:
All critical comments received were peer reviewed and when possible incorporated. All comments submitted by the peer reviewers are available at the following link: **http://lcinitiative.unep.fr/**

ANNEX 3

List of Background Literature
Available for Developing the 'Global Guidance Principles for LCA Databases'

Various LCA Guidance Documents were reviewed and information extracted prior to the Workshop in February 2011. The extracted text was entered into an Excel database and made available to all workshop participants. Not all documents have been published. The following documents were included:

Carlson R, Pålsson A-C, Notten P, Cappellaro F, Scalbi S, Patyk A. 2003. Guideline for collection, treatment and quality documentation of LCA data. Proceedings of an International Workshop on Quality of LCI Data; October 20 to 21, 2003; Karlsruhe, Germany.

De Beaufort-Langeveld ASH, Bretz R, van Hoof G, Hischier R, Jean P, Tanner T, Huijbregts M, editors. 2003. Code of life-cycle inventory practice. Pensacola (FL): SETAC Pr. ISBN 1-88061105809.

European Commission – Joint Research Centre – Institute for Environment and Sustainability. 2010. International Reference Life Cycle Data System (ILCD) handbook - General guide for life cycle assessment - Detailed guidance. EUR 24708 EN. Luxembourg: Publications Office of the European Union. [cited 2011 Feb 1]. Available from: http://lct.jrc.ec.europa.eu/pdf-directory/ILCD-Handbook-General-guide-for-LCA-DETAIL-online-12March2010.pdf.

European Commission – Joint Research Centre – Institute for Environment and Sustainability. 2010. International Reference Life Cycle Data System (ILCD) Handbook - General guide for life cycle assessment - Provisions and action steps. EUR 24378 EN. Luxembourg: Publications Office of the European Union.

European Commission – Joint Research Centre – Institute for Environment and Sustainability. 2010. International Reference Life Cycle Data System (ILCD) Handbook - Nomenclature and other conventions. EUR 24384 EN. Luxembourg. Publications Office of the European Union.

European Commission – Joint Research Centre – Institute for Environment and Sustainability. 2010. International Reference Life Cycle Data System (ILCD) Handbook - Specific guide for life cycle inventory data sets. EUR 24709 EN. Luxembourg: Publications Office of the European Union.

ESU-services Ltd. 2009. Electricity use and production in veolia environment activities - Scope dependent modeling of electricity in life cycle assessment, final report, v1.

FEFCO, GEO, and ECO. 2006. European Database for Corrugated Board Life Cycle Studies.

Flemström K, Pålsson A-C. 2003. CPM Report 2003:3 Introduction and guide to LCA data documentation using the CPM documentation criteria and the ISO/TS 14048 data documentation format.

Frischknecht R. 2010. LCI modelling approaches applied on recycling of materials in view of environmental sustainability, risk perception and eco-efficiency. Int J LCA. 15(7):666–671.

Frischknecht R. 2006. Notions on the design and use of an ideal regional or global LCA database. in Int J LCA, 11(1):40-48".

Frischknecht R, Jungbluth N. 2007. Overview and methodology, Eco-invent Report No. 1, Swiss Centre for Life Cycle Inventories. Dübendorf (CH).

Frischknecht R, Stucki M. 2010. Scope-dependent modelling of electricity supply in life cycle assessments. Int J LCA. 15(8):806-816.

Frischknecht R, Tuchschmid M, Gärtner S. 2007. LCA of background processes, Deliverable D15.1, New Energy Externalities Developments for Sustainability INTEGRATED PROJECT, ESU-services Ltd., Uster and ifeu Heidelberg.

Frischknecht R, Krewitt W. 2007. Final specification of software interfaces, requirements and technical realisation of exchange formats, Deliverable D1.2 - RS 1a, New Energy Externalities Developments for Sustainability INTEGRATED PROJECT, ESU-services Ltd., Uster and DLR Stuttgart.

Häggström S, editor. 2004. Database maintenance and development CPM phase III.

JEMAI, LCA Data Collection Methodology (chapter 6).

Lundie S, Ciroth A, Huppes G. 2008. UNEP-SETAC Life Cycle Initiative, Life Cycle Inventory (LCI), Task Force 3, Methodological consistency: Inventory methods in LCA: Towards consistency and improvement. Saarbrücken: VDM-Verlag.

National Renewal Energy Laboratory. 2010. Data Quality Plan for the US LCI Database – Discussion Draft.

National Renewable Energy Laboratory, Athena Sustainable Materials Institute, Franklin Associates, Ltd., Sylvatica. 2004. U.S. LCI Database Project – User's Guide Draft, February 2004, NREL/BK-35854. [cited 2011 Feb 1]. Available from: www.nrel.gov/lci/pdfs/users_guide.pdf.

Plastics Europe. 2009. Eco-profiles and environmental declarations - LCI methodology and PCR for uncompounded polymer resins and reactive polymer precursors.

Schmidt JA, Weidema B. 2009. Response to the public consultation on a set of guidance documents of the International Reference Life Cycle Data System (ILCD) Handbook.

Viebahn P, Kronshage S, Trieb F (DLR), Lechon Y (CIEMAT). 2008. Final report on technical data, costs, and life cycle inventories of solar thermal power plants, Deliverable n° 12.2 - RS Ia, NEEDS New Energy Externalities Developments for Sustainability INTEGRATED PROJECT, DLR, Stuttgart and CIEMAT, Madrid.
Externalities Developments for Sustainability INTEGRATED PROJECT, ESU-services Ltd., Uster and DLR, Stuttgart.

Unknown. 2009. ILCD Handbook Public Consultation Workshop.

Weidema B, Hischier R, Althaus H-J, Bauer C, Doka G, Dones R, Frischknecht R, Jungbluth N, Nemecek T, Primas A, Wernet G. 2009. Code of practice data, Eco-invent Report No. 02, Version 2.1.

Weidema BP. et al. 2009. Overview and methodology, (draft), Data quality guideline for the ecoinvent database, version 3.0.

worldsteel. 2008. Worldsteel – Methodology Report.

worldsteel. 2008. Worldsteel - Recycling Methodology.

WRI (GHG Protocol). 2009a. GHG Protocol Product and Supply Chain Initiative.

WRI (GHG Protocol). 2009b. Product Life Cycle Accounting and Reporting Standard, review draft for stakeholder advisory group.

WRI (GHG Protocol). 2009c. Product Life Cycle Accounting and Reporting Standard, Summary of Key Requirements review draft for stakeholder advisory group.

Various other documents were uploaded on the on-line workshop repository by the workshop participants both prior to and during the workshop:

Athena Institute & National Renewable Energy Laboratory. 2010. U.S. LCI Database Overview and Data Submission Requirements Version (DRAFT) 2.

CALCAS. 2009. Guidelines for applications of deepened and broadened LCA: Hybrid approaches combining IOA and LCA. Chapter for CALCAS deliverable D18, 2009. [Internet]. Available from: http://www.lca-net.com/files/Hybrid_IO-LCA_CALCAS_final.pdf.

Ekvall T, Weidema BP. 2004. System boundaries and input data in consequential life cycle inventory analysis. Int J LCA. 9(3):161-171.

European Commission - Joint Research Centre - Institute for Environment and Sustainability: International Reference Life Cycle Data System (ILCD) Handbook - Reviewer qualification for Life Cycle Inventory data sets. First edition March 2010. EUR 24379 EN. Luxembourg. Publications Office of the European Union.

European Commission - Joint Research Centre - Institute for Environment and Sustainability: International Reference Life Cycle Data System (ILCD) Handbook - Review schemes for Life Cycle Assessment. First edition March 2010. EUR 24710 EN. Luxembourg. Publications Office of the European Union; 2010.

Forschungszentrum Karlsruhe & UNEP/SETAC Life Cycle Initiative. 2003. Minutes of the International Workshop on Quality of LCI Data; 2003 Oct 20-21; Karlsruhe (DE).

Frischknecht R. 2000. Allocation in life cycle inventory analysis for joint production. Int J LCA. 5(2):85-95.

Frischknecht R. 2004. Transparency in LCA – a heretical request? Int J LCA. 9(4):211-213.

Frischknecht R, editor. 2005. Contents: The ecoinvent database. Int J LCA. 10(1):1-94.

Frischknecht R, Althaus HJ, Bauer C, Doka G, Heck T, Jungbluth N, Kellenberger D, Nemecek T. 2007. The environmental relevance of capital goods in life cycle assessments of products and services. Int J LCA 12 (special issue 1):7-17.

Frischknecht R, Althaus HJ, Doka G, Dones R, Heck T, Hellweg S, Hischier R, Jungbluth N, Nemecek T, Rebitzer G, Spielmann M. 2005. Selected modelling principles applied in the ecoinvent database. Journal of Life Cycle Assessment, Japan. 1(2):112-122.

Frischknecht R, Rebitzer G. 2005. The ecoinvent database system: a comprehensive web-based LCA database. J Cleaner Production. 13(13-14):1337-1343.

Hamans C. 2011. CEPMC note to UNEP-SETAC. Council of European Producers of Materials for Construction (unpublished).

Heijungs R, Frischknecht R. 2004. Representing statistical distributions for uncertain parameters in LCA: Relationships between mathematical forms, their representation in EcoSpold, and their representation in CMLCA. Int J LCA 10(4):248-254.

Hoekstra AY, Chapagain AK, Aldaya MM, Mekonnen MM. 2011. the water footprint assessment manual: Setting the global standard. London (UK): Earthscan.

IPCC. 2006. 2006 IPCC Guidelines for National Greenhouse Gas Inventories. Prepared by the National Greenhouse Gas Inventories Programme. Eggleston HS, Buendia L, Miwa K, Ngara T, Tanabe K, editors.. Japan: IGES.

Klöpffer W. 2008. Life cycle sustainability assessment of products. Int J LCA. 13(2):89-95.

Klöpffer W. 2009. Experiences with the critical review process of aluminium. Int J LCA. 14(Suppl 1): S45-S51.

Mekonnen MM, Hoekstra AY. 2010. The green, blue and grey water footprint of crops and derived crop products, Value of Water Research Report Series No. 47. Delft (NL): UNESCO-IHE.

Milà i Canals L, Sim S, Garciá-Suárez T, Neuer G, Herstein K, Kerr C, Rigarlsford G, King H. 2011. Estimating the greenhouse gas footprint of Knorr. Int J LCA. 16(1):50-58.

Mongelli I, Suh S, Huppes G. 2005. A structure comparison of two approaches to LCA inventory data, Based on the MIET and ETH databases. Int J LCA. 10(5):317-324.

National Institute of Advanced Science and Technology. 2005. AIST-LCA Ver.4, Research Center of life cycle assessment. Japan: AIST. [cited 2011 Feb 1]. Available from: http://www.aist-riss.jp/main/modules/product/software/nire.html?ml_lang=en.

Norris GA. 2001. Integrating life cycle cost analysis and LCA. Int J LCA. 6(2):118-120.

NREL, DOE & EPA. 2010. Supporting Life Cycle Inventory Data Development in the United States. NREL, DOE & EPA Workshop; 2010 Mar 2-4; Crystal City (VA) (unpublished).

Weidema BP, Bauer C, Hischier R, Mutel C, Nemecek T, Vadenbo CO, Wernet G. 2011. Overview and methodology. Data quality guideline for the ecoinvent database version 3. Ecoinvent Report 1. St. Gallen (CH): The ecoinvent Centre.

Weidema BP, Frees N, Nielsen AM. 1999. Marginal production technologies for life cycle inventories. Int J LCA. 4(1): 48-56.

Wiedmann T. 2010. Frequently asked questions about input-output analysis. York (UK): Centre for Sustainability Accounting [Internet]. Available from: http://www.censa.org.uk/docs/CENSA_Special_Report_FAQ_IOA.pdf.

List of Public Stakeholder Consultation & Outreach Events

1. 'International Stakeholder Engagement Meeting "Towards Global Guidance for LCA Databases"', Boston, U.S.A. – 30th September 2009

2. Presentation & consultation meeting, in conjunction with the Chinese Roundtable on Sustainable Consumption and Production, Beijing, China – 14th November 2009

3. 'Internationally Acknowledged Guidance for Life Cycle Databases – Indian consultation', Mumbai, India – 13th January 2010

4. International Stakeholder Engagement Meeting "Towards Global Guidance for LCA Databases", Tokyo, Japan - 9th February 2010

5. Presentation & short consultation at the CYCLE 2010 - 4th Canadian Forum on LCM, Montréal, Canada – 4th May 2010

6. '6th International Consultation on the 'Global Guidance Process for LCA Databases" during the SETAC Europe Meeting, Seville, Spain – 26th May 2010

7. Consultation in the context of the LCM Brazil Conference, Florianópolis, Brazil – 25th November 2010

8. Consultation meeting at the LCA X Conference, Portland, USA. – 4th November 2010

9. 'International Symposium on the LCA Global Database Guidance, Tokyo, Japan – 13th November 2010

10. Presentation & consultation meeting at the ALCAS 7th Australian Conference on Life Cycle Assessment Melbourne Australia – 10th March 2011

11. Presentation & consultation 'Process on "Global Guidance for LCA Databases"' at CILCA 2011, Coatzacoalcos, Veracruz Mexico – 4th April 2011

12. Presentation & short consultation at the Americana Event, Montreal, Canada – 23rd March 2011

13. Consultation meeting during the SETAC Europe Meeting, Milan, Italy – 18th May 2011

About the UNEP/SETAC Life Cycle Initiative

The Global Life Cycle Initiative was established by UNEP and SETAC. Among other things, the Life Cycle Initiative builds upon and provides support to the ongoing work of UNEP on sustainable consumption and production, such as Industry Outreach, Industrial Pollution Management, Sustainable Consumption, Cleaner and Safer Production, Global Reporting Initiative (GRI), Global Compact, UN Consumer Guidelines, Tourism, Advertising, Eco-design and Product Service Systems.

The Initiative's efforts are complemented by SETAC's international infrastructure and its publishing efforts in support of the LCA community.

The Life Cycle Initiative is a response to the call from governments for a life cycle economy in the Malmö Declaration (2000). It contributes to the 10-year framework of programmes to promote sustainable consumption and production patterns, as requested at the World Summit on Sustainable Development (WSSD) in Johannesburg (2002).

The UNEP/SETAC Life Cycle Initiative's mission is to bring science-based Life Cycle approaches into practice worldwide

Our current work is building on the Life Cycle Initiative's continual strength to maintain and enhance life cycle assessment and management methodologies and build capacity globally. As we look to the future, Life Cycle Assessment (LCA) and Life Cycle Management (LCM) knowledge is the Life Cycle Initiative's anchor, but we will advance activities on LCA and LCM to make a difference within the real world.

Therefore, the renewed objectives are the following ones:

Objective 1: Enhance the global consensus and relevance of existing and emerging life cycle approaches methodology;

Objective 2: Facilitate the use of life cycle approaches worldwide by encouraging life cycle thinking in decision-making in business, government and the general public about natural resources, materials and products targeted at consumption clusters;

Objective 3: Expand capability worldwide to apply and to improve life cycle approaches.

For more information, see **http://lcinitiative.unep.fr**

SPONSORS & STRATEGIC PARTNERS OF
THE UNEP/SETAC LIFE CYCLE INITIATIVE

Workshop Host

Government Platinum Sponsors and Strategic Partners

Private Sector Platinum Sponsors

International Plastics Associations & Chemistry Company

Academic Private Partnerships as Platinum Sponsors

13 Corporate Sponsors: Advisory Members within CIRAIG

Gold sponsors

Regional Networks & Partners

African Life Cycle Assessment Network (ALCANET), Red Iberoamericana de Ciclo de Vida, IBICT Brazil, Malaysian Palm Oil Board, National Metal and Materials Technology Center (Thailand), National University of Singapore, Sichuan University.

About SETAC

The Society of Environmental Toxicology and Chemistry (SETAC) is a professional society in the form of a non-forprofit association, established to promote the use of a multidisciplinary approach to solving problems of the impact of chemicals and technology on the environment. Environmental problems often require a combination of expertise from chemistry, toxicology, and a range of other disciplines to develop effective solutions. SETAC provides a neutral meeting ground for scientists working in universities, governments, and industry who meet, as private persons not bound to defend positions, but simply to use the best science available.

Among other things, SETAC has taken a leading role in the development of Life Cycle Management (LCM) and Life Cycle Assessment (LCA).

The organization is often quoted as a reference on LCA matters.

For more information, see **www.setac.org**